INNOVATIONS AND CHALLENGES IN APPLIED LINGUISTICS FROM THE GLOBAL SOUTH

Innovations and Challenges in Applied Linguistics from the Global South provides an original appraisal of the latest innovations and challenges in applied linguistics from the perspective of the Global South. Global South perspectives are encapsulated in struggles for basic, economic, political, and social transformation in an inequitable world, and are not confined to the geographical South. Taking a critical perspective on southern theories, demonstrating why it is important to view the world from southern perspectives, and why such positions must be open to critical investigation, this book:

- charts the impacts of these theories on approaches to multilingualism, language learning, language in education, literacy and diversity, language rights, and language policy;
- provides broad historical and geographical understandings of the movement towards a southern perspective and draws on Indigenous and southern ways of thinking that challenge mainstream viewpoints;
- seeks to develop alternative understandings of applied linguistics, expand the intellectual repertoires of the discipline, and challenge the complicities between applied linguistics, colonialism, and capitalism.

Written by two renowned scholars in the field, *Innovations and Challenges in Applied Linguistics from the Global South* is key reading for advanced students and researchers of applied linguistics, multilingualism, language and education, language policy and planning, and language and identity.

Alastair Pennycook is Distinguished Professor of Language, Society, and Education at the University of Technology Sydney, Australia and Adjunct Professor at MultiLing, Oslo, Norway.

Sinfree Makoni is Professor in the Department of Applied Linguistics and African Studies at Penn State University, USA and Extraordinary Professor at the University of the North West, South Africa.

INNOVATIONS AND CHALLENGES IN APPLIED LINGUISTICS

Ken Hyland is Professor of Applied Linguistics in Education at the University of East Anglia and Visiting Professor in the School of Foreign Language Education, Jilin University, China.

Innovations and Challenges in Applied Linguistics offers readers an understanding of some the core areas of Applied Linguistics. Each book in the series is written by a specially commissioned expert who discusses a current and controversial issue surrounding contemporary language use. The books offer a cutting-edge focus that carries the authority of an expert in the field, blending a clearly written and accessible outline of what we know about a topic and the direction in which it should be moving.

The books in this series are essential reading for those researching, teaching, and studying in applied linguistics.

Innovations and Challenges in Applied Linguistics from the Global South
Alastair Pennycook and Sinfree Makoni

INNOVATIONS AND CHALLENGES IN APPLIED LINGUISTICS FROM THE GLOBAL SOUTH

Alastair Pennycook and Sinfree Makoni

LONDON AND NEW YORK

First published 2020
by Routledge
2 Park Square, Milton Park, Abingdon, Oxon OX14 4RN

and by Routledge
52 Vanderbilt Avenue, New York, NY 10017

Routledge is an imprint of the Taylor & Francis Group, an informa business

© 2020 Alastair Pennycook and Sinfree Makoni

The right of Alastair Pennycook and Sinfree Makoni to be identified as authors of this work has been asserted by them in accordance with sections 77 and 78 of the Copyright, Designs and Patents Act 1988.

All rights reserved. No part of this book may be reprinted or reproduced or utilised in any form or by any electronic, mechanical, or other means, now known or hereafter invented, including photocopying and recording, or in any information storage or retrieval system, without permission in writing from the publishers.

Trademark notice: Product or corporate names may be trademarks or registered trademarks, and are used only for identification and explanation without intent to infringe.

British Library Cataloguing in Publication Data
A catalogue record for this book is available from the British Library

Library of Congress Cataloging-in-Publication Data
Names: Pennycook, Alastair, 1957- author. | Makoni, Sinfree, author.
Title: Innovations and challenges in applied linguistics from the global South / Alastair Pennycook and Sinfree Makoni.
Description: New York, NY : Routledge, [2019] | Series: Innovations and challenges in applied linguistics | Includes bibliographical references and index.
Identifiers: LCCN 2019018150| ISBN 9781138593503 (hardback) | ISBN 9781138593510 (pbk.) | ISBN 9780429489396 (e-book)
Subjects: LCSH: Applied linguistics. | Applied linguistics–Southern Hemisphere.
Classification: LCC P129 .P464 2019 | DDC 418–dc23
LC record available at https://lccn.loc.gov/2019018150

ISBN: 978-1-138-59350-3 (hbk)
ISBN: 978-1-138-59351-0 (pbk)
ISBN: 978-0-429-48939-6 (ebk)

Typeset in Bembo
by Taylor & Francis Books

CONTENTS

Acknowledgements vi
Preface viii
Foreword x

1 Introduction: Gazing from the South 1
2 The making of the South in applied linguistics 19
3 Southern multilingualisms 42
4 Language endangerment, vitality, and reclamation 63
5 Decolonizing language in education 82
6 Challenging the northern research gaze 102
7 Applied linguistics from a southern perspective 122

References *138*
Index *161*

ACKNOWLEDGEMENTS

The two of us (Makoni and Pennycook) first met around 20 years ago at a conference in Japan. During dinner, someone asked Makoni how many languages he spoke. He politely refused to answer, pointing out that languages could not be counted. Since that moment we have been in a long discussion about the implications of such moments – the provenance of such questions and the politics of such inquiries. This is our latest collaborative work, a project that has bounced back and forth across continents for a couple of years, a period of agreements, disagreements, suggestions, corrections, and much more. Aside from thanking each other for another fascinating intellectual journey, there are many others who need to be acknowledged, since there have always been multiple other participants in this sustained engagement.

Alastair is particularly grateful to the Advanced Research Collaborative (ARC) at the City University of New York (CUNY) for granting a fellowship to work there in 2018, with the perfect conditions to think, talk, and write (and for the two of us to meet up in New York). Amid the many scholars involved with the ARC, of great importance were Ofelia García, Ricardo Otheguy, Lourdes Ortega, Angela Reyes, Nelson Flores, Jorge Alvis, and the Glotopolitica group. Alastair would also like to thank colleagues at the Centre for Multilingualism in Society across the Lifespan at the University of Oslo, and particularly those who gave detailed feedback on a draft chapter from the book at a writing retreat: Haley De Korne, Kellie Gonçalves, Pia lane, Quentin Williams, Jorunn Thingnes, Olga Solovova, Unn Røyneland, and Liz Lanza. The important role such places – the ARC at CUNY and the MultiLing Centre at Oslo – play in fostering the conditions for serious scholarship should not be overlooked (and should ideally be emulated). Sylvia Owiny, the librarian of African Studies at Penn State University has also been extremely reliable and helpful, searching expeditiously for many references which we required at short notice in the writing of the book.

Many colleagues involved in the Southern Multilingualisms and Diversities Consortium have also been consistent interlocutors in this work, and we would like particularly to acknowledge the sustained discussions we have had with Ana Deumert and Lynn Mario de Souza, who are both outstanding scholars and generous collaborators, providing numerous references and ideas that enriched our writing. Also from that network, thanks to Ashraf Abdebay, Kathleen Heugh, Ryuko Kubota, Angel Lin, Beatriz Lorente, Reynaldo Macias, Tommaso Milani, Finex Ndhlovu, Cristine Severo, Shi-xu, Elana Shohamy, Chris Stroud, amongst others. And thanks to Rafael Lomeu Gomes for enabling a series of Skype discussions around Southern Theory over the past year. We have also benefited from a long engagement with the topics in this book with Dipesh Chakrabarty and Walter Mignolo.

Thanks to the series editor, Ken Hyland, who first approached us with the idea for the book, and who has been supportive throughout. And we are grateful to Lizzie Cox at Routledge for guiding this project through to completion. We owe a great debt to our partners – Busi and Dominique – both of whom provide multiple forms of support (as well as tolerance), not least daily critical conversations, and demands to engage better with questions of gender, slavery, other languages, different contexts, and more. Sinfree would finally like to thank mai Tino and Tsungi for their unwavering support of his academic career.

PREFACE

Applied linguistics investigates real-world problems involving language. As such it involves both academic study and lived experience, mediating between theory and practice and attempting to reconcile opposed interests and perspectives. Encompassing issues as diverse as speech pathologies, language teaching, and critical literacy, this is a socially accountable discipline which seeks to better understand and intervene in practical issues. It is a field central to understanding society and human responses to it.

The *Routledge Innovations and Challenges in Applied Linguistics Series*, as its name suggests, seeks to tap the large and growing interest in this area through a number of topic-based books focusing on key aspects of applied linguistics. Unlike many series, however, it does not set out to provide another overview of the field or detailed analysis of a single study. Instead, each book offers a strong personal view by a recognized expert of where the field is heading in a specific area. Volumes in the series give an accessible and structured overview of each area as a context for the topic, while the main part of the book takes up and develops this topic with a personal and cutting-edge perspective which points the way forward. Where necessary, to capture the diversity of a current and controversial issue, topics will be addressed by several authors in an edited collection. In every case, though, books in the series discuss a current and controversial issue surrounding contemporary language use and are authored/edited by leading authorities.

There are, in sum, five main goals guiding this series:

1. The series will address issues of contemporary concern in applied linguistics and related areas and offer *cutting-edge* theories, approaches, methodologies, and understandings to those issues.
2. Authors in the series will bring their *own perspectives* to issues rather than simply offering a general overview of the topic.

3. The series will be *comprehensive*. Each issue will be treated thoroughly and critically, taking account of various approaches, issues, and problems but always looking forward.
4. Each book will be *reader-friendly* with numerous examples and described cases and these will be closely related to research and theory.
5. All the books in the series will emphasise *connectivity*, helping readers understand the relationships between theory, research, and how language works in the real world.

The books, then, blend a clearly written and accessible outline with an appreciation of an expert's take on the field. Each is written for those keen to learn more and delve more deeply into a topic by understanding what we know of a field, where it is heading, and the challenges involved. We hope that the titles will generate discussion and debate within the academic community and will be read by teachers and researchers as well as by postgraduate students.

Ken Hyland
University of East Anglia

FOREWORD

In our contemporary context of applied linguistics, where mobility and diversity may have become household terms, many are the lingering theoretical and practical conflicts around issues related to these concepts:

- In the internationalization of higher education, who has the right to certify competence in the English language and why?
- In discussions around multi-, poly-, and trans-lingualism, who decides where one language begins and another ends (if at all)?
- In discussions centering around "native-speakerism" and English as a lingua franca, who decides what is English?
- In discussions around the limits of humanism and the blurring of the lines that separate epistemology from ontology, who decides what is or isn't a knowledge-producing subject and one that is capable of communication and expression?

That such conflicts are political and ideological is to state the obvious, but this can currently mean many things, from the politics of globalization to the politics of neo-liberalism. Back in 2006, Makoni & Pennycook had already raised the issue of the role of politics and ideology in the production of concepts of language through *metadiscursive regimes*. More recently, Heller & McElhinny (2017, p.xxii) sought to "develop an approach to linguistic analysis in which political economy, social difference, and social inequality are at the center". Carefully attempting to extract "alternative genealogies" of theorizing on language, they conclude that, because they are not hegemonic, these genealogies are exactly the ones that leave the least traces. The question begged here is whether these are unleft traces or whether they have been invisibilized.

Writing on political and ideological aspects of racism and diversity, Ahmed (2012, p.180), calls attention to what she sees as theoretical, discursive, and perceptive "walls" that she defines as "that which you do not get over. It is not over if you don't get over it". Ahmed suggests that certain categories, such as racism or sexism are seen as political and ideological "blockages of thought", hindering, like walls, the presumed free-flow of "normal" thought. Rather than unblocking or eradicating such walls, the role of critique should be to first account for and make visible such "blockages" and "walls" within institutional worlds. It is only when blockages cause the functioning and the flow to recede that the wall surfaces. Walls and obstacles are not just "there". They were produced by the same political and ideological thinking that defined what unobstructed flow was and what "normal" or "natural" functioning were; hence the need to critically account for their existence as products of the same institutions they are accused of obstructing. Not only were the walls institutionally (and hence politically/ideologically) produced, their *invisibility* was also produced.

All of this points to the need for what Grosfoguel (2011) calls *epistemological critique*. Grosfoguel and other Latin American decolonial thinkers point to the fact that since the 16th century, hegemonic Eurocentric paradigms have informed Western philosophy, science, and rationality and have attributed to themselves a neutral, objective point of view, which has hidden their locus of enunciation and with it the historical, sociocultural, political, and economic interests that traverse and color their perceptions and knowledges. It is from this, a-historical, body-less, abstract point of view that so-called Modernity and Western Science define themselves as universal, disqualifying other modernities, knowledges, and sciences produced from other historical and sociocultural locations. From this perspective, the histories in which language speakers, languages, and theorizing about language are embedded are inescapably traversed by political, economic, and other social issues of power. Like Makoni & Pennycook's *metadiscursive regimes* and Heller & McElhinny's *alternative genealogies*, it is a call for attention to the meta-theoretical dimension of thinking about language.

It may not be sufficient to understand that all knowledges are *situated* and contextual. It may be of crucial importance to understand that there are entangled embeddings in which certain levels of situatedness of certain knowledges, like the walls and blockages denounced by Ahmed, may easily go unperceived. Such is the case of the concept of *coloniality of power* as defined by Quijano (2007) which functions as a hierarchical organization of races, knowledges, cultures, languages, religions, genders, and sexuality that takes as its basis the concept of race. Rather than deriving from a biological factor, the concept of race derives from the relationship of inequality and dominance established between the colonizer and the indigenous Amerindian at the moment of colonial contact in the Americas. At the inauguration of that relationship, the inequality attributed to the colonized Amerindian formed the basis for assuming the inferiority of all that pertained to the colonized. This inferiority was then biologized as *race* which served as a visible, tangible (even rational) justification for the alleged inferiority of the Amerindian. Thus, from a *consequence* of the previous attribution of inferiority, race was transformed into the *cause and justification* of inferiority, and this inferiority was extended to all that pertained to the Amerindian. The result was *epistemological racism* or *epistemicide,* extended to the rest of the world as *coloniality*.

It is thus not sufficient to be aware only of the importance of one's historical and sociopolitical locus of enunciation when theorizing. Decolonial thinking, developed and proposed by Latin American scholars, consists of a strategy of interrogating and interrupting this paradigm of coloniality. Similarly, Santos (2018) embarks on epistemological critique, to replace universalized Western concepts such as globalization with a non-hegemonic *southern perspective* or *epistemologies of the South*. In this view, all processes of globalization are seen as movements from an unmarked original location to a newer location. However, the *located-ness* of the process is never lost. For Santos, the attempt to unmark certain locations of origin as *universal* and the marking of others as *local* are indicators of power, inequality, and injustice. For Santos, *an abyssal line* disqualifies the existence, subjecthood, and agency of non-hegemonic peoples, their knowledges and capacities, and results, like coloniality, in *epistemicide*.

Defending the existence of a non-hegemonic *southern perspective,* Santos challenges the hegemonic view and seeks to *make visible* the existence of multiple peoples, knowledges, languages, and so on, on the non-hegemonic side of the abyssal line where, rather than a vacuum of inexistent knowledges, there exists a complex plurality of *ecologies* of knowledges. Neither *decolonial thinking* nor *epistemologies of the South* claim to replace a previous incorrect paradigm with a correct one, but rather offer paradigms of complexity which, rather than seeking authenticity, seek justice and horizontality; rather than seeking new solutions as homogeneous products, they point to new practices as complex heterogeneously entangled processes. Following Ahmed (2012), one has to first *block* what the current hegemony establishes as the flow of normality, justice, and equality; one has to become the blockage points in order to make them visible. Such are the strategies of both *decolonial thinking* and the *epistemologies of the South:* Each seeks to first uncover the persistence of *coloniality* on the one hand, and *abyssal thinking* on the other. Once these have been uncovered, attempts to *interrogate* and *interrupt* them are then developed. Both decolonial thinking and epistemologies of the South are attempts at interrupting the normality of meta-theorizing to uncover unseen walls so that attempts may be made to get over them; such is the complex, commendable, and timely endeavor of epistemological critique and ontological exploration in which Alastair Pennycook and Sinfree Makoni engage in this book.

1

INTRODUCTION: GAZING FROM THE SOUTH

This book looks at applied linguistics from a southern perspective. This is not just a case of adding some perspectives from the South, or including various southern people who are often forgotten, or incorporating geographical areas or topics occluded from analysis in Global Northern applied linguistics. What we're addressing here, by contrast, is a much more far-reaching set of challenges to what applied linguistics means, what it encompasses, what its central concerns are, what it regards as its antecedents and historical pedigree, and what ideas and traditions it therefore draws on. The innovations and challenges we want to bring to applied linguistics in this book extend far beyond an agenda that seeks to redress various exclusions; rather, these are deep-seated challenges to some of the core tenets of applied linguistics as well as new directions for theories and practices in the field. Acknowledging the complicities of applied linguistics with a history of colonialism and capitalism and a range of contemporary inequalities, this book encourages us to rethink and remake applied linguistics at a global level in open-ended ways. This chapter lays out the basic concerns and background to the book, making a case for the need for alternative understandings of applied linguistics and the importance of the contribution of the Global South to Global North scholarship.

What, then, is the Global South? It is not, it must be said, an idea without its own challenges and contradictions, though it is no less important as a result. Simply put, the Global South refers to the people, places, and ideas that have been left out of the grand narrative of modernity. It may at times refer quite literally to the South, to regions of South America and much of Africa, for example, that have not been part of the upward march of economic, social, and political 'progress' in wealthier nations. More importantly, however, the Global South refers to broader histories of exclusion and disenfranchisement, and thus might equally refer to Indigenous communities in North America, New Zealand, Australia, China, Laos, or America. Indeed, the idea of the Global South may be applied to the urban poor in cities in the northern hemisphere rather than to wealthy elites in the southern hemisphere. The South, from Santos' (2012) perspective, refers both to the conditions of suffering and inequality brought about by capitalism and colonialism and to the resistance to such conditions. The South therefore also exists in "the global North, in the form of excluded, silenced and marginalized populations, such as undocumented immigrants, the unemployed, ethnic or religious minorities, and victims of sexism, homophobia and racism" (Santos, 2012, p.51).

Two of the important texts that instigated this move to think in terms of southern theories are Connell's (2007) *Southern Theory* and Jean and John Comaroff's (2011) *Theory from the South*. For Connell, focusing particularly on social theory, the central concern is "the erasure of the experience of the majority of human kind from the foundations of social thought" (p.46). Similarly, for the Comaroffs, the principal focus is the ways in which "Western enlightenment thought has, from the first, posited itself as the wellspring of universal learning, of Science and Philosophy" (2012 p.113). For both Connell and the Comaroffs the issue was not only a critique of the dominance of theory and knowledge from the North but also the fundamental need to reverse this relationship, to open up alternative ways of knowing from southern perspectives. On the one hand, then, is the tendency to universalize findings from WEIRD (Western, Educated, Industrialized, Rich, and Democratic) contexts to the rest of the world (Henrich et al., 2010) and on the other the concomitant exclusion of the majority world from social scientific theorizing. It is particularly in the work of Santos (2012, 2018) on *southern epistemologies* that these arguments have taken shape over the last decade, with his insistence on understanding the Global South in terms of multifaceted relations of global inequalities and on the need to develop alternative, southern epistemologies: "The epistemologies of the South concern the production and validation of knowledges anchored in the experiences of resistance of all those social groups that have systematically suffered injustice, oppression, and destruction caused by capitalism, colonialism, and patriarchy" (2018, p1).

From the outset, then, it is clear that the Global South refers not so much to a geographical region, and to more than merely a set of geopolitical inequalities. As is also evident, it brings in a range of other concerns, including Indigeneity, race, class, sexuality, poverty, gender, and colonialism. The idea of the Global South is heir to a range of previous forms of work that have sought to address global inequalities of both material and intellectual goods, from a focus on dependency theory (how so-called developing nations are forced to be dependent on so-called developed nations for anything from the price of coffee to the ways sociology is done), Third World scholarship, postcolonial theory, and much more (see Chapter 2). This also intersects with decolonial perspectives (Mignolo, 2011a; Mignolo and Walsh, 2018), Indigenous standpoints (Nakata, 2007), and other projects to both decentralize northern or western epistemologies and to construct intellectual sovereignty in the Global South. The challenges such a project faces are many. As Kwesi Kwaa Prah (2017) points out, any project to develop intellectual sovereignty in Africa has to escape the weight of intellectual neocolonialism that always defers to knowledge production from elsewhere, devaluing Indigenous knowledge systems in favour of received knowledge.

Such processes are compounded by institutional racism, the languages in which such knowledge is often expressed (received knowledge in received languages), and the interests of local elites in extending the life of colonial culture and knowledge derived from the metropolitan centres of culture and power in the contemporary world. For Prah (2017, p.20), the goal is to "achieve a universalism which has equal space for all voices, and not a universalism under restrictive Western hegemony", and to this end "the centre of gravity of knowledge production about Africa and Africans must be situated in Africa, so that the 'otherness' of the subject of scholarship which Western hegemony has imposed on Africa and Africans is eliminated". Such projects raise further complications, however: Should a project to include multiple voices rather than only those of a hegemonic North attempt to seek a more inclusive universalism, or should it seek to undermine calls for universalism? And if, as Santos (2018, p.3) asserts, southern epistemologies may be "ways of knowing, rather than knowledges", the question is not merely one of adding new ideas to the archives of existing knowledge but of changing what counts as knowledge, of developing a relation between existing knowledge and "artisanal knowledges" (p.43).

The challenge of thinking about applied linguistics from a southern perspective, therefore, raises questions that run far deeper than a set of additive concerns about contexts we may have missed out in our research. It asks much more difficult questions about that research itself, and who is doing it, with what assumptions, for whom, with whom, and for what purposes. The idea of the Global South therefore encompasses far broader issues than an attempt just to redress global exclusions: It addresses contemporary and historical ways in which forms of knowledge have been developed and valued, as well as the larger colonial, economic, and political forces that lead to these epistemological imbalances. For applied linguistics, the questions raised by southern perspectives address not only its colonial past and contemporary location in neo-liberal times, but also its key tenets about language, knowledge, and education. We shall return in much more depth to this background in the next chapter, and to concerns about language, education, and research in the following chapters. First, however, we shall consider in greater depth some of the tensions around the Global South framework, before outlining both some of the useful questions these perspectives can open up (innovations) as well as some of the challenges this poses for applied linguistics.

North and South: Geographical, geopolitical, and decolonial concerns

There is an immediate concern that emerges when we talk of the Global South: Although the term is intended geopolitically, metaphorically, and epistemologically, it cannot at times escape its geographical reference. While Global South scholars are insistent that it is a geopolitical concept referring to struggles against inequality, there is often at the same time a pull towards the South. This is not surprising both because the term 'south' is always likely to orient us in that direction and because, given the historical development of colonialism and capitalism, "the epistemological South and the geographical South partially overlap, particularly as regards those countries that were subjected to historical colonialism" (Santos, 2018, p1). Yet this becomes complex when regions that are clearly very far south geographically (Australia and New Zealand being obvious examples) are not considered to be in the Global South, or when regions considered north in relation to others (North Africa, for example) are considered part of the Global South, or indeed when regions that are almost defined by their geographical northerness (the lands of Indigenous people within the Arctic Circle, for example) may also be considered in political terms as part of the Global South.

In Levon's (2017) critique of the northern bias of Coupland's (2016) edited book on sociolinguistic debates, the problem is explained in terms of "the geopolitical positioning of the various contributions" (p.280) being almost exclusively in the North: The effects of the overwhelming majority of contributors being located in the Global North (and primarily in North America and Western Europe), he suggests, are twofold: On the one hand "it makes it seem as if sociolinguistics does not take place outside of North America and Western Europe, whereas this is clearly not the case". It is unfortunate and limiting that sociolinguists from elsewhere – Africa, South America, or South and East Asia – are not included. On the other hand, this absence perpetuates "a particular geopolitics of knowledge that privileges Northern perspectives and prevents Southern scholars from contributing a differently positioned interpretation of events and practices that concern them" (pp.280–281). This critique, which closely aligns with many issues we will be dealing with in this book, points to two kinds of omission: First, scholars from outside Europe and North America are not included, which means generally that these contexts of research are also not included; and second, alternative epistemologies that might derive from these southern contexts (southern epistemologies) are not as a result given any space.

It is important to note that the two issues are different: Scholars in the geographical South may well do research on local contexts but may do so from what might be called northern perspectives. Trained in the major institutions of the North (or in departments in the South that have nonetheless adopted these knowledge frameworks), these academics' intellectual capital is based on the goods they have gained through an elite education. Thus, being from the geographical South, and even looking at southern contexts, is by no means a guarantor of southern epistemologies. And in any case, if the Global South may include regions of the geographical North, then we need to consider this issue from a more complex perspective. Certainly on the one hand, there is a problem that a book such as Coupland (2016) – a book which from most other perspectives is a key text in the discipline – does not engage with southern perspectives, or include contexts from the Global South, even though it does include authors located geographically in the South. On this point Levon's (2017) critique seems equivocal as to whether the issue is geographical or geopolitical, since it suggests Australia and Singapore (this latter falling below the North–South line that is usually used to divide the world geopolitically) may be in the South. Yet should we not also consider, on the other hand, the focus of the texts themselves? Is perhaps a discussion of the inequality before the law of Indigenous Australians (Eades, 2016) a southern perspective, even if Australia is considered to be in the Global North and the author herself is not Indigenous Australian (we return to questions of positionality below)?

Here, then, we can see the complexity and challenges of the idea of the Global South: It is one thing to critique a sociolinguistics text for its exclusion of scholars, contexts, and frameworks from the geopolitical South, but it is a more complex question to decide what constitutes a southern context or perspective, once it is acknowledged that the South may also be in the North, and that the geographical South by no means guarantees a southern viewpoint. A book on the sociolinguistics of global cities (Smakman and Heinrich, 2018) approaches this slightly differently: The editors divide the book into North and South perspectives. This division (Archer, 2013) locates 'world cities' in the global North – "affluent and increasingly post-industrial countries" – and 'megacities' in the global South – "relatively poor and often post-colonial countries" (Smakman and Heinrich, 2018, p.6). From this perspective, Sydney sits firmly in the Global North – ranked 15th in the world (one behind Los Angeles) in terms of its 'magneticism' (its capacity to attract businesses and people from around the world) – along with London, Tokyo, Paris, the Randstad area of the Netherlands, Los Angeles, and Moscow. This makes a clear statement about the geopolitical framework of the book – the cities in the Global South are Cairo, Mexico, São Paulo, Dubai, and Kohima (India) – while also drawing attention to the point that the Global South does not mean south of the equator (Sydney is south of the equator while Cairo, Mexico, Dubai, and Kohima are to the north). Dubai, however, is a more difficult city to locate in geopolitical terms. Only São Paulo, as one of the vast, expanding, and troubled megacities of the world, is firmly in the South in all senses.

Just as the wealthy cities of the South may be positioned in the North, so southern perspectives may be brought to bear on places located in the North, nowhere more obviously than when dealing with the *circumpolar North* regions such as Finnmark (northern Norway) or Northern Canada within the Arctic Circle (Hayman et al., 2018; Lane and Makihara, 2017). This is where the issues shared by many Indigenous people (Indigenous Australians, First Nations people in North America, or Sámi in the far north of Europe) can come together under a Global South perspective (*Fourth World* was a related term within the First/Second/Third World framework; see Chapter 2). These are people sharing similar concerns of a settler colonial history – and for many the 'postcolonial' label is roundly rejected: As Indigenous Australian Bobbi Sykes asked, "What? Postcolonialism? Have they left?" (cited in Smith, 2012, p.25) – of continued poverty, battles over land rights, problems of health, substance abuse and unemployment, and struggles to maintain linguistic and cultural practices in the face of entrenched discrimination. The very commonality of Indigenous struggles points to the importance of a common term to describe them. Clearly, however, the Global South or southern perspectives terminology is straining here to refer to people whose geographical northernness, and solidarity with other Indigenous inhabitants of the circumpolar North, also seems to define them.

Relatedly, then, Indigenous Australians may be in the Global South while Sydney is in the Global North. It is a long journey from rural New South Wales to Sydney – and if this remark seems flippant, it is also very true for many people. This gets more complex if we try to allocate Indigenous Australians living in Sydney into a North/South categorization (about one third – around 70,000 – of the Indigenous population in New South Wales lives in Sydney; Australian Bureau of Statistics, 2018). We therefore have to be careful about lumping cities or countries into these broad categories. A similar and often unacknowledged problem occurs in the World Englishes framework, where alongside the lack of clarity as to whether we were dealing with history, politics, varieties of language, or speakers (Bruthiaux, 2003), the problem of placing countries into circles overlooks considerable internal variation. Malaysia, for example, has generally been located in the Outer Circle, with its colonial history and its recognizable variety of English used internally, but for whom is English a second-language variety? For a rural Malay or an urban Chinese middle-class family? It is on these grounds that Tupas and Rubdy (2015) urge us to think in terms of 'unequal Englishes' rather than nation-based varieties: Who has access to what kinds of English and how are different types of English valued? A problem for both areas of work – Southern Theory and World Englishes – is therefore the continuing states-centric focus of many studies of global relations. An emphasis on national GDP, for example, suggests that when it rises above a certain point, a country may move into the Global North (various South American countries, such as Chile, are sometimes now shown as part of the Global North), overlooking the deep internal inequalities within nations.

Likewise, then, we need to be cautious about placing cities or countries into our North/South divide. This became an issue in attempts to understand the *metrolingual practices* of a city such as Sydney (Otsuji and Pennycook, 2018). The argument about studying *metrolingual practices* – local language practices in the city – is that we have to look at specific sites of linguistic interaction rather than demolinguistic mapping of ethnic groupings. In that paper, we focused on Chinese market gardeners and Bangladeshi-owned stores. Of course, both groups of people benefited from the advantages of working in a global city such as Sydney (in the Global North), but these were also people very much at the lower end of the economy, working very long hours, struggling at times to get by. And as we looked at the networks of food production both within the local region (local vegetables grown for local markets) and internationally (dried fish imported from Myanmar), it was clear that these complex relations of economy and work intertwined with globalization from below (Mathews and Vega, 2012), ethnicity and migration. We thus seemed to end up with elements of the Global South (struggles to overcome conditions of inequality in the periphery) within a city of the Global North (a wealthy city with high indicators of social and economic privilege) located in the geographical South.

These tensions are evident throughout much of the writing on the Global South. Even when authors more explicitly point to the Global South, there may also be a tendency to locate it in an ambivalent geographical/geopolitical sense. Ndhlovu (2017), for example, argues for the importance of "the burgeoning scholarship from the Global South (Asia, Africa and Latin America) in calling for pluralization of toolkits we use to look at development discourse" (p.92). Thus, at the same time that he argues for southern epistemologies and a focus on the "affordances and promises that African linguistic diversity and cultural resources hold for creativity and innovation – the key drivers of sustainable economic development and social progress" (p.89), he also adds a geopolitical gloss (Asia, Africa, and Latin America) that locates these epistemologies in particular regions. To be clear, we are very much in accord with Ndhlovu's arguments here – innovation in applied linguistics can indeed be driven precisely by African linguistic diversity and cultural resources – but we also note that the overlap between the geographical South and the Global South may also be potentially exclusionary: The 'Asia, Africa, and Latin America' gloss also overlooks Indigenous and other disenfranchised people located in other parts of the world.

The issue that emerges, then, is that in many cases the 'southern' label is doing various kinds of work: It is a label of political economy that refers to impoverished regions of the world; it is a term for geopolitical relations, with the South starting not below the equator but somewhere south of where the money is (roughly along the Tropic of Cancer, running through Egypt, North India, Bangladesh, South China, and Mexico); it is a term for political struggle, including diverse clashes against poverty, patriarchy, environmental destruction, and discrimination; and it is a term for alternative ways of knowing, of different cosmovisions. As Mignolo (2011b, 2014) reminds us, while the East/West divide was based around a Christian/colonial partition of the world, the North/South divide is a post-WWII division of the world along developed/developing lines. Depending on the locus of enunciation, the Global South may refer to underdeveloped and emerging economies (from a Global North perspective) or, from a southern perspective, to "epistemic places where global futures are being forged by delinking from the colonial matrix of power" (2011b, p.184). Ultimately, however, for Mignolo, a decolonizing project has to step outside this framework since neither East and West nor North and South are positions that a decolonial project can sustain: "decoloniality will no longer be identified with the 'Global South' but it will be in the interstices of a global order that was once divided into 'East' and 'West' and more recently 'North' and 'South'" (2014, VII).

We raise these complications not by any means to undermine the idea of southern perspectives, but rather to draw attention to some of the complexities around the southern or decolonial turn in recent scholarship. Related points, or course, have been made about many other such terms: A positive spin can be put on the 'Third World' label, for example, though it already problematically positions parts of the world in historical, geopolitical, and numerical terms; or on 'underdevelopment' (the intention may be to point to the active processes of unequal development) though it is hard to escape the implications of relative scales of progress (for further discussion, see Chapter 2). Similarly, then, the 'south' part of Global South (not to mention the 'global' part) brings with it certain tensions. The 'decolonial' agenda also presents various concerns (Savransky, 2017; and see Chapter 6). So, let us try to be clear about the position we are taking. Pointing to these flaws, tensions, and contradictions around the North/South terminology does not mean that we are trying to show this is unworkable. It may perhaps be the case that in trying to address such a wide range of concerns – the struggles of precarious workers and the unemployed, of documented and undocumented migrants and refugees, of victims of sexism, homophobia, and racism, of ethnic and religious minorities (Santos, 2012, 2018) – within the idea of southern epistemologies, that the framework overreaches itself, that the concerns become too diverse to deal with. It may also be the case that the notion of the South, as some decolonial theorists argue, is one we need to escape, yet the issues of global inequality, institutional racism, and inappropriate application of inappropriate knowledge remain.

This brings to the fore important questions for applied linguistics: How can we deal with the inequalities in global knowledge production, the lack of inclusion of scholars from outside the dominant regions, the imposition of inappropriate frameworks to address language and education outside the central places and institutions? The point is that these things matter. They mattered to us when we wrote about *disinventing* language (Makoni and Pennycook, 2007) – northern ideas about language were doing damage to southern communities – and they matter to us now even more so in an era in which issues about globalization, truth regimes, race, and immigration have become such significant public concerns. They matter too because it may be the case that things are getting worse: Rather than becoming more inclusive, there is evidence that the field is becoming narrower (see Chapter 5). While processes of decolonization at least brought questions of southern multilingualism into the purview of language policy and planning (in nonetheless problematic and shallow terms), for many areas of applied linguistics, the rest of the world has become simply irrelevant. So we have chosen to stay with the idea of southern epistemologies or a southern view of applied linguistics, in order to open up for discussion ways in which applied linguistics needs to engage in much more profound ways with concerns about disenfranchisement, colonial histories, and global inequalities, with the exclusion of scholars and contexts from many parts of the world, with the need to reject claims to universalism and to seek instead a wider set of ideas and forms of knowledge. And this, as we argue in the next section, presents possibilities for innovation and renewal.

Innovations: Reinventing applied linguistics

When we talk of 'gazing from the south', there is more at stake than a shifting geographical perspective. Southern perspectives present a range of innovative possibilities and epistemological challenges for contemporary applied linguistics. In each chapter of this book, in line with the focus of this series, we will address these in sections labelled 'innovations' and 'challenges'. A southern perspective, we argue, does much more than merely challenge the North to be more inclusive: It brings "radical hope", creates opportunities for "balanced judgement and measured insight" and creates space for "imaginative excellence" (Heller and McElhinny, 2017, p.xv; citing Hannah Arendt, 1968, and Junot Diaz, 2016). For Savransky, it is not only a question of the development of epistemologies of the South but also the cultivation of a *decolonial imagination* (p.13) that "demands of us that we risk imagining an entirely different relationship between knowledge and reality" (Savransky, 2017, p.18). More specifically, this makes room for a renewal of applied linguistics founded on ideals not only of inclusivity but also, more importantly, of secularism, tolerance, diversity, equality, and democracy, a form of "bottom-up subaltern cosmopolitanism" in Santos' (2018, p.8) terms. The southern perspectives we discuss in this book offer fresh perspectives, new understandings, and alternative ways of doing applied linguistics.

These perspectives for renewal will become more evident throughout the book but can be sketched out briefly here. The next chapter lays out some of the background theoretical and geopolitical concerns, reviewing key ideas within southern, Indigenous, and decolonial theories, and explaining the implications of these challenges to northern, western, colonial, and modernist epistemologies. Also explored in this chapter are disparities within the Global South: There is no uniform or ideal Global South framework. Chapter 3 returns to more obviously applied linguistic themes, and in particular ways in which we understand language and multilingualism. Although some have noted a *multilingual turn* (May, 2014; Ortega, 2013) in applied linguistics – both English language education (viewing English from a multilingual rather than a monolingual perspective) and sociolinguistics (with a proliferation of studies of fluid language practices and new terminologies) – the politics of how we understand multilingualism remain complex and contested. Do new ways of talking about multilingualism, and the recognition that multilingualism is the global norm, really take us far enough in recognizing a diversity of ways of using language, or are they potentially retrogressive? Are the new translingual terminologies so new or rather perhaps an appropriation of ideas about language that have been circulating in the South for a long time (Heugh and Stroud, 2018)? Can reappropriations of these terminologies through ideas such as *ubuntu translanguaging* (Makalela, 2018a, b, c) take us forward in our thinking about multilingualism? At the very least, such questions suggest that innovation in applied linguistics cannot rest in self-satisfied contentment at having (re)discovered multilingualism: There are far more pressing concerns about what this means and for whom.

Let us try a brief reversal of possibilities to shed light on what is at stake here. Imagine for example, that global politics and colonial history had played out differently and what we are now calling the Global South had become a dominant political and economic force. Scholars from the Global South, located in their well-funded central institutions in Mumbai, Montevideo, Maputo, Manila, Mogadishu, and elsewhere would base their universalizing claims on languages with tones, clicks, and a wide range of structures, and their assumptions about language use on complex chains of multilingualism. Indeed they might not even be so inclined to talk about separate languages as distinct entities, and they would struggle to get their heads around the strange set of ideas in the North that it is possible to look at one thing called a language separate from its surrounds, its history, geography, and politics, or that people could speak only one language, or that you needed a special term to describe people that spoke more than one. No good reason to invite these backward northerners down South to participate in any discussion of language use. Now one might immediately object to this fantasy on the grounds that, say, the development of such institutions would require a particular path of modernity which would lead to similar language outcomes to those that now pertain in the North, but if there's one thing we've learned from the critiques of development discourse (see Chapter 2), there is no one pathway towards one notion of modernity, and certainly singularity, standardization, and submission are not necessary for being modern. Or one might, more interestingly, propose that such academics might not claim universalism for their ideas. There is no good reason to claim that universalizing is a necessary aspect of good scholarship. So perhaps those strange northern scholars would get off more lightly, and be able to continue their odd studies of isolated things called languages as the minority activity it really has always been.

But let us return to the world as it is. A major focus of northern scholarship in relation to southern multilingualisms has centred on language endangerment, language rights, and language revitalization. Indeed, one of the problematic ways in which a southern perspective is sometimes taken up is that it is assumed that a view from the South will involve 'diversity' (where the singularities of the North are multiplied in the South) and language endangerment (where languages are threatened by other languages). While much of this apparently well-meaning work has sought to develop language policies in favour of local languages (alongside other work and agencies promoting European languages), it has operated from several flawed premises. In Chapter 4, we argue that this understanding of language has been based firmly in northern epistemologies, promoting concepts of language choice and ethnicity that are alien to most southern contexts. By elevating languages over people, it has been unable to deal with the real issues of poverty, change, and discrimination faced by many language users in the Global South. This chapter points to the importance of rethinking the raciolinguistic frameworks (Rosa and Flores, 2017) that have informed this work for so long. It also points to ways in which recent work around the idea of *language reclamation* (e.g. Leonard, 2017) has started to open up some alternative ways of thinking about what is at stake when we talk about languages, revival, communities, and world views.

Rethinking language along these lines opens up a range of new possibilities for applied linguistics. One of the implications of this reorientation of northern concerns about language endangerment is that arguments about educational provision in European or local languages need to be rethought. Central to any applied linguistic endeavour are questions of language education. The issue for much of the

Global South is not just about developing multilingual and mother tongue educational solutions but also rethinking language for educational purposes. What is language and what roles can it play in the fast-changing educational domains of the Global South? The implications of a reframed understanding of multilingualism in terms of language vitality (Mufwene, 2017) make it possible to move forward from questions of choosing between one or other language of instruction or evaluation (Antia, 2018) and to consider instead the possibility of a more dynamic set of language-in-education provisions. This is part of the larger project of decolonizing the field. For Santos (2018, p.116), epistemologies of the South are "part of the vast current of decolonizing thinking". In Chapter 5, we engage with this topic in more depth asking both how different areas of applied linguistics – language teaching, second language acquisition, discourse analysis, and so on – might be decolonized, and what it means to decolonize educational institutions. Bringing together questions of southern education, southern knowledge, and southern language, we can start to see how applied linguistics may be renewed from alternative perspectives, as well as the importance of locally grounded solutions to educational problems.

Central to any project of renewal in applied linguistics must also be the question of research. The challenges of conducting research in and around Indigenous and southern communities has attracted considerable debate in anthropological and other domains. How, as an outsider, to access and avoid doing damage to those communities and their forms of language and knowledge, and how, as an insider, to bring alternative ways of thinking into mainstream domains without their dismissal or co-option? How can applied linguistics engage with alternative ways of knowing from particular standpoints? Looking at questions of research, ethics, and knowledge, Chapter 6 raises questions for how, by whom, and with whom research is conducted and who ultimately benefits from such research. The questions have direct relevance to issues about social ownership of languages, grammars, and dictionaries, particularly of minority languages. And for applied linguistics it raises the questions of how both research processes and research outcomes would look different if on the one hand more research emerged from the Global South and on the other if applied linguists learned to listen to other perspectives, to understand how language is understood differently in other contexts, to appreciate that whatever expertise in multilingualism, language policy, and language education we may be able to claim, it is only useful knowledge if it makes sense locally, a perspective that can only be achieved by understanding time-tested and accepted practice (Prah, 2017). This raises the further question of Indigenous forms of knowledge and we dwell at some length on the significance of alternative cosmovisions for thinking about language, place, things, and the world.

A central concern for this book is that applied linguistics has rather lost its way in recent years, becoming a somewhat moribund area of work marked by internal squabbles over models of language development, and interminable debates about the relation between linguistics and applied linguistics. One of our goals, therefore, is to make applied linguistics matter again by embracing the challenges of the

South. A tired discipline may be reinvigorated through southern insights. An applied linguistics that can embrace Global South perspectives needs researchers who are culturally grounded, political engaged, continuously self-reflexive, and capable of adopting dialectic and multiple perspectives on data. Part of the agenda here is to widen sociolinguists' and applied linguists' "epistemological repertoire" (Di Carlo, 2018, p. 140) so that research methods, interpretive tools, and interventionist and applied projects are far better attuned to social and cultural contexts that are outside the mainstream experiences of contemporary applied linguistics. Innovation in applied linguistics is not going to be achieved by yet another, even more complex model of second language acquisition, but rather by a renewal of the field by learning to *think otherwise*.

Challenges: On thinking twice and positionality

A project that seeks to undo many key assumptions of applied linguistics and to do so by drawing on less well-established perspectives from outside the mainstream wellsprings of intellectual work is clearly open to some challenges. While we might be critical of global knowledge hierarchies, some would argue that these exist for very good reasons: Not all knowledge is as good as any other. An argument that applied linguistics needs to be more inclusive of southern voices may be quite palatable, given the generally liberal orientation to inclusivity in the field (multilingual, multicultural, and even multimodal orientations, for example, can all be read as frameworks that seek to include people, cultures, languages, and modalities that have previously been ignored). But a more critical perspective that seeks not only inclusion but also questions many of the assumptions of northern applied linguistics on the basis that its frameworks are inappropriate for the majority world raises more difficult questions. The argument that southern voices need a greater place in the debates raises several concerns: Is this an issue merely of being more attentive to those linguists from the South who have often been overlooked because of the focus of their work (work on African languages "doesn't sell"), the places they publish (books and articles published outside the major publishing outlets do not reach the Centre), the style of their work (not always conforming to the academic norms of the Centre), or the languages they publish in (publish in a major language, and preferably English, or your work will be ignored), or is there more at stake here?

Once we start to think in terms of what Santos (2018, p.43) calls *artisanal knowledges* – "practical, empirical, popular knowledges, vernacular knowledges that are very diverse but have one feature in common: They were not produced separately, as knowledge practices separated from other social practices" – we are opening up a space not just for other, scientific facts, but for other ways of knowing. This means not only being attentive to those academics from the South who have been overlooked but also listening more broadly to popular understandings of language in the South. The issue is not merely of one set of academics (the North) overlooking another (the South) but also of the field more generally overlooking a different kind of voice: Local, everyday understandings of language and culture. This argument takes us partly in the direction of 'folk linguistics' (Preston, 1996), or what people think about language(s) themselves. From this perspective, it is important to understand how people orient towards different ways of speaking, while still contrasting such knowledge with how language varieties really operate (folk dialectologies as opposed to real dialectologies). A more political approach to global knowledge formation, however, takes the position not only that different ways of thinking about language from the South may be important, but also that we need to listen to other kinds of knowledge, other kinds of voices. Nowhere does this become more important than in questions of language reclamation, education, or research (see Chapters 4–6), where it has been strongly emphasized that unless academics from the North are able to listen, accommodate, and balance their knowledge of language with that of their southern interlocutors, their research or advice will have little hope of being either appropriate or accepted.

A strong epistemological politics challenges specialized knowledge more profoundly and makes a case for a greater role for local forms of knowledge about languages, their use, their social and cultural roles, their place in education. As Dasgupta (1997) notes, "the specialists in individual disciplines insist on thinking just once, and on ensuring only internal accountability" (p.24). This is akin to De Souza's (2017) discussion, drawing on Santos (2002, 2004a), of 'lazy thinking' (*razão indolente*) or what Dasgupta sees as an "overcodification that empowers only masters of accounting", reinforcing "the private arrogances of particular disciplines" (1997, p.24) and disenfranchising newcomers, outsiders, and the wider public. Dasgupta goes on to argue that linguists actually need the responsibility of "thinking twice and of representing the public interest in the realm of thinking" in order to avoid the narrowness of a disciplinary focus that is only engaged in discussion with itself (1997, p.24). In the context of applied linguistics from the South, this implies a major shift from treating southern others as research objects and informants to a more inclusive and disruptive role as knowledge creators and co-constructors.

Some may be sceptical about challenges to the "private arrogances" of disciplines since the whole point of developing a discipline, a set of theories, an academic domain, a body of knowledge, research methods, and so on is precisely to overcome ordinary people's ideas about things. People have all sorts of prejudiced, misguided, or simply ill-informed ideas about language and the point of applied linguistics is to present a much more careful account of what is going on. If this view perhaps sounds a bit elitist, we should also be careful not to dismiss it. Advising parents and teachers that bilingualism may be beneficial rather than harmful (even if done from a somewhat constricted vision of what bilingualism can mean), advising governments on the benefits of mother tongue education (even if the discussion often lacks insights into more complex language ecologies), explaining that language is always undergoing change and that alarms about deterioration are mistaken (even if such positions often fail to grasp the broader politics of such arguments) – these and many more roles played by applied linguists who know a lot about language and have studied it in depth are important and we'd be foolish to want to throw them out. And yet, the assumptions behind positions on bilingualism, mother tongue education, language change, and so forth also have to be understood as articulated from within a particular set of understandings of language and ideological views of society.

Orthodox applied linguistics takes a view of language as a given and thus assumes that it is dealing with "determinate rule-based systems called 'languages'" (Harris, 1990, p.49), rather than asking the more useful question as to how our beliefs about language derive from communicational processes. So, a first observation is that while expertise may be really useful, we should also be very sceptical about some of the unexamined premises on which such expertise is based and guard against expertise being tyrannical, colonizing our visions of language. Albury's (2016) study of folk linguistic attitudes to te reo Māori in Aotearoa/New Zealand points to the problem of "universal language revitalization theories that draw on Western European perspectives on language but assume universal relevance" (p.306) and shows instead how many assumptions about standardization, literacy, and corpus planning are questioned from Māori standpoints. From this perspective, "folk linguistic research methods can contribute to the decolonization of sociolinguistic theory and method by understanding, voicing, legitimizing, and ultimately applying more ontologies and epistemologies of language than those that generally premise current scholarship" (Albury 2017, p.37) As we shall discuss in greater depth in later chapters, this has major implications for how we think about multilingualism, language reclamation, and research more generally.

When we return to the question of what it means to try to understand language from a southern perspective, there are a number of issues at stake. The point here is not to dismiss northern canons of linguistic knowledge in favour of everyday ideas about language from the South. But neither is it to accept linguistic knowledge at the expense of such perspectives. The aim, first, is to become far more sceptical about canonical applied linguistic knowledge, based as it is on knowledge developed from a particular perspective, based on particular languages and contexts. A second goal is then to become far more attentive both to scholarly and everyday perspectives from elsewhere. This is about learning to 'think twice', to be open to different perspectives, and to learn to listen. An applied linguist who cannot hear other perspectives is not much of an applied linguist.

The question of positionality, as well as what has been termed the 'locus of enunciation' (Mignolo, 2000, 2002) is an issue that has circled uncomfortably around these discussions for many years. There are several difficult issues here: Who can speak for whom? What gives one the position to speak on these matters? How are academic legitimacy and credibility to be bestowed? Here we encounter the fraught territory of whether a 'southern' background (being from India, Latin America, or parts of Africa, for example, though as discussed above such a background is not a guarantee of perspective and southern localities may also be in the North) endows one with a particular position to speak, write, or research from a southern perspective. A Global South perspective already brings several challenges to such a proposition, since it might well be argued that academics moving from one privileged background in the southern hemisphere (an elite education in India, for example) to a position of privilege in the northern hemisphere (a generously-endowed professorship at an American university) are in fact little more than migrants within a cosmopolitan Global North. And once one has worked and studied for a number of years in these northern institutions, further challenges come from scholars who have remained in the South (Cusicanqui, 2012).

Would the late Braj Kachru ever have come up with a notion of Indian English, or World Englishes, if he had remained in India (Krishnaswamy and Burde, 1998)? This question cuts both ways: Perhaps one has to leave to see the picture – one can only conceive of an unlikely notion such as Indian English with the aid of the external gaze from elsewhere – but perhaps if one has left, one fails to grasp the local realities – the very idea that to talk of 'Indian English' is to operate with a particular set of nationalistic assumptions and to speak from the position of a "non-resident native who talks about 'Indian English' in some sort of native English" (Krishnaswamy and Burde, 1998, p.30). One can understand why the construct 'Indian English' becomes a usable idea to those "who live outside, and so elusive to those who look at it from the inside. Like Indian nationalism, 'Indian English' is 'fundamentally insecure' since the notion 'nation-India' is insecure" (p.63). The bigger problem, as Parakrama (1995, p.17) notes, is that linguists working within the World Englishes paradigm "cannot do justice to those Other Englishes as long as they remain within the over-arching structures that these Englishes bring to crisis". To take these new/other Englishes seriously, Parkrama continues, "would require a fundamental revaluation of linguistic paradigms, and not merely a slight accommodation or adjustment." So, as Parakrama urges, the issue is not just of an Indian speaking about Indian English but about the need to rethink the framework from which one does so.

The idea of the locus of enunciation can be helpful here since it points not only to the literal place and body from which one speaks but also the discourses that one takes up and challenges. White South African scholars should not be excluded from being able to write about South Africa (though the fact they remain the dominant voice needs to be challenged), and Black African scholars working elsewhere should not be assumed, by dint of their background, to have the last word on African concerns (though they should clearly have more of a voice than they are given now). Nor should African Americans be given the final say on African American studies (though surely their voice should be the dominant one). Who we should listen to and why we should listen are political questions about what is being said, in whose interests, and on what grounds. What, then, of our own positions as authors? What claims can we make to write as southern scholars, of southern contexts, for southern audiences, about southern concerns? It would be tempting, of course, to suggest that this book has emerged from a North/South dialogue between the two of us, either based on our geographical locations – Pennycook in the South (Australia) and Makoni in the North (USA) – or conversely based on our geopolitical origins – Makoni from the South (Southern Africa) and Pennycook from the North (UK or Australia). If the first proposition falls apart for obvious reasons (Sydney, as already discussed, may sit geographically in the South, but is better placed geopolitically in the North), the second is also problematic (geopolitical origins do not account adequately for current political alignments). So, let us avoid simplistic accounts of North/South dialogues and identity politics, and try to grasp a more nuanced account that also sheds light on the broader complexities of North/South relations.

As we have seen, the geographical and geopolitical locations of North and South are themselves complexly intertwined, and neither qualify nor disqualify either of us as writers about the Global South. We have both switched hemispheres for a major part of our academic careers, one, having lived and studied for many years in the northern hemisphere, now working in the South (Sydney) and the other, having moved in the opposite direction. Southern Theory should not depend only on ideas from or about the South – though as we shall see, this remains a constant site of contestation – but is concerned with the role of the Global South in the global present and in contemporary thinking (Comaroff and Comaroff, 2012). Sinfree Makoni sees himself as a pan-Africanist having grown up in southern Africa and studied for his junior degree in Ghana before working in southern Africa. In addition to being a pan-Africanist he regards himself as a diasporic Africanist constantly negotiating the construction of knowledge between the Global North and Global South. Although he professionally works in a major rural university, he has over the years developed a sedimented ambivalent relationship with his site of work, an ambivalence which filters through his interpretation of the nature of applied linguistics in the Global South. Makoni works at the interface between the North and South as part of a struggle to reduce academic hierarchies and to shift what knowledge counts in applied linguistics. It is the political project to develop African sociolinguistics that matters here, though it is one that cannot be disentangled from this life trajectory.

Pennycook's work has constantly sought to open up alternatives to the dominant paradigms of thought. This battle has emerged from an understanding of the politics of knowledge and a concern about what counts and what is dismissed in domains such as applied linguistics. Pennycook's critical applied linguistic project (2001) has always sought out alternative forms of knowledge: One aspect of this work that has often disconcerted readers is that it is a project of uncertainty, an endeavour to explore an open-ended politics in relation to a critique of language. He has also lived a life of (privileged) mobility, living and working in different parts of the world, and feeling, like Said (1999) always 'out of place' (Pennycook, 2012). In contemporary class terms and by dint of our established positions (however much we may critique that establishment and the hand that feeds us), we are doubtless many miles away from the disenfranchised of the Global South. And while that has almost always been the way of things – from Frantz Fanon to Cheikh Anta Diop, from Walter Mignolo to Gayatri Spivak, critics of racial and colonial orders have written from positions of elite educational privilege – it remains a tension without easy resolution. But it is also important to see this as a complexly collaborative project: Not merely a northern scholar based in the South working with a southern scholar based in the North, nor only discussions and debates and writing infused with the criss-crossing trajectories of North and South, but also long histories of listening to many others over the years. We like to think of ourselves in dialogue with a polycentric world of concerned others.

Conclusion

Let us try to reiterate what is at stake here. There remains in applied linguistics a deplorable blindness towards contexts outside the Global North. In book after book, conference after conference, article after article, academics from a narrow range of contexts – mainly European and North American – discuss research on specific contexts and generalize these to the wider world. Under claims of commonality – of a shared humanity, a universal language capacity, a collective interest in the discipline – classed, raced, and locality-based understandings of language use are assumed to be applicable to the majority world elsewhere. While the ways in which these differences are framed – the majority world, the Global North and South, the West and the Rest, First and Third Worlds, developed and developing societies – and the concerns that are highlighted within these frameworks – economic, political, social, epistemological, and other disparities – remain points of continuing discussion and dispute, it is nevertheless clear that an inequitable knowledge hierarchy ensures that certain assumptions about language, diversity, and education are given precedence over other possibilities elsewhere. And when this northern gaze does fall on its southern neighbours, such assumptions continue in ways of thinking about multilingualism, mother tongue education, language preservation, second language acquisition, discourse analysis, or research.

It is sometimes assumed that southern multilingualism must be about language endangerment or diversity. But this need not be the case at all. This is more about the northern rush to worry about saving languages for the good of humanity or to marvel at the complexity of language resources in southern contexts. To assume that the South is diverse or that languages are endangered is to continue to gaze from northern perspectives. This is not to say that many southern contexts aren't places of great diversity, nor that many languages may cease to be used. Rather, it is to challenge the assumptions both that such concerns are essentially what matter in the South and that the notions of diversity or endangerment make sense in such contexts. We want to raise more important questions than mother-tongue education or language endangerment, not so much because they don't matter, but rather because they are ill-framed. And to change this means not only listening to alternative questions, but listening to other ways of framing the world, other epistemologies and ontologies.

Our project of applied linguistics from a southern perspective seeks to address the *darker side of applied linguistics* (cf. Mignolo, 2011a): The deep ties of the colonial and neocolonial projects to language teaching; the exocitization of differences that reinforces the construction of racialized and ethnicized Others; the normative assumptions about gendered and sexual relations that obscure the politics of sexuality. In order to redress these deep-seated concerns, we need not merely to encourage a more inclusive applied linguistics that opens the doors to southern voices and encourages more research on and from southern contexts; we need to open up to a much wider range of possibilities (what we later call an *Ubuntu-Nepantla* way of thinking and doing). The challenge, therefore, is about more than an agenda of southern inclusion but rather of expanding epistemological repertoires, of opening up to the obligation to understand that inquiries into applied linguistic concerns elsewhere in the world must also be inquiries into other ways of thinking that offer possibilities of disciplinary renewal. Southern Theory is not a fixed body of knowledge but rather an emergent set of possibilities, and it is towards an engagement with these possibilities that we move in this book.

2
THE MAKING OF THE SOUTH IN APPLIED LINGUISTICS

This second chapter lays out some of the background theoretical and geopolitical concerns around southern theories. We draw attention to several important themes: If we are, as has been claimed, witnessing a 'decolonial turn' (Maldonado-Torres, 2007) in the social sciences – a recent (Nov 2018) open letter by 80 French intellectuals objecting to the emphasis on "racialisme, différentialisme, ségrégationnisme" in the decolonial movement in France (Le Point, 2018) points to the breadth of this movement and the strength of opposition to it – and if, as Santos (2018) suggests, *epistemologies of the South* are coming of age, it is nonetheless important to appreciate that the struggle for Southern Theory has a long history, from colonial opposition, through Third World solidarity, to postcolonial resistance. While contemporary Southern Theory and the decolonial option attempt to draw distinctions between their own current frameworks and their antecedents– suggesting, for example, that older work continued to derive from northern epistemologies – understanding this lineage is important if we are to see that Southern Theory hasn't just sprung into being in the 21st century as some scholars become more aware of the political and epistemological needs to engage more profoundly with diversity and global inequality.

Equally important is the need to consider the material conditions of inequality within which these discussions of epistemologies are occurring. As Castells (2000) made clear at the turn of the millennium, and as more recent analyses such as Piketty (2014) have also reinforced, global inequality has been on the increase. There are any number of figures to show both the extent of and the increase in global inequality: The income ratio between the richest 20 per cent of people in the world and the poorest 20 per cent, for example, increased from 30:1 in 1960 to 74:1 in 1997 (Castells, 2000, p.79). There are endless statistics such as these, though a better understanding of what is at stake here can often be understood in more tangible terms, such as malnutrition. Consider, for example, the educational implications of 150 million children under 5 (or about one third of children under 5 in the Global South) having stunted growth (largely irreversible effects of insufficient nutrient intake leading to delayed motor development, impaired cognitive function, and poor school performance) and a further 50 million being wasted (a strong predictor of infant mortality). Set against another figure of poor nutrition – the 38 million children under 5 who are overweight – and the picture becomes starker (Development Initiatives, 2018). The burden of these problems is felt across many parts of Africa, but it is important to remind ourselves too that malnutrition occurs across the world and may be seen in poor inner-city communities in the North.

To take another dimension – migration, displacement, and education – with complex implications not only for those who move but also for those who stay, as well as those who host migrants and refugees, the pedagogical ramifications are multiple (UNESCO, 2018). There are compound factors at play here, from international refugees fleeing conflict and natural disasters, to internal displacement (Syria and Venezuela currently sit high on both measures) – there are around 40 million internally displaced people around the world – and internal migration from rural to urban areas for work. All have major implications for the education of the often-young populations involved: Educational disruption in the area people are leaving, absence from school during processes of migration, and lack of provision in host countries. There are frequently further forms of exclusion from education affecting girls. Many other ways of looking at global inequalities, particularly in relation to education, are of concern, from educational infrastructures, materials, and teacher salaries, to local conditions of food, shelter, and employment, as well as economic and cultural practices that take children out of school. The point, briefly put, is that these are the real conditions of material inequality that have to be considered when looking at the Global South and North, and while questions of political economy are finally gaining some traction in socio- and applied linguistics (Block, 2018), these are still all too often framed in terms of agendas, concerns, theories, and geopolitical focus from a Global North perspective.

Pinker (2018) has argued for a more optimistic assessment of growing inequality, suggesting both that the calculation of inequality has been misunderstood, and that the social and ethical significance of inequality have been overstated. As in his previous work on violence (Pinker, 2011), he argues an optimistic account (placatory, at least for the Global North, though rather less so for those in the South suffering at the hands of malnutrition and violence), while also making a case for the Eurocentric Enlightenment values of reason, science, humanism, and progress. It is not that we ourselves want to argue instead a dystopian case, nor to reject the legacy of European thought, but rather that our optimism, like that of Santos (2018) or Mignolo and Walsh (2018) derives from the possibilities that come from challenging northern hegemony (and the Enlightenment values deeply allied with the colonial projects that have been a major cause of these inequalities) and from struggle and recognition of other possibilities amid a deeply inequitable world.

Opposition to inequitable global conditions has a long history, with a complicated interweaving of arguments among universalizing frameworks (such as Marxism) that point to global inequalities yet do so from a standpoint that projects their own position as applicable everywhere; approaches from the South that have sought a form of ethno-philosophy of, for example, Chinese or African thought; alternatives that have sought a more inclusive universalism; and frameworks that have pursued other modes of thought based neither in inclusive universalism nor in ethno-philosophical standpoints but rather in local understandings of difference. While the terms *decolonizing*, the *Global South*, and *southern epistemologies* may, at least in some quarters, have superseded other terms, such as the *Third World*, many of these terms overlap in current usage. Work in applied linguistics that tried from different perspectives to grapple with these concerns has therefore done so from a variety of standpoints. One of the most prominent was the centre–periphery model, which informed work such as Phillipson's (1992) view of linguistic imperialism, enabling the argument that "central" Anglo-American institutions had promoted the spread of English in the "periphery" for their own interests. The centre–periphery model is in part rooted in a general theory of underdevelopment that seeks to explain how the centre underdevelops the periphery (Frank, 1966, 1975). While providing a useful heuristic framework for understanding inequality between centre and periphery, this model has always struggled to tease out links between central centres and more local centres and their various peripheries, as well as concerns about how the so-called periphery may resist and appropriate the imposition of languages such as English (Canagarajah, 1999).

Also significant has been world-systems analysis, popularized by Wallerstein (2004) and his colleagues, that informed work such as Blommaert's (2010) *Sociolinguistics of Globalization*, providing a critical framework for understanding the world in terms of scales, from the micro-local to the macro-global. While providing a useful macro-picture of global inequality and avoiding a focus on nation states as the central operators, such work is confronted by the challenges of how to handle endogenous factors and cultural practices. Not so far distant from these orientations was the developed/developing/underdeveloped framework of development and dependency theory. While these terms came into general use (and it is still common to hear talk of developing or underdeveloped societies), from a more critical perspective, these terms were seen as highly problematic and applicable only to the extent that so-called developed societies actively caused the underdevelopment of others, as outlined in Rodney's (1972) *How Europe Underdeveloped Africa*. Important too was the First/Second/Third World distinction that emerged during the Cold War, with different blocs attempting to influence the Third World (or nations unaligned to capitalism or communism). This is not to suggest that Western aid (or contemporary aid by emergent powers such as China)[1] was unilaterally self-serving, but rather to suggest that any notion of underdevelopment has to be seen in terms of inequitable global processes and relational comparisons, and attempts to ameliorate such circumstances always involve particular interests with diverse local implications.

Before the emergence of the North/South distinction, the commonest framing of these issues was the East/West dichotomy, focusing on the political, economic, and cultural dominance of the 'West', while also addressing the West's construction of the East: Said's (1978) *Orientalism* was the key text in this line of critique. For Mignolo (2011b) both the East/West dichotomy (based on a Christian–colonial division of the world) and the North/South dichotomy (based on these northern analyses of global inequality) are frameworks we need to step beyond. More recently, we have seen the use of the minority/majority world distinction that has been useful insofar as it pointed to the fact that the conditions of the Global South were the conditions not of some distant 'minority' but rather of most people in the world. As Slater (2004) notes, despite the different ways in which these terms frame the world, they all draw attention to the dominance of Euro-American commerce, culture, and conceptions. As Connell (2014) puts it, the "normal functioning of the global economy of Knowledge" is a highly political economy that favours "theory produced in the metropole" and marginalizes any forms of knowledge "from the periphery" (p.527).

Awareness, opposition, and resistance to such inequalities also have a long history: "The present has history" Prah (2017, p.18) reminds us. "From the 1880s, the period of the high-noon of imperialist rivalries for colonial territories in Africa which historically panned out as the scramble for Africa, Africans started articulating their rejection of unbridled Westernisms" (2017, p.18). Opposition has persisted, manifesting itself in the Black Consciousness and *Négritude* movements. While on the one hand, "the quest for African self-identity and self-definition" led late colonial or early postcolonial thinkers such as Tempels, Mbiti, Kagame, and Mveng to focus on "African civilizational non-inferiority" and forms of "ethno-philosophy" (Prah, 2017, p.19), later postcolonial philosophers such as Hountondji (2009), Appiah, Towa, Gyeke, Ramose, Oguah, and Wiredu stressed "universals in their African cultural reference points and derivations" (p.19). These struggles can be seen equally in regions such as the Caribbean: It was Aimé Césaire (1913–2008) from Martinique – politician, Frantz Fanon's school teacher, and author of the denunciation of colonial rule, *Discours sur le colonialisme* (Césaire, 1955) – who, with Senegalese writer and politician Léopold Senghor (1906–2001) and Léon Damas from French Guiana (1912–1978), developed in Paris in the 1930s the idea of *négritude,* an affirmation of Black and slave identity (Kesteloot, 1991).

The idea has since been widely critiqued – overlooking at times the politics it articulated: "Je suis de la race de ce qu'on opprime" (Césaire, cited in Sistoeurs, 2008; I am of the race of those who are oppressed), a statement that resonates well with Southern Theory – for its supposed Black essentialism. Both the Nigerian Wole Soyinka, and Césaire's former student, Frantz Fanon, saw in *négritude* a necessary defensiveness about being Black: A tiger does not profess its "tigritude" but leaps on its prey, as Soyinka famously proclaimed in 1962 (cited in Ayobolu, 2017), and the idea of a Black soul, Fanon (1952) argued, was a product of the White gaze. Meanwhile, others in Martinique, such as Édouard Glissant (1981) – influenced by Césaire – developed related ideas such as *Antillanité* (Caribbeanness), emphasizing a shared Caribbean identity that could supersede language differences (Glissant might have much greater affinity with Nobel Laureate, Derek Walcott, than Walcott had with William Golding) while a different position was taken up by Bernabé et al. (1993, p.28), stressing *créolité* in terms of "une annihilation de la fausse universalité, du monolinguisme et de la pureté" (a destruction of false universality, monolingualism and purity). The important question that emerges from all this is *how* to oppose Western/northern/White domination rather than *whether*. The struggle to find ways to combat Western domination, free of Western frameworks, continues. Central to this chapter and book, therefore, is an understanding of knowledge economies and ecologies, and the related sociology of absences within global relations of inequality.

This chapter also emphasizes the point that there are many disparities within the Global South: There is no uniform ideal global South or global southern framework. We also discuss the complex politics of Indigeneity, which intersect with the politics of the Global South. And so, for a southern applied linguistics, the challenge has several facets: How has the discipline been implicated in the making of the Global South? Alan Davies (1996) mockingly accuses Phillipson's linguistic imperialism of suggesting that applied linguists going innocently about their work should feel guilty about what they may have wrought. Yet while Phillipson's (1992) framework has its weaknesses (as do all these frameworks), it at least insists on understanding our complicity in contributing to the support of inequitable language relations. A southern applied linguistics requires adequate accounts of the absences of other ways of thinking and the need for redress; it needs to decolonize many domains of its operation (see Chapter 5), and it has to grasp its moral accountability in terms of all that has been discounted as not important or relevant for the field. We do not have space here to provide a comprehensive overview of the history of global relations and the place of applied linguistics, but a brief account will allow us to see the traditions to which Southern Theory is heir. It also sheds light on the ways in which the focus of attention, from the Third World to the majority world, and from economics to cultural politics, shifts slightly as one framework takes over from another. This chapter goes on to review and explain key ideas within southern, Indigenous, and decolonial theories, and looks at the implications of these challenges to northern, Western, colonial, and modernist epistemologies.

Making the Third World

In order to grasp the contemporary nature of North–South relations, or put another way, how the North became North and the South became South, we need to explore the historical background, first through an understanding of colonialism and subsequently through an appreciation of the ways in which much that happened under colonialism continued, following the formal dismantling of colonial relations. Colonial relations between former colonies and European countries were maintained even after independence, through organizations such as la

Francophonie or the Commonwealth, for former British and French colonies, political alliances along old colonial fault lines, and broad economic settlements favouring particular forms of trade and commerce. This is important not only because of the significance of the long history of northern domination and exclusion of its southern Other but also because we also need to appreciate the long history of opposition. In many ways, Southern Theory is but the latest instantiation of resistance to imperialism, colonialism, and the hegemony of the West or North. While there is considerable debate about whether current conditions of globalization should be seen as another stage in the colonial enterprise – "the coexistence of successive global designs that are part of the imaginary of the modern/colonial world system" (Mignolo, 2000, p.280) – or a more radical break with the past – contemporary "Empire is not a weak echo of modern imperialisms but a fundamentally new form of rule" (Hardt and Negri, 2000, p.146) – it is important to understand both the continuity of colonial exploitation and ideology into the present and the particularity of current neo-liberal conditions.

Despite occasional and rather bizarre attempts to put a good spin on colonial history (Gilley, 2017), colonialism has to be understood as a systematic extraction of wealth and resources from colonized nations. While it is possible now to look with a certain fondness at some of the products of colonial exploitation – the grand colonial buildings, the growth of regional varieties of colonial languages, the emergence of hybrid cultures and religions – colonialism has to be understood as brutal (Walter, 2017), exploitative, and a core reason for the impoverishment of the Global South: European nations were not simply wealthy nations that expanded their capitalist enterprises but rather nations that became wealthy by exploiting their colonies (Blaut, 1993). Colonialism evolved from its early stages when Europeans set out on voyages of discovery, driven both by mercantile interests and a fundamental belief in their own religious rectitude, through a period where European assurity in their cultural and philosophical superiority formed the basis for an era of civilizing the world, to an era when the goal became to conceptualize the world and categorize the people, plants, languages, and cultures that were found, and on to the more recent periods of the late 20th century and early 21st century when globalization takes over from universal and international concepts of the world and the corporatization of many levels of society – the privatization of common ownership and state support for resources, education, health, and transport – has come to predominate within a new neo-liberal politics for the world.

Several concerns for this book need to be pulled out from this potted history. Colonialism and its aftermath produced a wide set of embedded and racialized images of the colonized, from the 'myth of the lazy native' (a view of native people as inherently lazy and thus justifying various forms of labour exploitation; Alatas, 1977) to assumptions that in comparison to the colonizers, the colonized were backward, primitive, superstitious, unclean, and many other things besides. Even some of the names the colonialists gave to the languages spoken by colonized communities reflected such views: The British named the language spoken by the Shona Masvina/Chiswina, meaning "dirty people" (Springer, 1909). From this perspective, as Europe orientalized other parts of the world, it was always constructing itself as the counterpart. Singh (1996) points to the "characteristic Orientalizing tropes of difference producing an ontological distinction between West and East, defining the Orient in terms of everything the Occident is not: decadent, weak, barbaric, feminine" (p.59). The British view of India, for example, "as a land of dirt, disease, and sudden death" (Metcalf, 1995, p.171) only became possible in relation to a construction of Britain as a land of health, cleanliness, and longevity: "Calcutta, one might say, became filthy only as London became clean" (Metcalf, 1995, p.173). This imagined West, of course, also erased social and economic class differences within the metropole, at least when it was convenient to do so, while at other times making clear links between all that was seen as inferior: Working-class people, women, femininity, and colonial subjects. Thus, while the West imagined the Orient as decadent and uncivilized, it concurrently imagined itself into being in terms of "the Western version of Western civilization (its own self-description) ingrained in the imaginary of the modern/colonial world" (Mignolo, 2000, p.328). As Venn (2000) makes clear, this process gradually established Western modernity "as the privileged, if not hegemonic, form of sociality, tied to a universalizing and totalizing ambition" (p.19).

In the latter part of the 20th century, colonial relations were transformed into a set of political and economic dependencies that were only partly mitigated by formal independence. With the major powers of the North locked in the 'Cold War' dispute between capitalism (the First World) and socialism (the Second World), former colonies and other countries that had been victims of colonial plunder were now caught up in a new battle to include the 'Third World' as part of a sphere of capitalist or communist influence. Closely associated with these struggles was a range of assumptions about "development" and "modernization". The picture of the world that emerged was one in which certain nations were considered modern and developed, and they had a duty, though often a very self-interested and market-oriented one, to help other nations to 'develop'. Linked to this view was an evolutionist understanding of the world, suggesting that modernization followed a linear path of upward progress, moving from one side of a series of dichotomous constructs – traditional, undeveloped, agricultural, rural – to the other – modern, developed, industrial, urban. These dichotomies could be resolved, these gaps could be closed, it was argued, through a process of "modernization".

Amongst the many problems with the evolutionary model of development, several need to be highlighted for the discussion here. While more recent views have shifted from the Keynesian interventionist policies of the 1960s to the marketplace orientations of monetarism and neo-liberalism, this central paradigm that bifurcates the world into developed and undeveloped, and prescribes an economic package for modernization, has stayed much the same in many circles (see, for example, Schultz, 1980). It became evident that most supposed development aid was based on the economic and political interests of the donor country rather than the recipient. The strongest criticisms of these policies came, not surprisingly, from

Third World countries themselves: "The Third World itself began to experience a measure of disenchantment, when it discovered that development aid was not really aid, but a business investment camouflaged to look like development aid" (Gibbons, 1985, p.40). The aid did not reach the most vulnerable, and at least in Africa aid has done little to change the economic trajectory of African economies, an argument well-articulated in Dambisa Moyo's (2009) book: *Dead Aid: Why Aid is not working and how there is a better way for Africa*. In many cases, aid forced local producers out of business because the easy availability of goods through aid militated against the development of local industries. While aid to many countries often produced limited benefits, donor countries, by contrast, gained in multiple ways through aid from former colonial countries. According to statistics released by the House of Commons (8 February 2018, *Business Ghana*), for example, there are a total of 976,288 healthcare workers in the NHS of whom 5,405 are Nigerians, 3,899 Zimbabweans, 2,345 Ghanaians, and 1,628 South Africans. Such aid is rarely categorized as such (it is instead cast in terms of migration, seeking new opportunities, and so on) so the aid that the Global South provides through a range of healthcare workers at all levels is overlooked.

Not only was the 'aid' that was provided to different countries part of a policy to secure political allies, either in the name of "socialism" or of the "free world", but modernization theory itself presented an "elaborated authoritative interventionist ideology of development" (Preston, 1986, p.174) that prescribed particular paths of social and economic development for these countries to 'catch up' with the modern world. Criticism of these inequitable and hypocritical practices came from several directions, notably from neo-Marxist Third World critiques of dependency, the underlying argument being that within a global capitalist system, development and underdevelopment are inversely related within and between societies. Frank (1966) argued that the expansion of the capitalist system over the past centuries had effectively created a world-embracing metropolis/satellite structure, the metropoles tending to develop and the satellites to underdevelop, this relationship being stronger in proportion to the closeness of the ties between metropolis and satellite. Galtung's (1971) structural theory of imperialism (on which Phillipson, 1992, also draws for his linguistic imperialism) similarly suggested that economic, political, military, communication, and cultural imperialism were all results of the unequal relationship between centre and periphery. From a different perspective, Escobar (1985) insisted on the importance of "examining development as discourse" if we are to "understand the systematic ways in which the Western developed countries have been able to manage and control and, in many ways, even create the Third World politically, economically, sociologically and culturally" (1985, p.384).

Such work pointed to the need to examine not only inequitable relations in terms of political economy, but also the discursive fields that divided developed and developing, traditional and modern along ethnocentric and monoparadigmatic understandings of change (Ciaffa, 2008). If the notion "modern" was based on a very particular understanding of the world, the other half of this equation, "traditional", was equally problematic, a residual category defined principally in negative terms, that is, defined by how it deviated from the normative and unquestioned 'given', "modern". The modern/traditional dichotomy also denied history to Third World nations: Only the developed nations had progressed from some assumed primordial state to the present. And when the history of so-called traditional societies was allowed, it was constructed along colonial lines: Pre-colonial, colonial, and postcolonial. It also implied that "traditional" societies were static and homogeneous and that the "traditional" and the "modern" were mutually exclusive, the only way of effecting change being through the replacement of the one by the other. A critical investigation of the concepts "modern" and "traditional" revealed them not only to be conceptually weak and empirically unsound, but also politically motivated. The barriers to development were not so much internal (traditional barriers to be overcome) but, rather, external (derived from the structural characteristics of the global capitalist system). Partly as a result of this framing of modernization, the relationship between tradition and modernity has been a central theme in postcolonial African philosophy, with several implications for the emergence of the Global South. What is the relevance of Indigenous African traditions to the challenges of contemporary life? Do traditional modes of thought and behaviour (Mengisteab and Hagg, 2017), and Indigenous African languages constitute resources or impediments to Africa's modernization projects (Ciaffa, 2008, p.121)?

A significant part of this 'aid' process was the provision of educational assistance with attendant language policies. Modernization theorists argued for the importance of education not only in training a workforce (the human capital side of the argument) but also in inculcating "modern" beliefs, values, and behaviours in the population, a process considered by some essential for modernization. Thus, Inkeles and Smith (1974) argued that "mounting evidence suggests that it is impossible for a state to move into the twentieth century if its people continue to live in an earlier era" (p.3). This process, they proposed, could be achieved through education. But once fundamental questions were raised about notions of development and modernization, the role of education in this process also came under scrutiny. As Carnoy (1974) pointed out, many education systems in Third World countries are a result of neo-imperial and neocolonial relations, continuing to serve the interests of the former colonizers and Central nations. Altbach (1981) argued that the major intellectual centres had a massive influence over the international academic system, providing educational models, publishing academic books and journals, setting the research agenda, and so on. The peripheral universities, while often playing extremely important roles in their own countries as central institutions, were often, according to Altbach (1981, p.602), little more than "distributors of knowledge" from the centre. Aspects of this process included models of research and forms of education inappropriate to the local conditions, the common use of Western languages (especially English), universities becoming consumers not producers of knowledge, the means of communication – journals, books, and so on – in the hands of the industrial nations, and the brain drain of well-trained people leaving the peripheral nations (Prah, 2017; Mazrui, 1975).

There are limitations to some of these critical discourses that emerged in the 1970s and 1980s since they tended at times to paint an image of the Third World as a passive victim of First and Second World oppression. This is why work such as Phillipson's (1992) account of "English linguistic imperialism", which draws on Galtung and other thinkers from this era, falls short. It fails to capture the ways in which so-called periphery communities used, appropriated, and subverted the use of English or French (the development of the notion of *négritude* by colonial subjects in Paris in the 1930s, for example) or other metropolitan languages to meet their local needs (Canagarajah, 1999). The key concept of "linguicism" in Phillipson's work refers to "ideologies and structures where language is the means for effecting or maintaining an unequal allocation of power and resources" (1992, p.55). Phillipson amply demonstrates how and why various governments and organizations promote the spread of English but rarely explores what the effects of that promotion may be apart from maintaining global capitalism. And when he does, this tends to be in terms of deterministic impositions: "What is at stake when English spreads is not merely the substitution or displacement of one language by another but the imposition of new 'mental structures' through English" (p.166). English linguistic imperialism, in conjunction with other forms of imperialism, remains the end point of analysis and leaves little space for consideration of how English is used in diverse contexts or how it is appropriated and used in opposition to those that promote its spread. And as with many of these over-determined, structuralist critiques, people in the periphery, Third World, developing countries, or wherever they were positioned, objected to the ways they were made into structural effects of global hegemony rather than agents operating in an inequitable world.

Southern Theory, therefore, needs not only a critical analysis of global inequalities but, above all, a space for alternative understandings of the world, an escape from Eurocentric critiques of Eurocentrism. It is this epistemological struggle that is central to Southern Theory. As Kothari (1987) pointed out, by "delegitimizing the notion of plurality of paths of truth" modern science threatened to overwhelm the world with a "homogenizing monoculture of the mind" (p.284). It is the universalizing tendencies of modernity that are so problematic here, assuming that academic thought based on particular frameworks in particular places is applicable anywhere else (Richard, 1987). Nandy (1983) showed how hierarchies were established within the modern world around a set of polarities such as the modern and the primitive, the secular and the nonsecular, the scientific and the unscientific, the expert and the lay, the normal and the abnormal, the developed and the underdeveloped, the vanguard and the led, the liberated and the savable. It is by countering these dichotomous constructions, the foundations of modernity's universalism, that a counter-politics of difference can be established. "The politics of diversity and plurality" Kothari (1987, pp.279–280) argued, "by rendering the mainstream monolith irrelevant, becomes the foundation of an alternative post-modern era of action and knowledge". If a call for postmodernism now seems both unlikely and outdated, the point, once again, is that this struggle for alternatives has passed through many stages, using the intellectual tools of the time to fight the longer-term political battles.

A southern applied linguistics, therefore, requires a relentless critique of North–South disparities, but in a way that avoids focusing in totalizing fashion on languages such as English. This is why more complex analyses of "global Portuguese" that acknowledge that "it is no longer possible to continue to use theoretical frameworks and analytical tools in the study of Portuguese which are typical of colonial modernity" (Moita-Lopes, 2015, p.10) and draw on scholarship from the Global South are more effective than dystopian analyses of imperialism. This brief overview of ways in which global inequalities have been understood – from dependency and centre–periphery theories to Third World and development discourses – has tried to provide some of the lineage on which southern theories draw, even if there are also arguments for a break from such theorizing. A southern applied linguistics is not a new invention but a reframing of old debates. At the same time, we have also tried to show how opposition to the West, the North, the First and Second Worlds – however this was framed – also took many forms, and this too needs to be understood from a southern applied linguistic perspective. It is to further aspects of these oppositional positions – orientalism, postcolonialism, and the decolonial option – that we now turn.

Postcolonialism and the decolonial option

While much of the work discussed in the previous section operated predominantly from theories of political economy, a related line of thinking has focused centrally on discursive constructions, or the ways in which the Others of the West/East and North/South divides have been portrayed. Postcolonial studies as it developed in the works of Edward Said, Homi Bhabha, Gayatri Spivak, and others, emerged principally as part of the shift of literary studies towards a broader cultural orientation (cultural studies), though with a specific interest in understanding how different texts – novels, travel writing, anthropological texts, colonial documents, maps, and images – were central to the discursive production of colonies and colonized peoples. Edward Said's (1978) work is often seen as paradigmatic here as it sought to show how the 'Orient' was a product of European writing. Under this critical gaze *Orientalism* shifted from its earlier meaning as the study and appreciation of Eastern cultures – Orientalists who studied oriental languages and cultures were often juxtaposed in the 19th century with Anglicists, who promoted English language and culture (Pennycook, 1998) – to a term used to critique the way the Orient was fashioned by Europeans (the two meanings are of course deeply connected).

Postcolonial studies have come in for criticism (particularly from critical social scientific rather than humanities orientations) because of the incorporation of literary modes of analysis and theory that have been seen as interested more in the development of literary theory than in political change. Kubota (2016) argues that postcolonialism "favors Eurocentric textual analysis and European theorists but overlooks social, economic, and political struggles experienced by the underprivileged" (p.481). The focus, she suggests, has been too much on discursive construction – from Said onwards, Foucauldian discourse analysis has been a key tool of postcolonial studies – and not enough on the racial, social, and economic struggles faced by colonial and postcolonial people. It is also a term often rejected by those who can't see where the 'post' part comes in: For a number of Indigenous Australians, the idea of postcolonialism obscures the point that they still live under colonial conditions (Heiss, 2003). Other scholars are sceptical of the term on the grounds that it is a "convenient invention of western intellectuals which reinscribes their power to define" (Smith, 1999, p.14).

Key postcolonial concepts such as *hybridity* were developed to avoid a colonized versus colonizer dichotomy, to escape essentialist accounts of either colonial imposition or colonized resistance, and to show how colonized people had taken up and appropriated colonial languages and cultures for their own uses. This is a key argument in the World Englishes movement, with its argument that "creativity in World Englishes" is based on "various types and levels of hybridity, both linguistic and cultural". This is a "type of hybridity in which African and Asian interculturalism and linguistic innovations and experimentation play a vital role" (Kachru, 2009, p.463). Kubota (2016) takes this current emphasis on notions of diversity, plurality, flexibility, and hybridity in applied linguistics to task for its lack of engagement with socioeconomic disparities and racial discrimination. Postcolonial theory, she suggests, along with the resultant celebration and romanticization of diversity and plurality in applied linguistics (Makoni and Trudell, 2006) is complicit with neo-liberal ideology, emphasizing diversity at the expense of equality (cf. Flores, 2013). Thus, even though the field has arguably long had as a central agenda the identification, dismantling, and overcoming of the regimes of truth produced by colonialism, and even though it has found a home in a number of institutions of the Global South (suggesting perhaps that the recent rejection of postcolonial theory may be yet another attempt by the new North to dismiss the old South), the take-up of postcolonial studies in northern academic institutions, and its focus on discursive rather than political economic formations, have rendered it suspect as an adequate critique of global relations in the wake of colonialism. Its time seems to have passed.

The notion of the *decolonial option – la opción descolonial* (Mignolo, 2008, 2011a) – has partly filled the space left by a decline in postcolonial studies. This work builds particularly around South American scholarship such as Dussel's (1977, 2008, 2013) liberation philosophy (*Filosofía de Liberación*) as well as *The Invention of the Americas* (Dussel, 1995; and compare Mudimbe's, 1988, *The Invention of Africa*). Central to this work has been Quijano's (1991, 1998, 2000, 2007) distinction between colonialism (colonial economic and political structures) and coloniality (*colonialidad*), "long-standing patterns of power that emerged as a result of colonialism, but that define culture, labor, intersubjective relations, and knowledge production well beyond the strict limits of colonial administrations" (Maldonado-Torres, 2010, p.243). This work seeks to reinvigorate the focus on the continued effects of colonial power, arguing for the need to find alternative ways of thinking beyond universal, modern, Western, colonial ideologies, and, following Quijano, to work towards *epistemic reconstitution* (Mignolo, 2018). Mignolo "flatly rejects the assumption that rational and universal truths are independent of who presents them, to whom they are addressed, and why they have been advanced in the first place" (2011a, p.99). The assumption that one can speak from an anonymous, generalizable, universal position – the "hubris of the zero point" Mignolo (2009, p.162) – has to be rejected in favour of an understanding of the place from which we speak. To achieve this, the decolonial option, Mignolo (2010) insists, needs a process of *delinking* from "Eurocentric categories of thought which carries both the seed of emancipation and the seed of regulation and oppression" (p.313), of delinking "from the colonial matrix of power" (2018, p.125).

In Maldonado-Torres' words, the *de-colonial turn* "introduces questions about the effects of colonization in modern subjectivities and modern forms of life as well as contributions of racialized and colonized subjectivities to the production of knowledge and critical thinking" (2007, pp.261–262). The decolonial option, then, offers another way forward in thinking about the effects of colonialism (coloniality) and capitalism on the world. While suggesting a generalizability of its position (the tension between specific forms of local knowledge and a generalizable framework that draws on them runs through many of these ideas), decoloniality has tended to be largely South American in focus. It tends to distance itself from Southern Theory (see next section) because the North/South divide is as equally problematic as the East/West one that it partly supersedes. It attempts to construct a critique of European thought from outside European ways of thinking: There are many European critiques of modernity and colonialism, but most fail to grasp their own positionality and to address the need to work with other ways of knowing. In order to do this, it seeks to delink from European thought, though as we suggest in Chapter 7 – particularly with respect to thinkers such as Dussel and his own engagement with philosophers such as Levinas – it can only ever be partly successful in such endeavours. With the collaboration between Mignolo and Walsh (2018), however, it has managed to bring a more grounded and pedagogical focus on *praxis* to its sometimes abstract claims to decoloniality. We shall turn in greater detail in Chapter 5 to a discussion of decolonizing and the decolonial option, particularly in relation to its significance for rethinking TESOL.

If the professional community is serious about changing, disrupting, and dismantling the hegemonic relations between native and non-native speakers, with their roots in colonial economics and epistemologies, we need to engage in what Mignolo (2010) calls *epistemic decolonization*, and *epistemic reconstitution* (2018) to enable an alternative way of thinking and doing in the profession (Kumaravadivelu, 2016, p.80). This requires what Mignolo calls a *grammar of decoloniality* if we are to do more than just argue that NNS teachers are as good as NS teachers, and instead aim at a more profound epistemological unwinding through research, material development, and strategic action designed to change the field in much more extensive ways. The positionality of the decolonial option suggests that this cannot be assumed to be a universal struggle against the hegemony of native speakers – this is played out very differently in different contexts and different languages – but rather that the colonial history and contemporary role of English and other hegemonic languages make such a call an urgent political imperative. Postcolonial theory and the decolonial option, then, provide another part of this picture of trying both to understand and change the relations that were produced by and continue to operate as a result of the long history of colonialism.

While this strand of thinking is sometimes seen as rather distanced from the political and economic struggles of people in the Global South, it nevertheless draws attention, as Kumaravadivelu (2016) points out, to the need for major changes to how we think and act. While for some, the focus on *translanguaging* (to which we shall return) does little more than substitute new, and perhaps infelicitous, terminology for perfectly good notions such as bi- or multilingualism, for others such as García (2014), the notion is tied to the broader decolonial struggle. García and Li Wei (2014) connect their own thinking on translanguaging to Mignolo's (2000) *bilanguaging*, which aims at "redressing the asymmetry of languages and denouncing the coloniality of power and knowledge" (p.231). For Cushman (2016) a

> translingual approach to meaning making evokes a decolonial lens with its focus on the ideologies implicit in any tool chosen for meaning making (be it mode, media, or genre), as these are always laden with cultural, historical, and instrumental import for the people who use them.
>
> *(p.236)*

While Jaspers (2018) may be quite right in questioning the idea that translanguaging is transformative in itself, clearly for some it is tied to a decolonial politics. As we discuss in the next chapter, however, a different critique (Heugh and Stroud, 2018) has suggested that translanguaging may also be seen as an appropriation of southern multilingualisms.

One of the important challenges to contemporary discussions of decolonial and Southern Theory, then, critiques the manner in which ideas from the South are appropriated by northern academics and institutions. "Ideas run, like rivers, from the south to the north and are transformed into tributaries in major waves of thought," argues Cusicanqui (2012, p.104). It is not only the case that the flow of ideas is always from the North to the South, as in the common critique of centre–periphery academic relations, for just as raw materials are exported from the Global South to be converted into manufactured products and resold to the South, so ideas flow to the North and "become regurgitated and jumbled in the final product" (Cusicanqui, 2012, p.104). These ideas are changed into a new canon of thought (decolonial theory is one of the targets of this critique) which is then re-exported back to its origins (with accompanying admonishments that southern scholars haven't cited the apparently new northern sources of knowledge). These new canons of thought become embedded in northern institutions, making visible certain themes and sources but leaving others invisible. This is particularly relevant as the North rediscovers a relationship to the environment (and discussions of the Anthropocene), and draws on Indigenous thought to do so (Hayman et al., 2018; Todd, 2016). A major concern, therefore, and one to which we return at various points (see below, and Chapter 6), is that the search for epistemic reconstitution or southern epistemologies always runs the danger of becoming yet another northern reappropriation of southern thought.

On these grounds, Cusicanqui (2012) proposes a *political economy of knowledge* rather than a *geopolitics of knowledge* because of the importance of

> the economic strategies and material mechanisms that operate behind discourses. The postcolonial discourse of North America is not only an economy of ideas, but it is also an economy of salaries, perks, and privileges that certifies value through the granting of diplomas, scholarships, and master's degrees and through teaching and publishing opportunities.
>
> *(pp. 102–3)*

This takes us back to the very real conditions of inequality outlined in the introduction to this chapter within which any of these discussions occur. It is also worth noting, as Savransky (2017, p.13) suggests, that epistemology – a pluralization of knowledges – remains "the ultimate horizon" of postcolonial and decolonial approaches alike. There are also deeper ontological questions (see Chapters 4 and 6) to be explored. These concerns, then, take us further in thinking through the politics of knowledge that lie at the heart of the development of a southern applied linguistics since we need to consider not only ecologies of knowledge but also economies of knowledge, not only alternative ways of thinking but also risks of their appropriation, and not only epistemological but also ontological questions.

Innovations: Theories of the South

If, as we have been arguing, a southern applied linguistics has to be located in this longer lineage of opposition to colonial relations (both material and intellectual), it is worth pausing to trace this notion of the *South* more clearly. As already noted, while the East and West have been (and still commonly are) used to demarcate one set of economic, political, and cultural differences, the notion of the Third World emerged during the Cold War to describe generally poorer and non-aligned countries. As the battle between capitalism and communism drew to a close (at least in the form in which it was being played out), "the ex-Third World" became "the Global South" (Mignolo, 2011b, p.183). One important moment in that process can be linked to the North–South line drawn in *The Brandt Report* (Report, 1980), written by the Independent Commission first chaired by former German Chancellor Willy Brandt, which drew attention to the deep-seated inequalities between the North and South hemispheres (adjusted somewhat). Also using the 'developed' and 'developing' terminology, the report interpreted the notion of hemispheres fairly freely: Much of the line runs north of the Tropic of Cancer before swooping down below the Tropic of Capricorn to include Australia and New Zealand.

This theme of global North–South inequality was picked up by Connell (2007), with a focus particularly on *Southern* Theory and, as the subtitle of the book suggested, *The global dynamics of knowledge in social science*. Focusing particularly on sociology (Coleman, Giddens, Bourdieu), Connell (2007) argues that this work has always seen the world through the eyes of the metropole. This involves four common moves: Making claims to universality – assuming all societies can be understood along the lines of metropolitan analysis: "all societies are knowable, and they are knowable in the same way and from the same point of view" (Connell 2007, p.44); reading from the centre – assuming that distinctions such as subjective versus objective ("alternative ways of picturing oneself at the centre of a world" p. 45) are important elsewhere or that the way time is understood applies universally; gestures of exclusion – ideas from the South are excluded, and if they are included, they are almost never considered as part of mainstream thought; and grand erasure – "the erasure of the experience of the majority of human kind from the foundations of social thought" (p.46).

In a similar vein, Comaroff and Comaroff focus on the ways in which "Western enlightenment thought has, from the first, posited itself as the wellspring of universal learning, of Science and Philosophy" (2012 p. 113) while at the same time the non-West – known variously as the ancient, primitive, Third, underdeveloped, developing world, or the Global South – has been constructed "primarily as a place of parochial wisdom, of antiquarian traditions, of exotic ways and means. Above all, of unprocessed data" (pp.113–14). Part of the Comaroffs' project is to suggest the benefits of reversing this order of things, of considering that the Global South may afford "privileged insight into the workings of the world at large" (p.114). Thus, unlike the "received Euromodernist narrative of the past two centuries" whereby the Global South tracks behind "the curve of Universal History, always in deficit, always playing catch up", (p.121) there are important reasons to take on board both Fabian's (1983) injunction to understand that the Global South is contemporary rather than behind, and that it is in fact the South to which we should be looking to the future. This argument also ties in with the position we outlined in Chapter 1 that our goal here is to seek ways of expanding the epistemological repertoires of applied linguistics by drawing on southern thought.

Theory from the South, Comaroff and Comaroff (2012) explain, is *not* based around an idea of theories derived from those who are from the South, nor theory that is only 'about' the South. Rather, it is concerned with the effects of the South *itself* on theory, of the role of the South in the global present. It is of course akin to terms such as the Third World, or to the postcolonial, but derives its meaning above all from its juxtaposition with the Global North. This is a key insight for the themes we explore in this book: The point of developing a southern applied linguistics is not merely to include research on people and places, or by academics from the Global South but to explore the effects of the South on applied linguistic theory and practice. The Global South cannot therefore be defined in a priori substantive terms but rather needs to be understood in relational terms. The South can be understood as a metaphor both for "the human suffering caused by capitalism and colonialism at the global level" and "the resistance to overcome or minimise such suffering". It can therefore be understood as "anticapitalist, anticolonialist, and anti-imperialist". This South also exists in "the global North, in the form of excluded, silenced and marginalised populations, such as undocumented immigrants, the unemployed, ethnic or religious minorities, and victims of sexism, homophobia and racism" (Santos, 2012, p.51).

Santos' influential arguments emphasize several important points: Southern Theory is above all political rather than geographical; it stands in opposition to capitalist and colonialist ideologies and practices; and it is concerned with marginalized populations wherever they are and on whatever grounds (race, sexuality, ethnicity, religion) they are excluded. It is on these grounds that Milani (2017) prefers to talk in terms of *marginality* rather than Southern Theory, arguing that it is global conditions of marginalization that are at stake rather than a dichotomous North/South distinction. As Milani and Lazar (2017, p.309) suggest, the term Global South "encapsulates the conflation between geographical positionality and political marginality" though they also acknowledge that it can be a useful "heuristic lens for the study of discourse, gender and sexuality, and the study of language and social processes more broadly" (Milani and Lazar, 2017, p.317). For Santos (2014) the question has to do with the development of *southern epistemologies (epistemologias do sul)* (Santos and Menenes, 2010). Dominant, Eurocentric concepts of what counts as valid knowledge have discounted other, southern ways of knowing as a form of *epistemicide* – the destruction of other ways of knowing, and thereby the rationales that different social agents use to explain their social practices. Emancipation, Santos (2016) insists, has to include an epistemological dimension, "an engagement with the ways of knowing from the perspectives of those who have systematically suffered the injustices, dominations and oppressions caused by colonialism, capitalism, and patriarchy" (p.18). For Santos (2014), the "understanding of the world by far exceeds the Western understanding of the world" (2014, p.viii).

In order to "reinvent social emancipation on a global scale" (Santos, 2016, p.18) we need to engage with these epistemologies of the South rather than northern or Western understandings of the world. This involves, amongst other things, a "sociology of absences" (Santos, 2016, p.21) that takes seriously the idea that whatever does not exist in our society is often actively produced as non-existent. This sociology of absences enables us to "expand the relevant experiences of the world" by seeing how "our present has been narrowed down to whatever exists on this side of the line" and that "whatever is on the other side of the line … is produced by people in their struggles against capitalism, colonialism, and patriarchy" (p.21). In terms of our more modest emancipatory project, a reinvigorated applied linguistics needs to engage with ways of knowing from those who have been marginalized and excluded. An expanded applied linguistic epistemological repertoire will not be achieved by growing from within (more research on the same topics) but from without (an expansion of possibilities). How this plays out in the context of multilingualism, language policy, education, and research will be the focus of the next four chapters.

Challenges: Indigenous politics and standpoints

One of the domains with which Southern Theory intersects is Indigenous politics. Indigenous people were accorded the status of the 'Fourth World' in the three worlds categorization of the mid-20th century (Castells, 2000): The Fourth World generally referred to people that didn't fit into the first three – marginalized populations of nomadic people and subsistence farmers within the Third World as well as Indigenous people within other regions of the world. As with Southern Theory, this Fourth World categorization also located questions of inequality not only within the more obvious North/South, First/Third World structures but also within the wealthier nations themselves. Indigenous or First Nations people have thus been understood not only as the super-marginalized within the Third World/South, but also as the extra-marginalized within the wealthier nations. There are of course immediate difficulties here, for although there is much to be gained through Indigenous solidarity, and although there are at times depressingly similar issues of health, unemployment, depression, and suicide among various First Nations people around the world (the Inuit of Canada and Aboriginal Australians share both positive and negative commonalities), the category itself, which may include Amazonian forest dwellers, the Sámi in the Arctic Circle, Orang Asli in Malaysia, or Māori in New Zealand, can also be a contentious categorization.

Important from the perspective of this book, however, is an understanding of where Indigenous concerns intersect with the broader North–South politics, and the difficulty posed by including Indigenous people within the Arctic Circle in the Global South. One of the commonalities of Indigenous people (leaving aside the negative commonalities of low life expectancy, unemployment, incarceration, and more) is the deep connection to the land (and, as we argue in Chapter 6, the sea). The struggle over land and sea rights is not only about place but about a much wider cosmology, and this is why, as Connell (2007, p.198) notes, "many indigenous communities' relationships with land showed astonishing tenacity in the face of pressures from pastoralists, missionaries, farmers, miners, the state, the tourist industry – indeed the whole of what Mudimbe (1988) calls 'the colonizing structure'". The term 'Indigenous' itself is controversial both in terms of who gets to claim such a position and whether this term adequately describes the people for whom it is intended. The idea of 'Indigenous people' is a relatively recent one that emerged in the 1970s out of the struggles of the American Indian movement and Canadian Indian brotherhood. It internationalizes the struggles and sufferings of Indigenous communities while not detracting from a concern with the local and unique challenges which Indigenous communities may face. 'First Nations', 'Aboriginal' and other such terms sometimes gain and sometimes lose ground in relation to Indigenous. In other contexts, such as New Zealand, terms such as Māori or *tangata whenua* are used much more frequently than 'Indigenous', while different origin and tribal terms are also used to differentiate between groups. The term Māori also works to define relationships between Māori and *pakeha,* the non-Indigenous settler population (Smith, 1999, p.6).

Around 3 per cent (about 670,000) of people in Australia identify as Indigenous, the largest proportion of whom (35%), contrary to popular belief, live in major cities. The Australian *Overcoming Indigenous Disadvantage Report* (SCRGSP, 2016) notes *as a success* that the gap in life expectancy between Indigenous and non-Indigenous Australians had narrowed "from 11.4 years to 10.6 years for males and from 9.6 years to 9.5 years for females" (SCRGSP, 2016, p.13). Life expectancy is of course a complex matter involving early child mortality (decreased), disability and chronic disease (increased), health, education, home environment, and more. Of the areas in which the report signals no change over the reporting period, the number of people learning an Indigenous language remained constant at 11 per cent, with 16 per cent of the population speaking an Indigenous language (the proportion is much higher in remote areas). Domains that were not reported as a success included incarceration rates which have increased, with Aboriginal and Torres Strait Islander adults imprisoned at 13 times the rate for non-Indigenous adults, and youth at 24 times the rate for non-Indigenous youth (SCRGSP, 2016, p.20). The figures above paint a very particular picture of Indigenous lives in Australia and do not really answer in any broader way what it means to be Indigenous. While commonalities across Indigenous populations point to similar conditions of inequality, it is also the case that there are wide differences across and within Indigenous communities. Again, we do not wish to paint a dystopian picture here, but when we consider the North and South, and the potential of Indigenous thought for global renewal, basic issues around education, language, health, and violence cannot be overlooked.

The power to claim the right to define oneself as Indigenous being in the hands of Indigenous people has been a long and difficult struggle. As Gomes notes, "Identification, classification, and certification are hegemonic tools or arts of governmentality whereby the complexity of Indigenous identities is invariably reduced to a grossly simplified and legible ontological and cartographical classificatory system that makes governing easier and more effective" (2013, p.10). Merlan (2009) points out that definitions of Indigeneity may be either 'criterial' – based on sets of inherent criteria that define the Indigenous, such as evidence of or belief in original inhabitation of a territory – or 'relational' – that is centred around relations with non-Indigenous others, such as distinguishing themselves from dominant social organizations. Such criteria are complicated by many other layers of relations, including competing questions of belonging. In Malaysia, for example, the Malay struggle for dominance in what they saw as their own country required the co-opting of the *Orang Asli* as fellow *bumiputera* (sons of the soil), thus claiming political rights over later arrivals from China and India but ignoring the history of relations between Malays and those who had been there before they arrived.

Questions such as race also complexify the situations, where racial identifications may play both exclusionary and inclusionary roles (Gomes, 2013). A particular set of insidious racial identifications played out in the Australian context where a group of Indigenous activists won a court case against a conservative commentator on the grounds that his claims about 'fair-skinned' Aboriginal people taking advantage of their claimed heritage had contravened the Racial Discrimination Act (Heiss, 2012).

Indigenous people also have to struggle with competing views about their linguistic and cultural heritage and how they deal with this in a world where such heritages may have commercial potential for impoverished communities. Monaghan (2012) explains how "reconstructed Wirangu language has been both a product of the need for distinction and a vehicle for the establishment of a range of ethno-commercial activities" (p.48) among the Scotdesco community in South Australia. As part of their attempt to attract visitors to their small community, they have built a giant, concrete wombat. While this does bring in some income, it also presents various challenges, among them "the strains of performing Aboriginality to strangers" (p.59). As De Korne's (2017) study of Diidxazá in southern Mexico shows, Indigenous languages may be both marginalized and co-opted because of certain values they are now seen to hold. We therefore need to be wary of assuming either that they are always discriminated against or newly valued but instead recognize "local social and symbolic capital and the ongoing struggles through which Indigenous communities have gained increased rights and recognition within structures of inequality and exploitation" (2017, p.55). Indigenous communities are not of course themselves homogeneous, and so while the accrual of certain rights and recognition always occur within inequitable structures of inequality and discrimination, their distribution within communities may also be uneven.

At least in some contexts, however, "Indigenous ontologies in which place has agency irrespective of human presence or awareness" (Larsen and Johnson, 2016, p.150) are being taken up and contributing towards what Escobar (2011, p.137) refers to as "narratives of transition" involving "radical proposals for moving towards the pluriverse" or a world in which many kinds of knowledge and understanding are given a place. One of the challenges therefore for Indigenous people, and for the themes we are addressing in this book, is both to develop an Indigenous position that is not tied to suffocating notions of 'authenticity' but is nonetheless seen as emergent from Indigenous ways of knowing, and at the same time to find ways to be heard and to participate in broader conversations without this standpoint always being reduced to an Indigenous point of view. Various standpoint theories (and note also the locus of enunciation discussed by Mignolo above) have been developed "by a diversity of marginalised groups whose accounts of experience were excluded or subjugated within intellectual knowledge production" (Nakata, 2007, p.213). An Indigenous standpoint, as Nakata explains is not just a "simple reflection of experience" or some sort of "hidden wisdom that Indigenous people possess" or an assertion of truth "beyond the scrutiny of others on the basis that, as a member of the Indigenous community, what I say counts" (p.214). Rather, it requires complex analytic and writing skills in order to investigate "the actualities of the everyday and discover how to express them conceptually from within that experience" instead of using predefined categories (p.215).

There have, of course, been numerous critiques of attempts to establish such standpoints, with challenges of epistemic relativism (anyone's knowledge is as good as anyone else's), identity politics (only certain people can make knowledge claims), the reification of identities (what defines Indigeneity), and forms of politics focusing on recognition rather than redistribution. Yet these are all concerns, suggests Nakata, that Indigenous scholars need to engage with as Indigenous people recognize that they are "entangled in a very contested knowledge space" (2007, p.215). Indigenous researchers have to be aware that they are engaged in "researching back" in the same tradition of "writing back" or talking back that has been one of the features of "postcolonial" or "anti-colonial literature" (Smith, 1999, p.7; for further discussion, see Chapter 6). From this point of view, Nakata goes on to argue, the point is not just to try to "overturn the so-called dominant position through simplistic arguments of omission, exclusion or misrepresentation" but to develop "better arguments in relation to my position within knowledge" (2007, p. 216).

One difficulty, however, is that as northern academics rediscover space, place, things, affect, and the significance of embodiment, they turn to northern sources, forgetting that Indigenous people have known all this for a long time. As Todd (2016) describes it

> I waited through the whole talk, to hear the Great Latour credit Indigenous thinkers for their millennia of engagement with sentient environments, with cosmologies that enmesh people into complex relationships between themselves and all relations, and with climates and atmospheres as important points of organization and action.
>
> *(pp. 6–7)*

And she waited in vain, for while the northern academy re-engages with the climate, with the earth, with people and places, Indigenous knowledge is almost always still absent. As she goes on to describe this process:

> here we were celebrating and worshipping a European thinker for "discovering", or newly articulating by drawing on a European intellectual heritage, what many an Indigenous thinker around the world could have told you for millennia: the climate is a common organizing force!
>
> *(p. 8)*

The challenge is to develop a form of *radical Indigenism* which assumes that Indigenous "philosophies of knowledge are rational, articulable, coherent logics for ordering and knowing the world" (Garroutte, 2003, p.113). This radical Indigenist perspective both challenges Western science and knowledge and calls for Indigenous perspectives to inform language and other projects. An Indigenous standpoint can help "unravel and untangle ourselves from the conditions that delimit who, what or how we can or can't be, to help see ourselves with some charge of the everyday, and to help understand our varied responses to the colonial world" (Nakata, 2007, p.217). This articulation of Indigenous standpoint theory is a useful way of understanding the broader perspective on Southern Theory. As we have been suggesting, it needs to go beyond an identity politics of the South (I'm a southern scholar, so listen to me), particularly since the Global South is a more complex idea than simple global southernness. It also needs to get beyond the simple charge of omission and misrepresentation (southern contexts are not sufficiently discussed or fairly dealt with). Rather, it points to a compound engagement with the implications of marginalized knowledge for contemporary theorizing.

Conclusion

We have tried in this chapter to outline some of the lineages as well the disjunctures, some of the ways forward as well as the pitfalls, around Southern Theory and related frameworks. Simply put, the point is this: In an inequitable world – a world made inequitable by particular political economic policies and practices – there is also an unequal divide in knowledge production. Certain people from certain places (the Global North, formerly the minority world, the West, the developed world, the Centre) produce the vast amount of knowledge about the rest of the world and make generalized or even universal claims to the applicability of that knowledge to the rest of the world. This knowledge is also not merely vaguely inappropriate in some way, but more importantly linked to what Mignolo (2018) calls the *colonial matrix of power* (coloniality/modernity) or Santos (2018) sees as the struggle against colonialism, patriarchy, and capitalism. This struggle requires an understanding of the absences that such knowledge implies and a renewal of southern epistemologies. For Mignolo (2018 p.106), "decolonial thinking and doing aim to delink from the epistemic assumptions common to all the areas of knowledge established in the Western world since the European Renaissance and through the European Enlightenment."

What does this mean for applied linguistics? As we shall argue through the rest of this book, there is an equal need for a decolonizing of the field, a delinking from (not a rejection of) a range of assumptions about language and language users. We will focus in Chapter 5 on decolonizing particular aspects of applied linguistics (from discourse analysis to second language acquisition) but our focus over the next two chapters will be on decolonizing language. We have already noted elsewhere (Makoni and Pennycook, 2007) that current approaches to diversity, multilingualism, language policy, and learning all too often start with the enumerative strategy of counting languages and romanticizing a plurality based on these putative language counts. While opening up questions of diversity from one perspective, at the same time such strategies also reproduce the tropes of colonial invention, overlooking the contested history of language inventions, and ignoring the collateral damage that their embedded notions of language may be perpetrating. By rendering diversity a quantitative question of language enumeration, such approaches continue to employ the census strategies of colonialism while missing the qualitative question of where diversity lies. They continue to use the underlying ideology of countability and singularity, where language-objects are physically located in concepts of space founded on a notion of territorialization. Heller and Duchêne (2007, p.11) remark that we need to "rethink the reasons why we hold onto the ideas about language and identity which emerged from modernity". Addressing the question of language preservation, they suggest that rather than assuming we must save languages, "we should be asking instead who benefits and who loses from understanding languages the way we do, what is at stake for whom, and how and why language serves as a terrain for competition". Questions around language preservation and reclamation will be a particular focus of Chapter 4.

For the terms of this book, we have to appreciate that "imperialism lay at the heart of ideas about linguistic and racial difference and inequality" (Heller and McElhinny, 2017, p.90). The development of linguistics and anthropology as part of the colonial enterprise, as well as the overlapping history of the development of nation states, produced models of language that were intertwined with definitions of racial difference, nations, and whose knowledge counted. The implications of these ties will be explored in much greater detail in the next chapters as we look at the ways that work on multilingualism, language revitalization, and educational policies all too often fail to escape their colonial heritage. This leads to both a narrow knowledge base and inapplicable knowledge, a major concern to an area such as applied linguistics with its injunction to engage with local contexts. In order to broaden the epistemological repertoire of applied linguistics, therefore, we need to listen to and engage with a wider world of languages and ideas. The challenge for a book on southern approaches to applied linguistics is to seek out ways to escape this history, to develop other forms of knowledge, to look at the world differently, to expand our applied linguistic epistemological repertoires. We shall return to many of these questions in the following chapters: To questions of colonial linguistics and multilingualism in Chapters 3 and 4, to concerns around decolonization, northern knowledge, and linguistic and educational interventions in Chapter 5, and to questions of knowledge and research from Indigenous and southern perspectives in Chapter 6.

Note

1 It is rather ironic, but also revealing of the troubling processes of historical forgetting and political myopia, to note in the contemporary world complaints by politicians that China is giving aid to poorer countries in Africa, the Pacific, and central Asia as part of an attempt to secure economic and political cooperation, as if this was not precisely what the powerful post-war nations were doing during much of the 20th century.

3

SOUTHERN MULTILINGUALISMS

Across the fields of socio- and applied linguistics there is general agreement that multilingualism is and always has been the global norm. Multilingualism, viewed from this perspective, is an indomitably good thing (and not, as it was seen before, a problem or an aberration), and the task of linguists, sociolinguists, applied linguists, and educational linguists is to enhance the understanding and practice of multilingualism. At the same time, our understandings of multilingualism have been greatly affected by and filtered through monolingual ideologies – a condition that has been called a 'monolingual habitus' (Gogolin, 1994, 2002) or 'monolingual mindset' (Clyne, 2005). As a result, as has been widely noted over the past decade, bi- and multilingualism have been misconstrued through a monolingual lens as the capacity to use separate languages (Heller, 2007), as an ability to learn and operate in distinct enumerable codes. There is a growing sentiment that we need to overcome the monolingual blinkers of Anglo- or Eurocentric thought, to see monolingualism as an invention (Gramling, 2016), a strange and possibly irrelevant or impossible condition. As Busch (2012) puts it: *niemand ist einsprachig* (no one is monolingual).

All this is well and good, and rapidly becoming a normative position for sociolinguists. We want to suggest, however, that the straitjacket of monolingual thought is not so easily thrown off. Monolingual mindsets go far deeper than favouring monolingualism over multilingualism, or viewing multilingualism in monolingual terms: The issue at stake is a set of deep-seated language ideologies that are in need of a much more profound decolonizing. One step in this direction has arguably been made by the claim that languages are far more fluid and unstable than common accounts allow, thus unsettling a notion of 'multiple monolingualisms' by suggesting that language boundaries are artificial artefacts. The moves to talk in terms of *polylingualism* (Jørgensen, 2008), *translanguaging* (García and Li Wei, 2014), *translingual practice* (Canagarajah, 2013), and so on suggest ways forward from older visions of stable and separate languages. And yet this work too has been critiqued on the grounds that to "lay claim to an uncovering or (re-)discovering of multilingualism as more than the sum of languages understood as monolingual entities" by scholars from Europe and North America (and writing predominantly in English) "appears ahistorical and dislocated from the experiences and scholarship of marginalised and minoritized people who live in both the geopolitical north and south" (Heugh and Stroud, 2018, p.2). This recent scholarship, they argue, not only appropriates, and claims as new, ideas that have been long circulating in the Global South, but also does so from a position that views multilingualism as a "singular phenomenon" rather than embracing the full implications of a "plurality of multilingualisms" (pp.6–7).

In this chapter, we shall explore these arguments in more depth as we seek to understand both the ways in which multilingualism has been constructed, and the need to understand multilingualisms as plural and diverse, a discussion that will be taken further in Chapter 4 through an exploration of language ontologies. In the first section, we will review some of the arguments about the ways languages have been constructed as singular entities. These language myths that insist that language use is an instantiation of pre-existing languages, we suggest, have things the wrong way round: Languages are second-order abstractions from the everyday practices of communication rather than first-order entities deployed in different contexts (Love, 2017). We will then look in more depth at the processes by which languages have been invented, before making an argument that the pluralization of languages may not be a useful way of capturing diversity. We argue that it is time for more sophisticated models that capture as far as possible the full panoply of contexts in the Global South, from urban to rural, formally educated to informal, and contemporary to historical sociolinguistic. Such models need to go beyond simply replacing monolingualism with multilingualism, as both concepts emerge from the same intellectual context. We need instead models that question the very foundations that underpin such linguistic simplifications.

Language myths

Assumptions about the existence of languages, and therefore about multilingualism, are so deeply embedded in predominant paradigms of language studies that they have until recently rarely been questioned. It is important, however, to consider several important points: First, that sociolinguists rarely believed that languages were as fixed and as stable as sometimes portrayed; second, that there has also been a sustained critique of the 'language myth' from within linguistics; third, that these critiques may contribute to, but are not the same as, a southern position on language. And so, finally, as we hope to make clear in this chapter, as well as at a number of other points in this book, if we are to talk in terms of northern and southern views on language, we need to see them as deeply intertwined. To deal briefly with the first of these issues, we should note that the idea of languages in fixed, structural terms was already seen by many as simply a useful fiction in order to be able to make some sense of the complexity of language events. As Haugen, for example, observed,

> [t]he concept of languages as a rigid, monolithic structure is false, even if it has proved to be a useful fiction in the development of linguistics. It is the kind of simplification that is necessary at a certain stage of a science, but which can now be replaced by more sophisticated models.
>
> *(1972, p.25)*

If a problem was nonetheless ways in which these language myths congealed within sociolinguistic orthodoxies (as with the idea of code-switching which solidified from a flexible idea to a more rigid notion of alternating between languages; Pennycook, 2016, 2018b), so that language became seen as a "solved problem, a stable and determined entity" (Harpham, 2002, p.ix), these were not necessarily so much beliefs about language as pragmatic tools for doing sociolinguistics. The search for 'more sophisticated models', however, was greatly hampered by the ossification of these pragmatic accounts of language.

There has nonetheless been a long history of critique of the various language myths that circulate in both popular and academic circles. Different intellectual traditions, from philosophy to anthropology (Davidson, 1986; Whorf, 1988) have dealt with the existence of languages with some scepticism. A number of theoretical positions coalesce around a critique of languages as discrete, unified natural systems: "Languages are not natural objects" (Love and Anslado, 2010, p.592). Prominent among these has been the integrational linguistic position that the idea of languages is a "myth" (see Harris, 1980, 1981, 1998, 2009; Harris and Taylor, 1997; Pennycook, 2007b). From an integrational linguistic point of view, "people use signs in order to communicate", but signs are not pre-assembled or agreed upon by mutual consent. Language from this point of view is so deeply embedded in context that it cannot be separated from it. Language can only emerge through a process of abstraction, leading integrational linguists to talk in terms of 'first-order' and 'second-order' activities, the first referring to real communicative activity, and the second to the kind of abstraction that leads to the naming and claiming of languages. For Thibault (2011, p.7) such 'first-order' activities include "a whole range of bodily resources that are assembled and coordinated in languaging events together with external (extrabodily) aspects of situations, environmental affordances, artifacts, technologies, and so on." It is the process of rendering "first-order activities as users of language amenable to contemplation and inquiry conducted by means of language itself" that leads to the abstraction of languages as "objects" and "decontextualized reifications we recognize as linguistic units" (Love, 2009, p.44).

This is akin in some ways to Haugen's earlier observation about linguistic reifications: It is when we start to believe that our second-order reifications and abstractions are really what language is about that we have started to lose the plot. The problem comes when we get this sequence the wrong way round and assume that language use is a second-order instantiation of the first-order things called languages, rather than understanding languages as second-order abstractions of communicative activity. A related point derives from the work on *emergent grammar* (Hopper, 1998) where the notion of systematicity embedded in the concept of grammar is understood as a product of repeated social activity. Language use draws on "lingual memory" shaped in part by each individual's life experiences (Becker, 1995; Johnstone, 1996). Hence, as Hopper (1998, pp.157–8) argues,

> there is no natural fixed structure to language. Rather, speakers borrow heavily from their previous experiences of communication in similar circumstances, on similar topics, and with similar interlocutors. Systematicity, in this view, is an illusion produced by partial settling or *sedimentation* of frequently used forms into temporary subsystems.

Communication occurs through a process of mutual adjustment: "when we speak or write, we take those imperfectly remembered prior (a priori) texts and reshape them into contexts" (Becker, 1995, p.15). This 'determined indeterminacy' (Khubchandani, 2003, p.241) is a position quite at odds with a sender/receiver model of "fixed-telementation" in which the thoughts of one person are transported to another through the use of a particular code (Toolan, 2009; Pennycook, 2018a). As Harris (1990, p.45) remarks, "linguistics does not need to postulate the existence of languages as part of its theoretical apparatus". Once we make communication central to our thinking, languages may be a "variable extra" (Harris, 2009, p.44).

The immediate relevance of sociolinguistic concepts such as multilingualism thus becomes suspect in diverse contexts (Love, 2009). Multilingualism from such a perspective is not therefore a universal category; indeed, the very idea that multilingualism could refer to the same thing in diverse contexts of communication is revealed as an absurdity. Linguistic anthropologists and others studying creole languages have also cast suspicion on the ways in which languages have been described and mapped onto communities. Le Page and Tabouret-Keller (1985), for example, argue that in extremely complex heterogeneous contexts not every speech event or language will necessarily belong to a nameable language system. Furthermore, speakers may not necessarily have a clearly defined idea of what language they are speaking, and what does or does not constitute "a language". As a result, rather than focusing on languages and their users, we would be better off focusing on the "acts of identity" (Le Page and Tabouret-Keller, 1985) involved in different interactions. In a related vein, Schiefflien's (1990) research on Kaluli literacy suggests that children are not taught language or verbal behaviour as such, but rather are taught appropriate social behaviour during interactional movements. This perspective echoes research into other post-colonial contexts (see Makoni and Makoni, 2010) that suggest that to study languages we always need to incorporate social activity, location, movement, interaction, and history, as well as, wherever possible, users' perspectives (Pennycook, 2010).

The focus of such work is therefore on multilingualism as part of wider social and cultural practices, making the social grounding of human interaction central, as opposed to language-centred multilingualism, which assumes a multiplicity of language systems as central to the analysis. From the perspective of linguistic anthropology, with a particular interest in the notion of language ideologies, or regimes of language (Kroskrity, 2000), the question becomes one of asking how it is that languages are understood locally in schools, in communities, in workplaces, in families, and in diverse social interactions. We are obliged to take account of whether people believe they speak languages, what they believe about those languages, and to analyse the beliefs about language which they hold passionately even if those languages have been invented. These beliefs are part of the language ideologies of language users, and as Woolard (2004, p.58) notes, such work has shown that "linguistic ideologies are never just about language, but rather also concern such fundamental social notions as community, nation, and humanity itself." For linguistic anthropologists, the problem has been that the "surgical removal of language from context produced an amputated 'language' that was the preferred object of the language sciences for most of the twentieth century" (Kroskrity, 2000, p.5). In order to construct itself as a respectable discipline, linguistics had to make an extensive series of exclusions, relegating people, history, society, culture, and politics to a role external to languages (Nakata, 2007).

By studying language ideologies as contextual sets of belief about languages, or as Irvine (1989, p.255) puts it, "the cultural system of ideas about social and linguistic relationships, together with their loading of moral and political interests", this line of work has shown the significance of local knowledge about language. At the very least, this sheds light on Mühlhäusler's (2000) point that the notion of "a language" "is a recent culture-specific notion associated with the rise of European nation-states and the Enlightenment. The notion of 'a language' makes little sense in most traditional societies" (Mühlhäusler, 2000, p.358). Because of the centrality of Eurocentric concepts of language, mother tongues, and other monoglot perspectives, "what has passed for a science of language (*including multilingualism*) over the past 150 years has been nothing but an exercise in culture maintenance" (Love, 2009, p.31, emphasis ours).

Inventing languages

Given these various critiques of the ways in which language has been constructed in the Western/Northern tradition, it is now much less controversial to suggest that languages are inventions (Makoni and Pennycook, 2007) or at least, in a milder version of this idea, that languages are social constructs. The implications of this insight, however, that "not all people have 'a language/languages' in the sense in which the term is currently used in English" (Heryanto, 1990, p.41) are less widely appreciated. The construct of "language itself as an all or nothing affair" (Rajagopalan, 2007, p.194) as well as many ideas that are part of this metalinguistic package can be understood as inventions. Sabino (2018, p.109) argues that the "languages ideology" that has congealed over many centuries promotes an unwarranted belief in uniform "grammatical systems", the "normalcy of monolingualism", grammaticality judgements, a congruent model of linguistic and ethic/racial identity, lists and enumerations of languages, and a host of questionable constructs including bilingualism, code-switching, first languages, language death, fossilization, interlanguage, revitalization, native and non-native speakers, World Englishes, and so on. Languages themselves are excellent examples of 19th-century social and scholarly invention in Europe and colonial contexts (Errington, 2008; Mudimbe, 1988; Rajagopalan, 2020; Spear, 2003).

Importantly for the arguments in this book – and particularly the focus on coloniality (see Chapter 2) and decolonization (see Chapter 5) – the colonial origins of language invention need to be appreciated. An important challenge that Southern Theory throws up for applied linguistics is the realization that linguistics has deep roots in colonialism/coloniality and that some of its contemporary practices may be reinforcing contemporary dominant neo-liberal interests. More broadly we need to understand how disciplinary knowledge – Western academic knowledge and disciplines such as anthropology, linguistics, and economics (Cohn, 1996) – developed during and as part of the colonial process. The development of an understanding of language and of speakers of languages has therefore to be understood in the context of the systematic denigration of alternative forms of knowledge. According to Monaghan (2012), discussing Indigenous communities in South Australia

> before anthropologists and linguists came along people engaged in fluid speech practices and arguably did not have, or indeed need, the concept of a formalised language. Language in this sense is part of an imposed Western analytical framework that is underpinned by scriptist notions of the primacy of the written word over speech.
>
> *(p.52)*

Silverstein (2014) makes a similar point, suggesting that the idea of language as a bounded system discrete from other such bounded systems was never evident among the Worora people in northwestern Australia. As Errington (2001) explains, colonial authorities and missionaries

> shared a territorial logic that was similarly inscribed in colonial linguistic work, presupposing mappings of monolithic languages onto demarcated boundaries ... Within these bounded confines were conceived to be ethnolinguistically homogeneous groups that were localized, and naturalized, as "tribes" or "ethnicities".
>
> *(p.24)*

Linguists "can be regarded as a small, rather special group of colonial agents who adapted European letters to alien ways of talking and, by that means, devised necessary conduits for communication across lines of colonial power" (Errington, 2008, p.4). As a result, the description of languages was intimately linked to the wider colonial emphasis on human hierarchies (Rajagopalan, 2020), so that "the intellectual work of writing speech was never entirely distinct from the 'ideological' work of devising images of people in zones of colonial contact" (Errington, 2008, p.5). This also entailed the use of language difference "in the creation of human hierarchies, such that colonial subjects could be recognized as human, yet deficiently so" (2008, p.5).

Research was shaped by nationalist and imperialist ideas that had an impact on the geographical location where the research was conducted and on how speakers of the languages being studied were framed. Carl Meinhof, the famous German Africanist, for example, preferred to work with African informants in Germany (Pugach, 2017). In fact, his research on Duala and on comparative Bantu vowel systems were published before he had ever set foot on the African continent. Meinhof felt strongly that the most important work could be conducted only in the metropole. Fieldworkers who resided in the colonies, he thought, were too close to their own particular subject matter. Only in the metropole could the necessary analytical distance and scientific objectivity be reached, producing research that would contribute to Germany's global intellectual influence and domination. Based in Hamburg after 1909, Meinhof established a laboratory for studying African languages with the most sophisticated scientific equipment of his time. Even though African speakers were necessary to this enterprise, Africans were always positioned more as objects of study than as agents who create and recreate signs, within a flow of time and against a background of contingency and indeterminacy (Adejunmobi, 2004). While linguistic research has largely moved on from such colonial assumptions, the legacy of how languages and their speakers are understood is still with us.

Language descriptions cannot be abstracted from the colonial imperatives to control, subdue, and order. The description of languages, therefore, has to be seen not so much as a scientific division of a language spectrum along natural lines but rather a colonial project in the defining and dividing of colonized people. As Irvine and Gal (2000, p.47; Gal and Irvine, 2019) describe the process of 'linguistic description' of Senegalese languages by 19th-century European linguists, "The ways these languages were identified, delimited, and mapped, the ways their relationships were interpreted, and even the ways they were described in grammars and dictionaries were all heavily influenced by an ideology of racial and national essences." In his discussion of the imposition of Bahasa Indonesia, Heryanto (2007, p.43) argues that it was through the introduction via European colonialism of "the idea of 'language'" that "the old word *bahasa* came to articulate this newly-acquired concept. The adoption of a pre-existing word in East Asia to articulate a new concept from modern Western Europe helped make the concept appear universal."

Since language was taken to be a universal human property, it was also assumed that the word 'language', or the local words, such as *bahasa,* that came to be used as translations of this concept, likewise referred to a shared linguistic property tied to nation and culture in similar ways. This introduced concept, Heryanto suggests, did not accord with local understandings of language. In Malay and Javanese, the two most widely spoken and influential languages in Indonesia, "there was no word for 'language'. More importantly, there was neither a way nor a need to express its idea until the latter part of the 19th century" (2007, p.43). This newly introduced concept of language entered "a world with no language", in the process replacing vernacular views of language and how it worked. In speaking of 'a world with no language' the point, to be sure, is not that these contexts involved any less language use, but rather that these language users did not speak 'languages'.

The process of invention is not restricted to colonial history or to the geographical South. In recent years, the term 'Roma' has been established throughout Europe to encompass diverse populations (who we might nonetheless classify as part of the geopolitical South – the disenfranchised within the Global North) that have been called in everyday life by a variety of often denigratory names (Gypsies, Manouches, Tziganes, Bohemians, Sinti), according to place, time, authority, economics, and politics. This process of categorization (aimed at times to avoid the already derogatory terms in use) served to homogenize diverse people on the assumption that they share common cultural values, in which nomadism is the most frequently imagined similarity (Canut 2011). Such processes of homogenization are a founding principle of European policies toward European populations that face discrimination. The current ethnicization of the Roma derives from the historical reinvention of a 'Roma' people and the Romani language (Canut 2011). European processes of invention are closely tied to discourses of endangerment and preservation, as we shall see in the next chapter.

Language invention happens at several levels: the very notion of languages as entities linked to nations, ethnicities, people, and territories is first of all transported into unfamiliar places. The local linguistic 'chaos' is then sorted out to fit languages into categorizations of people, and, where extra work is needed, languages are specifically created and renamed in order to fit preferred linguistic conditions (this is why we prefer to talk of *inventions* rather than *social constructions*). Shona in Zimbabwe, for example, was created on the basis of a two-stage process: First, a codification of dialects associated with different missionary stations, and second, the unification of dialects by colonial linguists (Makoni et al., 2007). Beck (2018) draws attention to the contemporary effects of such inventions, particularly in the case of ongoing controversy among the different stakeholders with respect to Afrikaans at the University of Stellenbosch, South Africa, and the status of kiSwahili as the language of internal communication at a Tanzanian university. "The emergence of invented languages", she points out (Beck 2018, p.231), "are a result of an existential onto-epistemological dislocation stabilized through the hegemonic project of colonialism". Such examples direct our attention not only to the colonial invention of languages, but also to their continued disruptive presence in education systems.

Mannheim (1991) points out that prior to the Spanish invasion, the Quecha in South America did not need a construct of language – indeed like many other communities they did not have specific names to refer to what they spoke – and thus Quecha emerged as a product of colonial conquest. Once this sorting out has been achieved, this invented world of languages and ethnicities is reported as if it were an objective reality that has always been in place (Harris, 2009). It is assumed to be a natural phenomenon. We also have to appreciate in these and other contexts that many languages, such as Igbo or Yoruba in the 19th century, had different meanings prior to colonial encounters (Irvine, 2009) and that what was understood by many people as their language was simply their description for how they spoke (Crowley, 1999). The process of invention transforms dialogical and "heteroglossic" material into "monological texts" (Blommaert, 2008). The invented linguistic artefacts were textualized in a wide range of genres: Grammatical outlines, grammatical sketches, word lists, orthographies, and so on (Blommaert, 2008; Errington, 2001, 2008; Makoni, 1998). In this codification process, the serious complexities of different sociolinguistic contexts were reduced through the technical apparatus of monological sociolinguistics into "equally serious simplicities" (Dasgupta, 1997, p.21). In most colonial contexts, local languages were standardized by outsiders without direct involvement of the local population, except as informants based on a series of texts, folklore, narratives, and so on (Blommaert, 2008). The objective was to produce European bilingual speakers "competent" in the varieties of African languages, which they had created in conjunction with European languages (Fabian, 1986; Jeater, 2002.

The overall effect of this intervention was the creation and appropriation of standardized African languages by Europeans. In such contexts, what should be construed as colonial languages are not only English, French, Spanish, or Portuguese, as is generally accepted, but also standardized African languages that were constructed on the basis of linguistic templates whose origins were in European languages. Uncritical advocacy of standardized African languages, therefore, may serve as a retrospective legitimation of the colonization of these languages. In a bid to regain control of how their languages were represented by colonial grammarians, African dictionary makers and local language users invented a form of monolingualism (Bonfiglio, 2010) that enabled them to subsequently resist, at a later stage, ways in which their languages had been represented. The ideologies of resistance were thus most strongly manifested in the production of Indigenous monolingual dictionaries and grammars. Attempts to regain representation of sociolinguistic situations were limited by the resistance of linguistic elites to the use of multilingual grammars and dictionaries. These elites, as Khubchandani (2003) explains, served as mediators between "western language values and indigenous language patterns", claiming for themselves the right to arbitrate which language varieties should be approved, without being fully aware of the indifference of the majority of the citizens to such efforts in their everyday speech activity (Khubchandani, 2003). From this point of view, it is not solely European languages that are colonial while African languages are Indigenous tools of resistance, since both can be seen as colonial artefacts.

The unilingual/bilingual state projects in much of the Global South are thus "pursued, entrenched and safeguarded by politico-administrative elites in government and a compliant and non-reflexive intelligentsia" that have become little more than "purveyors of Northern epistemologies, most of which have little applicability in the complexly multilingual contexts of the developing world" (Mwaniki, 2018, p.30). This process then becomes naturalized so that, for example, the sociolinguistic truism that multilingualism is the natural and common condition for the majority world obscures the implicit language categorizations that lurk behind such apparently descriptive categorization. What is often overlooked is that multilingualism as commonly understood is a way of thinking, a world view, an intellectual orientation that forces us to operate under the burden of a backward-looking metalanguage that was never designed "for our modern priorities" (Harris, 2009, p.33). Sociolinguists and applied linguists have revelled in their 'multilingual turn' (May, 2014), their discovery that multilingualism is the normal state of humanity, their denunciations of monolingual mindsets among both colleagues and a broad range of policy makers and the wider public, without pausing to examine the ideological underpinnings of the version of multilingualism that they are proposing for the world.

Multilingualism and plural monolingualisms

A central argument in many contemporary accounts of multilingualism is that language research has tended to work with monolingualism as a norm, and that such a construct is inappropriate because a majority of, if not most, people, are multilingual. This line of argumentation, which celebrates the shift from monolingualism to multilingualism, does not, from the point of view of a renewed southern perspective, do enough to question the underlying premises of its own position. It underestimates the social impact and intellectual resilience of monolingual ideology. Although we share many of the concerns over the monolingual bias at the heart of much research on language, we are also concerned that the resultant idea of enumerable multilingualism does not take us far enough. Even if we accept that there has been a conceptual and administrative shift from a focus on monolingualism to multilingualism as reflected in the discourses of much established scholarship (Martin-Jones et al., 2012), the problem still remains that the idea of 'a language' (albeit a product of a complex interplay between sociohistorical factors and politics) makes possible the idea that multilingualism may be made up of different autonomous objects, a plural or multiple monolingualism. If, however, we grasp the full implications of the impossibility of the central construct of 'a language', it becomes clear that we cannot in fact critique and then pluralize monolingualism as there can be no such thing. Rather than the monolingualism-as-bad and multilingualism-as-good position, we would be better off seeing all these language-countability frameworks – from the pernicious 'zerolingualism' (Jaspers, 2011) through the problematic semilingualism (Stroud, 2004; Salö and Karlander, 2018) and monolingualism (Gramling, 2016) to the vaunted bi- and multilingualism (May, 2014) – as problematic.

Many students in the early years of schooling in different parts of the world (though particularly in the Global South) attend school without knowing they are 'multilingual'. Being multilingual is something they discover at school through a radical process that alters their self-perception and identity when pedagogy forces them to discover languages as separate entities. Pedagogy entails teaching a specific view and understanding of language. In such cases, pedagogy creates objects: Language reinforced by the presence of "subjects" like English, Shona, or Yoruba on the timetable alongside mathematics, biology, health, and science. The northern understanding of multilingualism as "multiple monolingualisms" insists on ideas such as a mother tongue or a medium of instruction so that "African languages, which have existed side by side for significant periods of time, complementing each other in multilingual symbiosis, are suddenly cast as competing for spaces" (Banda, 2009, p.2). The idea of 'a language' as an educational construct is also reflected in debates as to whether Caribbean Creole (CC) is a variety of English or a separate language. Nero (2006) cites examples of Jamaican speakers of CC who assumed they spoke English until they were assigned to ESL classes, thus challenging their sense of being native speakers of English. Although sociolinguists have long had to acknowledge the messiness of the category 'language', and have used, for example, notions such as *continua* to account for the impossibility of imposing borders between creoles and related languages, the Caribbean Creole (CC) example illustrates further how languages are constructs of the frameworks that make them.

Clearly, for Jamaicans, Caribbean Creole (CC) was English, whereas their experience when assigned to an ESL class undermines that very same belief. So CC gets caught between speakers' beliefs about what they speak (English), creole studies' affirmation that it is a fully fledged creole language, institutional language ascriptions as a second language or dialect (ESL classes for CC speakers), and a classification as a subvariety of English that cannot be counted as a World English on a par with Indian or Singaporean English from the point of view of the World Englishes framework. As Mufwene (2001, p.107) has noted, "the naming practices of new Englishes has to do more with the racial identity of those who speak them than with how these varieties developed and the extent of their structural deviations". In Liberia, speakers of what some linguists might call Liberian Pidgin are adamant that what they speak is a variety of English. In Ghana, educated Ghanaian speakers find the reference to what they speak as Ghanaian English offensive since they perceive their English to be indistinguishable from standard English. The example of Ghanaian English also draws our attention to the need to incorporate local perspectives and the locus of enunciation into any analysis of language use: When Ghanaians and indeed other Third World-educated individuals insist that what they speak is English, this does not suggest that they are unaware of linguistic differences between them and other users, but rather that at times the differences are insignificant to them (Rajagopalan, 2007).

These examples point to several concerns about the linguistic analyses on which many accounts of languages in the contemporary world rely. Although the serious study of creoles by linguists and the concomitant acceptance of creoles as languages like any other has been a great advance from earlier views of creole languages as somehow deficient, the incorporation of these languages into a standard linguistic framework has also caused what Grace (n.d.) calls "collateral damage". By turning them into languages like any other, the very distinctiveness, diversity, and creativity of creoles is reduced to questions of uniformity, origins, and substrata. A similar point is made by Branson and Miller (2007) with respect to sign languages. Although much was gained initially by finally treating sign language as languages like any other, rather than as mere gesture or the gestural representation of pre-existing languages, much has also been lost by the inability to see their uniqueness as gestural languages that operate spatially and temporally in ways quite different from other languages. While both creoles and sign languages have gained from the dedicated work by linguists to show that they are equal to other named language, they have also suffered as a result, being reduced to the same normative structures created to describe other languages. Sign languages can help us see how communication operates in spatiotemporal and embodied terms. By understanding how sign languages work, we can rediscover "the multi-dimensional nature of spoken language – its strategic use of time, of space through gesture and body language, and of tone" (Branson and Miller, 2007, p.119). As Kusters and Sahasrabudhe (2018, p.62) note, certain academic ideologies about gesture and signing "have de-localised and de-contextualised fluid language practices; simplified and essentialized their difference; or made distinctions where language users typically do not experience such distinctions".

Lurking behind many of the arguments made in this chapter is the perennial controversial notion of the native speaker and expertise. If languages were invented, then they cannot have native speakers. They will, however, have people who may claim to be experts in them, and others who resist their formation. Global South scholarship aims to challenge the power structures behind many claims to expertise in language which in some cases is encapsulated and reinforced under categories such as native speakers or the international publishing industry. The idea of a native language and by extension, a native speaker, is to a large degree, a product of the rise of the 19th-century nation state (Bonfiglio, 2010), during which the emergence of language as local, organic, and rooted in a homeland became popular. Thus, native language and nationality were configured by metaphorical extension from the physical environment and biology. The constructed languages may be legitimate in the eyes of political administrators and those who are experts in them, but the notion of a native speaker is a deeply troubling term, tied to racial identifications of speaking subjects (Bonfiglio, 2010; Rosa and Flores, 2017). As Flores and Rosa (2015) explain, raciolinguistic ideologies link "the white speaking and listening subject to *monoglossic language ideologies*, which position idealized monolingualism in a standardized national language as the norm to which all national subjects should aspire" (p.151). The myth of the native speaker is reinforced by plural monolingual models.

Plural monolingualism is a powerful ideological position because it is supported by powerful discourses. Plural monolingual discourses are mutually reinforced and complemented by discourses of language rights, (May, 2005; and see next chapter). The individuality and autonomous nature of language is further consolidated by such discourses in which individual languages have rights assigned to them, which then creates an impression of a language-centred universe where human concerns are of secondary significance (see Blommaert, 2008; Mufwene, 2010). If the idea of independent languages is not readily applicable, advocates of language rights find themselves in an invidious position of supporting very specific and culturally grounded views of both language and right as if they were universal (Ndhlovu, 2018; see Chapter 4). By promoting 'alien' concepts without accommodating the specificities of local interpretation of variants of those concepts, advocates of language rights undermine interests of the communities they seek to serve (May, 2005). The language rights discourses sidestep the language they are seeking to preserve by not examining how language rights are interpreted by the vernaculars whose rights they are seeking to advance, and thus stand accused of their own imperialistic stance insofar as they override other world views and discourses. As Heller and Duchêne (2007) remind us, the question we need to address is why we continue to retain modernist ideas about language and identity, particularly in the face of other realities. We will explore these questions of language rights, discourses of endangerment, and language revitalization and reclamation in the next chapter.

Innovations: Remixing multilingualism

Despite the burden of current research tending towards a pluralization of monolingualisms in its rediscovery of multilingualism, there are a number of different ways in which we can move towards a more productive understanding of language use. Fardon and Furniss (1984) propose that multilingualism is "Africa's lingua franca". In plural monolingualism, the starting point is singular languages that may be used together, whereas in lingua franca multilingualism languages are so deeply intertwined and fused into each other that the level of fluidity renders it difficult to determine any boundaries that may indicate that there are different languages involved. While plural monolingualism is consistent with a model that renders it possible to choose between languages, multilingualism as a lingua franca, or what we have elsewhere (Makoni and Pennycook, 2012) called a *multilingua franca*, by contrast, militates against this trend and conjures up a very different notion of language. In lingua franca multilingualism language is viewed as a multilayered chain that is constantly combined and recombined and in which "secondary" language learning takes place more or less simultaneously with language use. In describing lingua franca multilingualism, Fardon and Furniss point out that language is conceptualized as a multilayered and partially connected chain that offers a choice of varieties and registers in the speaker's immediate environment, and a steadily diminishing set of options to be employed in more distant interactions, albeit a set that is always liable to be reconnected more densely to a new environment by rapid secondary learning, or by the development of new languages

(1984, p.4). In many southern contexts, Global North concepts of languages, mother tongues, or multilingualism, simply do not reflect the ways languages are used and understood, which can be better described as forms of *multilanguaging* (Makalela, 2018a).

The grassroots multilingualism that we are trying to bring to the fore is evident in popular culture, the study of which creates opportunities to advance an analysis of multilingualism that links music, language, painting, and public transport. An analysis that combines diverse modalities has to be transmodal (Pennycook, 2007a; Makoni and Makoni, 2009) rather than multimodal (Kress, 2003; Kress and van Leeuwen, 2001) because meanings or communication in such situations are carried by diverse modalities (and not multimodalities, which echoes plural monolingualism). A transmodal analysis should capture the dynamic and evolving relationship between languages and other modalities. Meaning is an evolving art and drama because semiotic systems are constructed in context and are always in a state of becoming, inchoate, fragmented, and historically contingent. From this point of view, an understanding of *multilingua francas* incorporates not only the linguistic resources speakers draw on but also elements of the accompanying soundtracks. Language use in parts of South Africa may be interwoven with *Kwaito* (a version of South African hip-hop) and its various associations. In such contexts, sampling of sounds, genres, languages, and cultures is the norm (Pennycook, 2007a; Alim et al., 2009; Makoni et al., 2010).

As Williams (2017) shows in his work on hip-hop in South Africa, the styles and performances of hip-hop bring about a *remixing* of multilingualism, new and creative ways of doing multilingualism. Thus, Williams shows not only how hip-hop artists may draw on a variety of language varieties in their performances (Kaaps, isiXhosa, isiZulu, Sabela, SeSotho, Tsotsitaal, and various types of English from both South African and African American sources), but also that these artists create new ways of doing multilingualism, requiring in turn new ways of thinking about multilingualism. In hip-hop spaces, Williams (2017, p.4) explains, "languages converge, clash and intermingle to create resources of uptake and exclusion." A focus on "single and countable languages", therefore, cannot capture the "multilingual repertoire of speakers"; indeed, study of hip-hop performances requires a broader understanding of "complex semiotic webs within and across which speakers move, comprising not just languages as we know them, but bits of language such as registers, accents, words, and assemblages of form-meaning elements, such as rap rhythms and embodied performances" (2017, p.4).

This view of language takes social activity rather than language structure as central and explores how individuals and communities express "voice" (Blommaert, 2005), playing around with semiotics with fragmented and open designs, which can be manipulated to clarify, obfuscate, or make meanings ambiguous (Khubchandani, 1997, p.70; Makoni et al, 2010). This ambiguity or meaning obfuscation contrasts sharply with the type of multilingual school language practices "which puts premium on the explicit, unambiguous, overt manifestation through language by laying undue stress on its rationale and overt use" (Khubchandani,

1997, p.226). "Words and alternative ways of talking (...) have served as weapons against oppressive, vehicles for solidarity, among all manner of disenfranchised peoples, and instruments of extraordinary art" (Ana Cara, 2011 in Anne Storch, 2018, p.48). Linguistic creativity, Storch reminds us, "doesn't have to be playful and amusing; it can also be about experiences of marginalization, injustice and pain. There are consequently, different creativities and different indexicalities of creatively manipulated speech" (Storch, 2018, p.48).

The astute creation, decreation, and recreation of words and their meanings is, at times, used, as Storch (2018 illustrates, to

> evoke ideas and memories of what cannot always be seen or heard (such as spirits) of a performer's feelings and healings. Noisy and messy communicative practices such as "gibberish", screaming, and swearing need to be seen as performance rather than as deviations from "proper linguistic practice".

It is these created, decreated, recreated, 'gibberish' communicative practices that are re-centred in a sociolinguistics of the Global South and have to be analysed, using alternative frameworks. This dynamic fluidity calls for a need to imagine new metaphors to describe multilingual density, or to borrow from Illich and Sander's description of vernacular grammars in the late 15th century: "Lingua or tongue was less like one drawer in a bureau than one color in a spectrum. The comprehensibility of speech was comparable to the intensity of a color" (1988 pp.62–3). The rise of new forms of urban multiple language use has a long and complex history (Mazrui, 2017). These new *urbilingualisms* pose challenges to the study of multiple languages and render it necessary to construct new metaphors to capture the unfolding social, political, and linguistic complexity. They draw on and use a wide range of local and non-local languages and create new and fragmented semiotic systems; they are constantly in flux; they are predominantly oral; they are street languages, and as such are often linked to popular culture, crime, and urban unrest. To speak these languages, it is necessary to draw on multilingual resources, and yet these urban languages are also multilanguages in themselves, diverse, shifting, constantly evolving, and unpredictable in their usage. They vary according to who is using them to whom, and are constantly part of a creative *remixing*, as Williams (2017) puts it.

There is a danger, nonetheless, of treating youth languages as special cases, an approach that can misleadingly suggest that multilingual juggling, semantic manipulations, and phonological processes such as truncation or abbreviation, are unique to youth languages. The exoticization and commoditization of youth languages is exploited in popular media and in advertisements, including films such as "Tsotsitaal" (2006), "Nairobi Half Life" (2012), and "Kinshasa Kids" (2012), which draw on creative bricolage based on Tsotsitaal, Sheng, and Yanke. The popular media and, to some extent, academic research on youth languages tends to stylize and decontextualize the creative bricolage, thereby exaggerating their uniqueness (Nassentein et al., 2018). A related case has long been made by de Graffe (2019) in terms of what he sees as *creole exceptionalism*, a framing of creole languages as inherently different and extraordinary. We also need to be cautious lest this focus on urbilingual renewal suggests that more rural areas are less dynamic (Di Carlo et al., 2019; May, 2019): Southern applied linguistics can by no means afford to overlook non-urban contexts. The nature of multilingualism in rural areas is facilitated by a wide array of factors which include exogamy, child fostering, and economic interdependence (Lüpke and Storch, 2013, p.347). Indeed, a closer look at such communities suggests some escaped the weight of colonial control and exhibit

> small-scale multilingualism, referring to communicative practices in heteroglossic societies in which multilingual interaction is not governed by domain specialization and hierarchical relationships of different named languages and lects used in them, but by deeply rooted social practices within a meaningful geographic setting.
>
> *(Lüpke, 2016, p.35)*

Such communities, according to Lüpke (2016) are found across the globe, including West Africa, Amazonia, Northern Australia, and Melanesia. The communicative practices in such small-scale multilingualisms have been described using a number of terms, including 'egalitarian multilingualism' (Francois, 2012), 'balanced multilingualism' (Aikhenvald, 2002), and 'traditional multilingualism' (Di Carlo, 2016).

Lüpke argues that researchers cannot effectively describe the sociolinguistic practices in these small-scale communities through the use of conventional, sociolinguistic, psycholinguistic, or named hierarchical relationships between languages. While we of course need to subject accounts of such small-scale multilingualism to critical scrutiny (lest balanced or egalitarian multilingualism becomes a new form of exceptionalism), there are indications in this research that alternative ways of doing multilingualism are happening across the world. This lends support to our argument that for applied linguistics to advance it needs not only to expand the repertoire of sociolinguistic contexts in which socio-applied linguistics research is conducted but also to reorient to these contexts in new ways. A Global South framework needs to ensure it looks not only at rapid remixing in hip-hop performance but also differently-paced and differently-realized forms of linguistic creation in many other contexts.

Challenges: New ways of thinking

The arguments we have been making in this chapter present several major challenges, not only, and very obviously, to what we are here characterizing as mainstream/northern linguistics, but also to the broader southern project. If part of the decolonial project is to *delink* from European thought (Mignolo, 2018), it is nevertheless clear that to do so we need to engage in a sustained critique of northern conceptions of language (the deconstructive or disinventive stage). We cannot move straight towards alternative visions of language without establishing what they are alternatives to, yet in doing so we inevitably bring a lot of northern baggage into the discussion. This is a point of continuing debate in the development of a southern applied linguistics: There is no South without the North. While Mignolo (2018) eschews this terminology because of this very problem, it remains difficult to proceed without the prior critique. We need at the same time to be cautious lest the critique fills too much space (a critique of northern linguistics can still be seen as an internal debate). It is essential therefore that we seek alternative forms of knowledge for renewal of our discipline, a focus that develops much more in the following chapters. This remains, of course, a profound challenge as we try to evaluate new ideas, their provenance and their take-up, particularly when, for example, scholars such as Makalela (2018c) talk of "*ubuntu translanguaging pedagogy*" to refer to "African worldviews of interdependence and general use of languages without boundaries" (p.262).

We have returned in part in this chapter to some of our earlier arguments (Makoni and Pennycook, 2007, 2012) about languages as inventions and the need to engage in a project of disinvention as part of any critical language project. This project of disinvention, aside from its less than felicitous terminology, has always caused discomfort. Are we arguing that languages do not exist? When it is clear that people – particularly Indigenous and marginalized populations fighting battles for land, food, health, jobs, autonomy, and less incarceration – often organize political resistance around cultural and linguistic identities, what use is it to claim that languages are inventions? In answer to the first point, we would argue that we cannot pursue a southern project simply by jumping ship, and taking up alternative ways of thinking (though neither can a southern perspective be developed without such perspectives). Our point is that part of any such project has to engage with the dominant modes of thought and investigate how they came about and why they are flawed, and can employ both northern scholarship (integrational linguistics, for example, has few southern pretensions, but can be useful nonetheless) and southern scholarship to do so. If a goal of *decolonial thinking and doing* (to which we return particularly in Chapter 5) is to "delink from the epistemic assumptions" (Mignolo, 2018, p.106) that have come to define languages and their use, then we need to understand those modes of thought and how and why they developed. We cannot engage with a southern project without establishing what it is we are trying to supersede, and we cannot proceed with a southern project without acknowledging the deep connections across ways of thinking.

We do not argue that languages do not exist: To say they are inventions is to point both to the specific processes by which particular languages have been created out of the range of speech styles and resources available across communities, and to the general processes by which the notion of separate languages has been produced in the conjunction between political and academic work on languages. This does not mean they do not exist: Like many aspects of social life that are clearly socially constructed – gender and race are two clear examples (Haslanger,

2012) – they exist in social life and have major implications particularly in forms of discriminatory practices based around the distinctions these ideas create. We do not argue that languages do not exist but rather that they are not natural kinds, they are not things that exist beyond human activity. This can help us see why it is of course important that people mobilize around concepts of language, not as a result of 'false consciousness' (deluded political action based on a myth) but as a particular type of political activity. The disinvention argument, therefore, is by no means aimed at destabilizing liberatory projects based around languages but rather to open up a space for alternative ways of thinking about language.

Treating languages as socially and historically constructed provides space and latitude for social and political change and takes cognizance of individuals' social and adaptive strategies, as well as their resistance to some constructed languages. If Indigenous languages are socially constructed through a complex interplay of philosophy and politics, they are akin to other constructs such as customary law, which is a form of codified traditional law rather than any naturally occurring tradition. Joseph's (2006, p.1) reminder that languages are "political from top to bottom" is useful here as it draws attention yet again to the point that both the invention of languages and their disinvention are steeped in relations of power and politics. As Kusters and Sahasrabudhe (2018, p.62) explain, processes of "disinvention and reconstitution of the distinction between gesture and sign" can enable a more multifaceted understanding of (sign) language that is better "connected to fluid everyday language practices" and the ways these are "experienced, and expressed/processed in language ideologies". This does not, they suggest, mean that a struggle for language rights is no longer possible; rather it depends on what one is trying to do, when, and for whom. Both a better understanding of language practices and political activism to promote languages are "grounded in language ideologies and promote or produce ideologies" (Kusters and Sahasrabudhe, 2018, p.62)

Where, then, do we turn in the search for alternative ways of thinking about language? We have outlined some of these in the previous section: *remixing multilingualism, multilanguaging*, and *multilingua francas* all suggest different ways of conceptualizing multilingualism. This is also part of the longer project of this book (we will discuss Indigenous cosmovisions in Chapter 6), so we will return to this question particularly in Chapter 7. Clearly, however, the changing realities of urban (and rural) life, with enhanced mobility, shifting populations, social upheaval, health and climate crises, and increased access to diverse media and forms of popular culture, as well as the political imperative to redress northern hegemony, suggest we need to rethink, and therefore possibly rename, the ways in which language has been conceptualized. It is therefore necessary to develop local metalanguages: If current dominant metadiscursive regimes are a product of Western/northern philosophy intensified by colonial and postcolonial scholarship, they will not be able to bear the weight of renewed southern multilingualisms. Simply translating metalanguages from English into local languages or creating applied linguistics tied to particular languages, does not resolve the global domination of the South by northern applied linguistics because the underlying problems are assumptions about the nature of language.

So, what, finally, to do with the emergence of new terminologies and ideas derived from what are arguably northern contexts? On the one hand, neologisms such as *translanguaging* (García and Li Wei, 2014), have been used to take us beyond the assumed frameworks of bounded languages, while on the other hand older terminology such as *heteroglossia, repertoires*, and *registers* have been mobilized to do similar work (Pennycook, 2018b). García and Li Wei's (2014, p.2) explanation of translanguaging captures this current trend well. For them, translanguaging is

> an approach to the use of language, bilingualism and the education of bilinguals that considers the language practices of bilinguals not as two autonomous language systems as has been traditionally the case, but as one linguistic repertoire with features that have been societally constructed as belonging to two separate languages.

As noted at the beginning of this chapter, however, Heugh and Stroud (2018) take exception to the claims to have developed a new approach to multilingualism based on the idea that multilingualism is more than the sum of monolingual languages. This, they suggest, is a typical northern move that ignores work from the Global South (and see the critique by Todd, 2016, in the previous chapter, of northern appropriations of southern thought), and is disconnected from the lived experiences of marginalized people in the Global South (whether this is in the geographical North or South). Yet while we agree with much of the argument here – northern scholarship is all too often a process of dislocation and forgetting – we also suggest the need for a greater appreciation of the complexity at stake here.

It is not that we wish to reappropriate these terms for a southern project, but rather that we need to grasp the intricacy of intertwined strands of intellectual work. To what extent, for example, should Canagarajah's (2013, p.6) suggestion that a focus on *translingual practice* constitutes a paradigm shift – on the basis that "communication transcends individual languages", and "communication transcends words and involves diverse semiotic resources and ecological affordances", – be castigated similarly as northern disconnectedness when his own work has sought repeatedly to draw these connections? Or what do we do with García's (2014) consideration of Mignolo's idea of *bilanguaging* (see previous chapter) to link her translingual framework to decolonial theory? And what, to complicate things further, should we make of Makalela's (2018a, p.4) use of the idea of *ubuntu translanguaging*, the view that in the context of complex multilingualism, "no language is complete without another"? We need to be cautious not to argue either that this is inherently southern because of the locus of enunciation or the use of the idea of *ubuntu*, nor, heaven forbid, that it is a hybrid South/North idea, nor that it is a southern reappropriation of a northern appropriation of southern ideas about multilingualism (though this is the most promising of these options).

Rather, the point is that by insisting that neither people nor languages can be complete without each other, this term suggests a fresh way of looking at language and language use, and by grounding these concerns in Southern African educational contexts, this emerging body of work (Makalela, 2018a, b, c) opens up new possibilities for southern applied linguistics. Heugh and Stroud (2018) are right that too much northern scholarship appropriates ideas from the South, claiming as new what has been known elsewhere for a long time. They are right too that we need to move beyond a rediscovery of multilingualism to focus instead on the possibility of multiple multilingualisms.

> With the ascendancy of communication pursuits in linguistic enquiry viewed in the light of the "universal" and the "unique", there is a growing awareness of the plurality of cognitions, structures, and institutions which have a great bearing on human activity as such.
> *(Khubchandani, 1995 in Khubchandani 2003, p.241)*

In order to move towards an understanding of multiple multilingualisms, however, we need to do more than pluralize multilingualism (as if this were much better than just pluralizing monolingualisms). If pluralizing monolingualisms to create multilingualism has been a failed northern project, so a pluralized multilingualism will not suffice as a new southern project. We will discuss in the next chapter how a move towards ontological questions opens up a space for further thought on this.

Conclusion

We have sought to shed light in this chapter on the concern that the monolingual/multilingual dichotomy "misdirects and misrepresents the notion of language diversity" (Ndhlovu, 2018, p.118). In order to understand the metadiscursive regimes used in the construction of "languages", we need a critical history of linguistics which does not revolve around the Global North (Heller and McElhinny, 2017). There is a need for more work in linguistic anthropology in order to understand the ways in which languages are locally used and understood, as well as the effects of particular metadiscursive regimes on the working of local languages. Canut's (2011) work on the invention of Roma (the Global South in the geographical North) illustrates that the processes of invention are not only historical and located in the geographical South, but are current and on the North's doorstep. These entanglements have to be understood historically, so that the violence and horror of WWII can in part be understood as European colonialism revisited upon itself (Césaire, 1955; Fanon, 1952) and in turn the ways race and language were constructed in Nazi Germany carried over into apartheid South Africa (Pugach, 2017).

The assumption that monolingualism and multilingualism are two important pillars which might be used to frame sociolinguistic analysis, or that studies of multilingualism are attempting to move beyond the blinkered monolingualism that has constricted a lot of thought about language use, takes us a certain way but then stops short. For many people across the world, the critical issue is not whether one is monolingual or multilingual but that one uses language. This is why the ultimate move here may not only be from monolingualism to multilingualism but also back to monolingualism, where the latter is understood in very different ways from both the monological, one-variety concept that linguistics has been trying to escape, or the fantasy of a universal language capacity that underpins all languages. This is the monolingualism of multilanguaging, of multilingua francas, where people simply use language, drawing on whatever resources are available. Those people who we now see as deeply multilingual in the Global South rarely see themselves in the same way, and may not acknowledge this label of multilingualism. If we can do away with our language enumerations that sit so often at the heart of multilingualism, a great deal of productive research could start to open up the real complexities of grassroots multilingualism.

The next step, therefore, is to move towards an understanding of the relationships among language resources as used by certain communities (the linguistic resources users draw on), local language practices (the use of these language resources in specific contexts), and language users' relationship to language varieties (the social, economic, and cultural positioning of the speakers). From this point of view, therefore, we can start to move away from both mono- and multilingual orientations to language and take on board insights from outside the mainstream of language studies. The liberal linguistic consensus that sees "so-called 'heritage', 'ethnic', 'minority', and 'migrant' languages" threatened by the monolingual mindset and dominant languages misses the point that it is the way language is being understood here that is the problem (Ndhlovu, 2018, p.123). This will be part of the discussion in the next chapter, where we seek to explore in more depth ways in which a southern applied linguistics can break free from assumptions about separate languages, endangered languages, and language rights, and instead move towards a more complex and appropriate understanding of language in the Global South, which may also liberate the Global North from its rigid notions of language.

4
LANGUAGE ENDANGERMENT, VITALITY, AND RECLAMATION

One of the major areas of tension around North-South scholarship is in the field of language policy, language endangerment, and language rights. A northern applied linguistics orthodoxy has decried the death of languages as communities have abandoned lesser-used languages in favour of more widely used ones, suggesting that the languages themselves, the users of those languages, and humanity as a whole would all be better off if these languages were maintained, revived, or revitalized. The gradual disuse of languages has been denounced as language death or even *linguistic genocide* (Skutnabb-Kangas, 2000) when particular actors or particular majority languages are seen as responsible for killing off others. We shall deal in the next chapter with some of the educational issues that ensue from language policies that favour majority or minority languages, but here we shall examine questions around different understandings of multilingualism, and the implications for language policies, and language reclamation projects. These are difficult questions since it is clear that identifications with particular languages matter for many communities in profound ways. And yet, as Mufwene (2016) notes, the "linguistics discourse on language endangerment and loss has been marked by a number of disputable assumptions about what languages are and about the terrible price humanity incurs in losing linguistic and cultural diversity as some of them die" (p.115).

While attending to the complexities of relations between language, community, and the broader world, we also want to draw attention here to the extent to which the understanding of language on which many of these arguments has been based is all too often firmly rooted in northern epistemologies, promoting concepts of language choice and ethnicity that are alien to many southern contexts. Crucial in this context has been a failure to understand the complexity of multilingual southern contexts, inappropriately constructing the battle as one between dominant, majority languages and weaker minority languages or between European languages and local languages (Ebongue and Hurst, 2017). There has also been a tendency to link languages to particular world views and to argue that the loss of a language implies the loss of a culture and epistemology. This isomorphism between language and culture has been upheld widely across linguistic and applied linguistic domains, though gained most prominence in the language ecology movement (Skutnabb-Kangas, 2000, 2003; Pennycook, 2004; Romaine, 2015), and its arguments for causal links between environmental and linguistic decimation, and between language and cultural loss. As Ndhlovu (2018, p.118) explains,

> although the high-sounding metaphors of human rights, anti-imperialism and biodiversity resonate with contemporary international conversations around social justice and equity issues, passionate appeals to them have not done much good because the standard language ideology remains ensconced as the only valid and legitimate conceptual framework that informs mainstream understandings of what is meant by "language".
>
> *(Ndhlovu, 2018, p.118)*

If few sociolinguists would endorse some of the most resolute ecological frameworks – such as a model that "idealizes languages as fixed, and as competing with each other for speakers" and assumes "a highly connected population, with no spatial or social structure, in which all speakers are monolingual" (Abrams and Strogatz, 2003, p.900) – the tendency is nonetheless shared in these discourses on language endangerment to reify and elevate languages to a station above people, and thus to obscure the real issues of poverty, change, and discrimination faced by many language users in the Global South. While we will also carefully consider both the questions of what is lost when languages are no longer used, as well as the concern for some applied linguists that the critiques of discourses of language endangerment have made it difficult to argue for language-in-education projects that seek to support local language initiatives, this chapter points to the importance of rethinking the frameworks that have informed language preservation work for so long. Following some of the key arguments we have already established in the book – and centrally the need to decolonize language, to delink language from northern thought – the aim of this chapter is to look critically at issues of language endangerment, language rights, and language revitalization, with an aim to finding productive ways forward for alliances between linguists, applied linguists, languages, and communities.

Language misrecognized

As Stebbins (2014) makes clear, the linguistic criteria by which linguists make decisions about languages are ideologically driven. It took a long time for features not present in Indo-European languages (such as ergativity) to be recognized in other languages. It is crucial, she points out, "to engage with alternative ideologies of language" in order to "address the underlying power structures that have created the conditions for language endangerment" (p.294). In recognizing the long-term complicity between linguistics and colonialism (see Chapter 3) – a complex intertwined relation involving colonial accumulation, missionary endeavours, and language ideologies (Errington, 2001, 2008) – we need to open up for examination the extent to which linguistic descriptions and language policy interventions are as much part of the problem as they can ever be part of any solution. Analysing the assumptions on which linguistic descriptions and policy implementations are based matters because they are social interventions that have knock-on effects on the conditions of people's lives. The development of a 'standardized' version of a language, for example, that is markedly different from the variety that is actually spoken, or that is too simplified or too complexified, may render the development of literacy more difficult than is necessary. Standardizing languages, as Costa, De Korne, and Lane (2018, p.1) point out, may be a "Faustian bargain", with "language advocates" and state authorities assuming its inherent emancipatory and empowering potential, while confronting speakers with "linguistic standards that speakers themselves cannot meet, together with new hierarchies that give advantage to some speakers over others" (p.2).

Such disabling repercussions for literacy may be part of the material consequences of both linguistic descriptions and educational implementations (Makoni and Meinhof 2003 p.119). Other linguistic and applied linguistic processes with material consequences include the ways in which language/dialect distinctions are drawn, the ways a language or language in general are understood (what is a language like?), and notions such as authentic speakerhood. This becomes more complicated when linguistic descriptions by the lay public are taken into account (which they must surely be) since ordinary people are unlikely to use categories that correspond with those of the linguist (see Chapters 1 and 3). Bamanankan, the most widely spoken language in the Republic of Mali in West Africa, for example, has no lexical distinctions between 'language' and 'dialect', a distinction that varies greatly across different languages (see Chew, 2010; Dong, 2010, for Chinese) and which is based frequently around Eurocentric views of language and literacy. For Bamanankan, however, the productive suffix *-kan* may be translated as a manner of speaking – something like language variety, though perhaps also style – and linguists need to be wary not to map a language/dialect distinction onto such terminology. We shall return to some of the ways in which applied linguists can work more productively with communities (and communities with applied linguists) towards the end of this chapter.

Introductory books on linguistics establish what counts as language, with both a focus on what is to be included (signs and rules) and what excluded (animal communication, for example). Applied linguistics has tended to leave such descriptions unchallenged and to seek ways of using these already-described languages in educational and policy domains. As has been argued elsewhere (Pennycook, 2018a), the humanist drive to render language a property that belongs exclusively to humans – with a further unlikely proposition that language just appeared in evolutionary history – led on the one hand to the exclusion of animal communication as part of this history and on the other necessitated the construction of an arcane version of language that only humans could use. If this was something that only humans could do, it had to be something in the head, made of complex structures, separated from the world. Missing from this account were many other cultural modes such as music, dance, and drama as well as "the gestural, pictorial, sculptural, sonic, tactile, bodily, affective and artefactual dimensions of human life" (Finnegan, 2015, p.18). Such moves are highly problematic for an understanding of language in many communities since not only do they miss the point that language is something felt, experienced, embodied, practised, and related to the environment in complex ways, but they also exclude many aspects of language and its relation to performance, voice, social structure, and location.

The Global North version of language, with its origins in Enlightenment thought, its deep ties to colonialism and modernity, and its emphasis on literacy as a tool of rational thought, created a "cognitive language-centred model of the nature and destiny of humanity" (Finnegan, 2015, p.18). The myth of human language and literacy, Finnegan (2015, p.18) continues, "echoes that Enlightenment ideology in which language, and especially written language, is the condition of rationality, civilization and progress, attaining its apotheosis in the alphabetic writing of the West" (Finnegan, 2015, p.18). This is not to say that such ideologies and processes went unchallenged or unchanged: Colonialism may have "shaped the early standardization of isiXhosa (and other African languages)" though it never fully defined the process since language users resisted and changed these emerging literacy projects (Deumert and Mabandla, 2018, p.217). Once this model of language was refined through the colonial era – with its particular assumptions and divisions between civilized and uncivilized, rational and irrational, literate and oral – language as the precondition for humanity became a raciolinguistic category (Rosa, 2018; Rosa and Flores, 2017) as the precondition for rational, white, literate thought. Amongst several key assumptions behind this model of language are a stress on language as having a primary function as a conveyor of information (rather than, say, tied to bodies and affect). Languages are seen as having an ontological status outside the communicative event (they exist separately), as made up of discrete and discernible units, and, of particular concern to the discussion in this chapter, as representational systems, repositories of culture and knowledge that disappear if a language is lost to posterity (Mufwene, 2016).

Linguistics developed hand in hand with colonialism (Errington, 2001, 2008), and the field "adopted a practice of writing (i.e., documenting) Native American languages in ways that served Euro-American needs, particularly in the choice of what was described and the categories employed in doing so" (Leonard, 2017, p.18). As Leonard (2017) points out, the typical practice in these attempts at language "salvage work" is that "good speakers", whose legitimacy is determined by the linguist-researcher, are encouraged to produce language that is then transformed into "data", which in turn is conceptualized in terms of a "language as object" metaphor emphasizing structural properties over social practices (p.18). As long as "colonial definitions, categories, and methods are imposed onto Indigenous language work" (p.32), language projects will continue to be unsuccessful – in terms of not providing either expected linguistic or broader social, cultural, and economic outcomes – and to be viewed with suspicion by local communities. In order to develop more successful language reclamation projects, Leonard (2017) argues, we need to *decolonize language* (p.32). A central task of this book is to explore ways of decolonizing linguistics and applied linguistics (and see Chapter 5 for a more extended discussion), an endeavour that involves rethinking language and the ways it is described and implemented in a range of language-oriented projects. In the following section, we examine the discourses around language endangerment, before looking at different language ontologies.

The dangers of endangerment: Zombie linguistics

Discourses of language endangerment have come in for substantial critique, not least because of the ways that ecological arguments have sought to map languages as representational repositories of the surrounding world. From there the goal is to try to preserve language, culture, and knowledge on the grounds that this is good for both humanity and the environment. Just as we need to protect delicate ecologies, to fence them off, to create national parks, to collect DNA, so the solution to unbalanced language ecologies is to protect and classify endangered languages in order to preserve them. As Muehlmann (2007) makes clear, discourses of language preservation put very particular ways of understanding Indigeneity into play: "The endangered language movement builds its discourse on the assumption that safeguarding indigenous languages helps protect nature because indigenous people have a natural interest in sustaining ecological relations" (p.30). A romantic dream of ecological sustainability as the bedrock of Indigenous life becomes a key part of an argument for language preservation. As well as this "vernacularist nationalist organicist strain" in language preservation discourse, there is also, according to Cameron (2007), "an exoticizing or 'orientalist' strain" leading to "the implicit exoticism of images like 'our rich human landscape', and more generally, the discursive depoliticization of preservation and revitalization movements" (p.281).

Preservationist rhetoric, with its exoticizing and romanticizing view of local people locked in time, runs the danger of overlooking the language practices and language ideologies of local populations. As De Souza and Andreotti (2009) argue in the context of Brazil, 'preservation' may be seen by Indigenous communities not so much as the maintenance of the same but rather as the constant need to acquire difference and newness in order to remain the 'same'. Staying the same may be a process of renewal, and repetition may be a practice of difference (Pennycook, 2007c). While outsider views focus on the preservation of language and culture, particularly through education, from a local perspective, survival may be guaranteed by constant change, through the acquisition of newness, through difference. Part of the problem, as Duchêne (2008) makes clear, is that minority languages that need to be preserved are constructed as the flip-side of majority national languages, a view that tends to "reify language in its fixed and delineated dimension" and is thus incapable of "integrating the complexity of the social, economic and political factors that are involved in any process of linguistic, cultural or other minorization" (p.9). For Martin Nakata (1999, p.14), describing the linguistic prescriptions he encountered as a Torres Strait Islander,

> the most damaging aspect of the principle of culture preservation and promotion ... is that it has not only become a panacea for all our ills but has also become so regulatory that it precludes Islanders such as myself and Indigenous people all over this country from pursuing the issues that we want to pursue.

Discussing the revival of Wirangu, a South Australian language, Monaghan (2012) points to the dilemma that the discourse of endangerment "posits individual languages as denotational codes residing in a bounded ethnic group with a distinctive culture and inhabiting its own ecological niche" (p.52). This "ecologising discourse", he goes on, is underpinned by what Harris (1981) identified as the language myth, "the notion that there are languages, as fixed codes, out there in the world waiting to be discovered, documented, saved, or revived. The language myth is ubiquitous, a foundational myth and ideology in orthodox linguistics" (2012, p.52). As Heller and Duchêne (2007) suggest, rather than assuming we can and should save languages, perhaps we should be asking instead who benefits and who loses from understanding languages the way we do, what is at stake for whom, and how and why language serves as a terrain for competition. Wirangu, Monaghan (2012) points out, is a recent construction, an artefact of the colonial encounter. Before the arrival of linguists, whose aim was to fix languages, people's language practices were fluid and the formal concept of a language was quite unnecessary. Language in this sense, he explains, is therefore "part of an imposed Western analytical framework" with a particular focus on writing over speech (p.52). If language revival projects are based on these colonial-missionary constructions, the outcomes at best involve community alienation from these language inventions, and at worst further despair at another round of failed northern intervention.

As Lüpke (2019) notes, the "preoccupation with endangerment goes hand in hand with an essentialist focus on languages, rather than on communicative repertoires" (p.469), a focus that stems from "the history of language description and documentation" with its links to "colonial practice". Several interrelated concerns with these discourses of endangerment and preservation emerge: As a renewed focus on multilingualism and the disappearance of languages has engaged people at many different levels (from local activists, through academic linguists to international bodies), a set of northern discourses about languages and language death have come to predominate, backed by powerful institutions that are "constraining the discourses produced" as well as "the possibility of action on language issues by influencing world policy, global laws, and ultimately resource allocation" (Muehlmann and Duchêne, 2007, p.97). Processes of objectifying, counting, and documenting languages have been widely critiqued as practices of reification that have little to do with how languages are experienced by those communities; such documentary practices may indeed be harmful to those communities (Moore et al., 2010; Muehlmann, 2012).

The northern version of language had led to the understanding that we can document languages through literate means, or put another way, the languages we write down as grammatical and lexical systems are indeed the core of the language itself. As Perley (2012) argues, however, the idea that documentation of a language can save that language has several problems: "Documentation as language salvation" becomes the "operative metaphor used by language experts" and misplaces "expert attention on the language as a code rather than language as the conduit and catalyst for social relationships." The focus is on "the language as a code, but not the speakers who use the code" or the activities which they use the code for. The metaphors of endangerment and death that are central to this discourse posit language as "a biological organism that is undergoing species endangerment from outside forces" and thus allows for the uncoupling of "endangered languages from the community of speakers" (p.134). This "zombie linguistics", Perley argues, has various consequences for languages and communities, bringing communities working to revitalize their languages into conflict with experts, and on a larger scale putting the interests of experts above those of others.

As Mufwene (2016) puts it:

> Linguists who argue that all living languages must be maintained for the sake of linguistic diversity have to make a more convincing case, especially when the relevant populations feel they are disadvantaged by them. Those who argue that maintaining linguistic diversity is useful to linguistics as a profession should feel ashamed of themselves if they ignore the odds that the relevant populations are facing. The reason is professionally selfish. Well-intended linguists face ecologically what is literally a wicked problem: what is good for the survival of a particular population in the face of a changing socioeconomic ecology versus what is ideal for the practice of linguistics.
>
> *(140–141)*

The adoption of such models of language endangerment into applied linguistic attempts to construct policy based on language rights has also encountered serious criticism (Makoni, 2012; Makoni and Trudell, 2006). The dependence of language rights on a broader understanding of human rights is a problem in itself, since there has been a sustained critique from the Global South that the notion of universal human rights has always been a Western/northern construct (Peterson, 1990). For Santos, since post-Marxist critical theory remains anchored in a western-based discourse of universal human rights, it "reduces the understanding of the world to the western understanding of the world" and ignores "decisive cultural and political experiences and initiatives in the countries of the global South" (Santos, 2014, p.21). As critical legal theorists have argued, the institutional practices of human rights depend on an imagined "homogenous world society, in which the extension of formal equality and negative freedom and the globalisation of Western capitalism and consumerism" are tied together in an ideal model of society based on northern ideals (Douzinas, 2000, p.375) a position also echoed by African political scientists and historians (Zeleza and McConnaughay, 2007). Such critiques, it might be argued, ignore both the benefits that can be gained by appeals to human rights, as well as the often-forgotten role played by significant actors from the Global South (from Ghana, Jamaica, the Philippines, Pakistan, Sri Lanka, and Venezuela amongst others) in bringing extensive influence to the formation of these ideas (Jensen, 2016). Nonetheless, for many in the Global South, human rights (or language rights) are always exclusive. A critical analysis of the UN *Declaration on the Rights of Indigenous Peoples* (2007) suggests that it "will benefit the colonizers more than the nations it was designed for – the Indigenous nations" (White Face, 2013, p.4).

Similar problems have been identified with the notion of language rights, with its universalizing tendencies for both language and rights. As Pupavac (2012, p.20) notes, "assertions of global law in a world of international inequalities are problematic for emancipatory politics." The advocacy of "highly prescriptive" regimes of governance (p.25) that assume rights of intervention by global elites, the applicability of global governance to local contexts, the importance of language preservation over human emancipation, and the reification of languages as unitary entities, all raise questions for any language rights movement that operates under the banner of human and linguistic universality. For Mufwene (2010), languages cannot have rights, and linguists are all too often insufficiently clear

> about how countries that are rich in ecological, cultural, and linguistic diversity but are economically poor can, with their limited financial means, satisfy both the human rights of their populations to evolve out of poverty and the alleged rights of their languages to each be used in the education system and/ or other cultural domains.
>
> *(p.914)*

A great deal has been written on language rights (May, 2001; 2012) but in simple terms the problem can be seen as projecting a universalizing northern solution onto the complexities of the Global South. As Sonntag (2003) explains in the context of the global spread of English, "the willingness to use the language of human rights on the global level to frame local linguistic demands vis-à-vis global English may merely be affirming the global vision projected by American liberal democracy" (p.25).

Such critiques do not imply that languages do not matter to different communities: They are often the most central, symbolic, and organizing feature of any movement to reclaim space, autonomy, and decent modes of life (along with land, health, work, and cultural practices). And as Muehlmann (2009; 2012) shows, a loss of language may also have implications for other rights: For the Cucapá people of northwest Mexico, the decline in use of their language has led the government to claim they are no longer sufficiently 'Indigenous' to warrant preferred fishing rights. The question, however, is what is meant by language in the lives of different people and whether this understanding accords with outsiders' perspectives. Do notions of language loss, death, or endangerment, or ideas such as language rights help people to mobilize decolonial efforts around language? There can be no definitive answer to such questions outside the contexts in which language activists are working. Discourses of language rights and endangerment may become part of local initiatives to work with languages as part of broader emancipatory projects, but the ideas of endangerment, rights, and language will have to become locally inflected, will have to find a home in the languages involved, to be of use. This is why we need to push further into different understandings of language before looking at how reclamation projects may be possible.

Innovations: Towards multiple language ontologies

An inquiry into the nature of what language is might seem to be first of all an inquiry into language ideologies (Kroskrity, 2000): The "structured and consequential ways" we think about, or our "entrenched beliefs" in, language (Seargeant, 2009, pp.26–7). The notion of language ideologies, however, as Hauck and Heurich (2018) note, potentially leaves intact the object of inquiry: These are beliefs about things (languages) whose ontological status we have already established. A deeper inquiry into the nature of language requires us to ask ontological questions about what these things are. These are broader questions about what constitutes language in general, as well as the nature of languages themselves. This leads on to a review of the nature of this division itself, so steeped as it is in particular ways of thinking about the ways a supposed underlying human capacity for language can be separated out along cultural, ethnic, or national lines. When we observe that a response to the question as to what language people speak may simply be formed in terms of a general answer meaning 'language', we can follow the route of colonial linguistics and suggest that this naïve answer is a consequence of the respondents being unable to see the wood for the trees: "few natives" are able to grasp the idea of 'a language' since "their minds are not trained to grasp the conception so familiar to us, of a general term embracing a number of interconnected dialects" (Grierson, 1907, p.350). Or we can turn the question back on itself and ask what the basis for this distinction is in the first place.

This takes us in a new direction, a consideration of whether the normally pluralizable term 'languages' (different languages: *langues*) is the only one of this dichotomy open to pluralization, or whether language itself (*langage*) might not also be seen in terms of different ways of understanding the "multiple natures of language" (Hauck and Heurich, 2018, p.2). The notion of *southern multilingualisms*, therefore, recognizes not only that there are many different kinds of multilingualism, many different ways in which language resources may be interwoven – and that it is therefore important, for example, to talk of "Indigenous multilingualisms" (Vaughan and Singer, 2018, p.84) – but also that there may be multiple language ontologies. Before we ask what a particular language is, we need to ask what language is, and whether we want to accept, for example, the supposed truism that language is what separates humans from non-humans. This "mobilization of language for human distinctiveness and from a decidedly human perspective … relies on a particular linguistic nature that radically distinguishes language from nature and culture or society" (Hauck and Heurich, 2018, p.3). This assumption, which echoes through European thought, is based on a set of distinctions (human and non-human animals, culture and nature) that necessitated the creation of a very particular and esoteric version of language, one that only humans could possess and that was separated from bodies, gestures, senses, and social worlds (Pennycook, 2018a).

The answer to the question "what is language?" must, according to Hauck and Heurich, 2018, p.5) "remain plural". Based on studies of language in the Amerindian imagination, they argue that language "must remain an equivocal term, that is sometimes virtual and sometimes actual, sometimes part of pan-spiritual communication and sometimes confined to intra-kin-conversation." Looked at from an ethnographic point of view, the Americas are not only a region of great linguistic diversity in terms of what are usually known as "languages" but also in terms of different genres, styles, chants, songs, dreams, wailing, and narrative conventions within and across communities. "These diverse phenomena", they argue, "should not be understood as easily commensurable instances of a general phenomenon 'language'" since they "all may have different linguistic natures" (Hauck and Heurich, 2018, p.5). As Course (2018, p.5) suggests, the idea of 'language' possibly "obscures a fundamental diversity of ultimately irreconcilable practices, that Mapudungun and Spanish are understood to be fundamentally different kinds of things." From this point of view, the question is not only whether Mapudungun and Spanish "are two different kinds of the same thing" but also whether "they are two different things".

This view derives both from deep ethnographic understandings of language practices and language beliefs but also from the 'ontological turn' in anthropology. The argument concerns a critique that the central assumptions about culture in anthropology – that different people have different cultures that produce different world views – while appearing to some to suggest a form of cultural relativism, nonetheless imply a problematic universality of both humanity and the world: This position assumes that humans all have different cultures but are the same underneath, and that different world views cut the world up differently but that this world is itself consistent: The "modern, anthropological multiculturalist ontology" is based on "the unity of nature and the plurality of cultures" (Viveiros de Castro, 2014, p.6). An alternative, *perspectivist* way of thinking, by contrast, drawing on Amerindian philosophies, suggests "a constant epistemology and variable ontologies". The same point can be made about languages: The common argument is that languages cut the world up differently (languages have different words for the same thing as well as words for things that other languages do not) but both the reality of that world as well as the common property of language are shared and given. The critique of this assumption suggests that we need to consider not only different epistemological positions on the world – different ways of knowing about the world – but also different ontologies: It is not just world views but worlds that may in themselves vary (Holbraad and Pedersen, 2017; Viveiros de Castro, 2004a, b, 2014). This position is not so much multicultural as multinatural (Viveiros de Castro, 2014), not so much multilingual as multilanguage.

What if it is not just "epistemological Eurocentrism" that is at stake, but also a deeper ontological Eurocentrism that "opposes what these noncolonial languages assume, and does not understand that what is at stake is not only cognitive but existential justice – the cry that a different world is possible, and not just a different knowledge?" (Savransky, 2017, p.16). If the reference to opposition to what noncolonial languages assume looks at first glance to be a neo-Whorfian proposition (different languages cut the world up in different ways), it is important to see why this is in fact so different: The argument here is not one of a known world divided up differently by known languages, where to lose a language is to lose a culture or world view, nor does it suggest, on the other hand, that the physical world may be radically different when we step across some cultural or linguistic divide. The point, rather, is that the ways different people understand their worlds challenges the ways the categories of nature, culture, or language may be understood. Tlingit perspectives on glaciers, for example, offer "an alternative ontological awareness of glaciers as well as a nuanced Indigenous empirical scientific knowledge that moves away from the Eurocentric models of categorizing and understanding the natural world" (Hayman et al., 2018, p.77). So, the question of what may be articulated in noncolonial languages (and mixes of noncolonial languages, and of colonial and noncolonial languages, and of noncolonial languages and other artefacts) may be not so much an alternative epistemology but an alternative ontology. For Savransky, "pluralising other knowledges can never be enough unless their emergence calls into question the metaphysical structures of the imagination that keep the very relationship between epistemology and ontology intact" (2017, p.17).

This ontological turn in anthropology has, not surprisingly, been met by a range of critiques, including the ways in which particular versions of the world are privileged over others (Graeber, 2015), and questions about the focus on a radical ontological alterity obscuring common struggles faced by many Indigenous and minority people, such as climate change, incarceration, loss of land and habitat, neo-liberal economic policies, and so on (Bessire and Bond, 2014). Todd (2016) critiques the ontological turn – along with other recent trends such as posthumanism – for once again becoming a Euro-American dialogue even when many of the insights that inform this thinking have been drawn from Indigenous ways of knowing. When it is clear that many insights about ecology – such as the climate being a common organizing force, or the interlocking relations of people, plants, animals, and land – have been common knowledge in Indigenous communities for millennia, the people given credit for such "insights into the 'more-than-human' sentience and agency" were once again intellectuals of European heritage credited with 'discovering' such insights, rather than the people "who built and maintain the knowledge systems that European and North American anthropologists and philosophers have been studying for well over a hundred years, and predicating many of their current 'aha' ontological moments (or re-imaginings of the discipline) upon" (Todd, 2016, pp.7–8).

As Todd (2016) goes on to argue, there is a double bind here, both that the importance of Indigenous thought for posthuman and ontological discussions be overlooked, and that when not overlooked, it is appropriated in a way that "distorts and erases the embodied, legal-governance and spiritual aspects of Indigenous thinking" (p.9). It is not that posthumanist or ontological-turn thinking cannot serve useful purposes in rethinking language and knowledge but rather that these ways of thinking absorb Indigenous knowledge without accounting for location (Sundberg, 2013) or Indigenous place-thought (Watts, 2013). This is, as Todd (2016) argues, centrally about the continuation of colonial relations: Indigenous peoples, she argues, "are fighting for recognition – fighting to assert their laws, philosophies and stories on their own terms" (p. 18). When anthropologists or other social scientists select "parts of Indigenous thought that appeal to them without engaging directly in (or unambiguously acknowledging) the political situation, agency, legal orders and relationality of both Indigenous people and scholars, we become complicit in colonial violence" (p.18). When we cite European thinkers as the source of thought about the 'more-than-human' without also discussing "their Indigenous contemporaries who are writing on the exact same topics, we perpetuate the white supremacy of the academy" (p.18).

Here, then, are several deep challenges for this book and for thinking from southern perspectives. If we accept the importance of the ontological challenge to language (while remaining mindful of the pitfalls of too zealous a plunge into this way of thinking), we are confronted by the possibility that language may have multiple natures, that questioning the pluralizability of languages themselves as named and enumerable entities may come hand in hand with a need to entertain the pluralizability of the idea of language itself. We have been pluralizing the wrong idea all along. And yet, as we take up some of the challenges of looking at local ways of knowing and situated ways of thinking about language, we need to be cautious lest this becomes again a European dialogue with itself. But further, once we do acknowledge the alternative sources of such ideas, how to avoid their appropriation? How do we avoid this becoming yet another misuse of Indigenous thought and instead a real engagement with and acknowledgement of that thinking? We return to some of these questions in Chapters 5 and 6 on education and research, but in the next section we take up this issue in the context of language reclamation.

Challenges: Ways forward

When Indigenous people reject government provisions for Indigenous language and education and opt instead for 'White' curricula (including, for example, languages such as Portuguese in Brazil), this is often critiqued from a well-intentioned and pro-Indigenous standpoint as naïve and uninformed. For De Souza (2017, p.206) the problem with such critiques is that "the posture of some mainstream social scientists who claim to be pro-indigenous, and in favour of the preservation of indigenous languages and epistemologies" remains all too often "trapped within the bounds of their own Enlightenment epistemologies". When these researchers "claim to listen to the indigenous other, they apparently only hear their own voices and values" unable to escape from the "bounds of lazy thinking, and thus liable to waste the wealth of experience of the ecology of knowledges that surrounds them but remains invisible to their eyes". De Souza (2017) is here taking up Santos' (2004a) notion of 'lazy reason' (*razão indolente*) – the critique that dominant modes of thinking cannot understand or engage with alternative modes of thought – to critique ways in which Indigenous education has been understood in Brazil. This "lingering inheritance of coloniality and its unequal distribution of knowledges, bodies, and languages" persists and may be something that applied linguistics, in its focus on education, needs to be aware of in order to "avoid, albeit unwittingly, continuing the legacy of coloniality" (De Souza, 2017, p.206).

De Souza's point that too many social scientists hear only themselves echoes a long history of sociolinguistics of the South being *about* the South but not *with* the South. Rather than attempting to think *about* difference, the ontological turn "seeks to think *with* the difference that thinking from the South itself makes" (Savransky, 2017, p.19, italics in original). As Nakata (2007, p.32) observes of Ray's (1907) study of languages in the Torres Strait Islands, while at first sight these linguistic descriptions are impressive, closer scrutiny tells us "more about Ray and the emerging discipline of linguistics than they do about the languages he was studying". Thus, although Ray's work on these languages was in a number of ways an exemplary demonstration of field linguistics, and although the details of these languages he recorded remain useful to this day, the focus was also one that treated language "as a static entity in a temporal space, contextualised only by its grammatical rules" (p.35). The problem here at this important point at the beginning of the 20th century and the beginning of linguistics as a scientific discipline was that languages were turned into things that existed beyond their speakers, outside time and place. "If the history of a language and its users is not factored into the theory as a primary standpoint", argues (Nakata 2007, p.37), "then any knowledge generated about that language is flawed".

This is not, as Nakata points out, to reject the work of such linguists and the knowledge of language they produced, or the importance of the arguments that showed that the languages of such people were as complex as any others, but it is to point to the problem that a linguistic focus on formal aspects of a language "fundamentally separates the language from the people; it falsely separates the act of speaking from what is being spoken". It is for reasons of not being heard, of languages and ideas being taken and twisted, that the North American First Nation Hopi, for example, have started to "struggle with experts from anthropology and linguistics who have in some ways appropriated for their own purposes Hopi language, Hopi cultural principles" (Gal, 2018, p.238). As we discuss further in

Chapter 6, for many Indigenous people, research has become a bad word, a term reflecting their constant status as objects of inquiry whose knowledge can be appropriated for academic purposes but whose active role in knowledge production and ownership is overlooked. The Hopi struggle to regain control over Indigenous knowledge practices has led to a ban on linguists reporting their words and expressions. For Nakata, at the heart of the problem is the linguistic assumption that languages are "floating in a vacuum, 'ready-made' within a system of phonetic, grammatical and lexical forms and divorced from the social context in which the speech is being uttered" (2007, p.37). The dilemma, even for activists trying to gain recognition for minority languages, as Gal (2018, p.235) points out, is that once a particular version of language came to dominate academic and institutional domains, there was little choice but to turn their "linguistic practices into a 'language' as defined in the modernist ideology".

As Albury (2016) remarks in the context of te reo Māori in Aotearoa (New Zealand), if current theories "continue to define language vitality in western ontological terms, then they will enjoy less applicability in the revitalisation of te reo Māori in Aotearoa" (p.30). We can identify several key northern ideas about language that are at best inappropriate when applied to southern contexts and at worst are downright harmful. These include a legacy of considering languages in terms of cognitive, literate systems rather than embodied and embedded cultural processes; a tendency to reify languages as if they exist outside human relations; and a set of assumptions about languages as repositories of knowledge that once lost, lead simultaneously to the loss of shared forms of culture and knowledge. While many may agree that looking at languages in ecological terms is a useful way forward, this depends very much on the versions of languages and ecologies that are deployed. If this means mapping languages and species as quasi-biological categories (Perley, 2012), reifying languages as species-like entities (Pennycook, 2004), we become stuck in a narrow set of linguistic and ecological metaphors. Ecological metaphors can of course be helpful for understanding how language and knowledge are bound up in relational terms (different languages and different knowledges exist in complex distributions). There is no overarching reason to reject such metaphors but when connections are drawn too closely between languages and species, we find ourselves on dangerous territory.

Expressing frustration at the quandary these critiques suggest – that too much work on language preservation operates with inappropriate and inadequate understandings of language use – various language activists have sought a way forward that still acknowledges the very legitimate concerns about community languages as part of Indigenous projects to claim a space in the contemporary world. The problem, as De Korne and Leonard (2017, p.6) remark, is that attempts to revitalize endangered languages have become associated with "language documentation, categorisation, and ethnic essentialism" and the common practices of "objectifying, counting, categorizing, and 'purifying' languages (or cultures)". The challenge, given that there are nonetheless very real reasons why communities want to work on language projects, is how to avoid these "narrow perspectives on language use and knowledge that are potentially harmful to speech communities" and how to support the "promotion of minoritised languages by ground-level participants [as] fundamentally a political act through which participants negotiate control over linguistic authority, knowledge production, and self-definition through their linguistic practices" (De Korne and Leonard, 2017, p.7).

Arguing that linguistics may reinforce its colonial legacy when researchers focus on linguistic rather than cultural units that "categorise and theorise Indigenous languages using norms for major global languages, or default to Western constructs of what 'language' is when engaging in Indigenous language research, teaching, and advocacy," Leonard (2017, p.15) proposes a paradigm of *language reclamation*, which focuses on community engagement with language practices, rather than *language revitalization*, which tends to focus on the language itself. *Language reclamation* aims to address community needs and perspectives and to "incorporate community epistemologies such as how 'language' is defined and given sociocultural meaning" (p.15). Reclamation can thus be understood as a type of *decolonization*:

> Rather than exhibiting a top-down model in which goals such as grammatical fluency or intergenerational transmission are assigned, it begins with community histories and contemporary needs, which are determined by community agents, and uses this background as a basis to design and develop language work.
>
> (p. 19)

Language work from this perspective has to involve a much broader array of concerns than many linguistic approaches manage. One of the challenges for linguists from outside these communities is to learn to work "effectively with people whose models of language differ from our own" (Stebbins, 2014, p.302). As Stebbins (2014) notes, "the ideologically driven approaches of linguists to language impact on both our analyses and our advice to communities" (p.304). The challenge for linguists, she notes, is to recognize the perspectives on language developed by community members for what they are and "to find ways to make our own meanings in relation to them" (p.305).

The idea of reclamation also arguably allows for a more flexible understanding of what is at stake here: Not so much the revival of or even revitalization of a language that is no longer used, but rather a reclaiming of language for varied purposes. As Couzens and Eira (2014, p.313) note, because of the loss of a language from a community, the limitations of historical records, and the forms of language mixing both during and after the colonial-missionary era, "at many levels, revived languages in present-day use are not going to be the same as their historical counterparts". Languages in the present "reflect the means and priorities by which they are reclaimed" and are different in many ways, including genres, modes, domains, and conceptual systems that relate to contemporary language use, as well as inevitable changes to pronunciation, syntax, and lexicon. Language reclamation, we should recall, always occurs in contact with other languages. Even with some of the celebrated cases of language revival – Hebrew (Israel and elsewhere), Cornish

(Cornwall, UK), Kaurna (Adelaide, South Australia), and Wampanoag (Cape Cod, Massachusetts, USA) – we have to understand that these new versions of the language can only be very different from their historical counterparts. As Zuckerman suggests, "the revival of a no-longer spoken language is unlikely without cross-fertilization from the revivalists' mother tongue(s)" (2009, p.41). Revival efforts always therefore end up producing something different again, and certainly not the original language (as if that idea were itself a definable entity).

Working on language reclamation, then, is "deeply cross-cultural" (Couzens and Eira, 2014, p.314) both because the language itself must be so and because the collaborative work of linguists needs to engage across the different language ideologies and ontologies of communities. This perspective resonates with Santos' (2018, p.16) discussion of the centrality of "intercultural translation" as the challenge of articulating "a conversation among different knowledges" that are based in different cultural frameworks. This requires "a productive understanding and connection between sets of ideologies formed for very different purposes, from within very different social and intellectual heritages" (Couzens and Eira, 2014, p.314). Their project sought to find meeting points between Western epistemologies and ways of knowing developed through linguistics and Aboriginal ways of knowing. From the point of view of culture, for example, while linguistics can posit various relations between language and culture, for Indigenous people this is often a relationship of great profundity that also brings in questions of land. Many operate with "a broader definition of 'language', responding to our linguistically oriented questions in terms of family, education, understanding of the land, song, and so on" (p.318). Important here is the need to "alleviate the risk of reductionism which a linguistic approach to language revival appears to pose" (p.320) so that any revival project can open up to a much broader domain of relations in which language is involved. These relations around land (and also sea, Ch. 6), culture, nonverbal communication, and identity can no longer be perceived as peripheral domains to the core of language; they are, rather, central aspects of a broader notion of language.

To operate from this perspective requires an alternative framing of language from the standard linguistic or applied linguistic approaches, based as they are in quite different ideological frameworks, including "different lines of authority, the importance of relationships both past and present, and of certain cultural meanings" (Couzens and Eira, 2014, p.332). This requires a "much broader view of what is involved in linguistic analysis. It requires a deep listening at discipline level, to hear what other ideologies are important and relevant to our understanding" (p.332). It is this kind of 'deep listening' that southern epistemologies demand of us, echoing what Watkins and Shulman (2017, p.27) expect of the *Psychologies of Liberation*: "psychologists relinquish their role as authorities and experts who have the final word, developing new capacities for listening, questioning, and facilitation of group processes". Hence Block's (2008) concern that the metaphor of language loss may often be quite inappropriate, and his call to "listen to the voices of those who have actually lived through language maintenance and loss, so as to avoid romantic depictions of such experiences" (p.201). For Sarkar (2018, p.503), working on language revitalization projects with the Mi'gmaq in Canada, the question became one of how to "work together without it turning into the old colonial story of white people from the outside trying to be helpful but winding up doing more harm than if they had never come". As she goes on to argue, we all too often assume in applied linguistics that our patchy knowledge of second language acquisition and pedagogy based in "the usual Western contexts" will be applicable to all other contexts. We need instead to spend a lot of time learning and listening, understanding what matters, and how to fit in.

It is this kind of "*wangan ngootyoong* [1]-informed methodology – the practice of engaging respectfully with diverse ideologies – that gives us the tools to develop broader epistemologies, intertwining the best of Western scientific traditions with current and reclaimed Aboriginal approaches to knowledge and research" (Couzens and Eira, 2014, p.322). We shall return in Chapter 6 to some of these concerns about respect and collaboration in the context of research (Smith, 1999). For Lüpke (2019) the way forward may be through a three-pronged approach that draws on local, grassroots practices, seeks to empower local people as knowledge producers, and focuses on *supporting vital repertoires* rather than *revitalizing languages*. This ties in with the broad arguments we have been making in this book that the goal of a southern applied linguistics is to broaden the epistemological repertoires of the field. One such broadening is to shift the focus away from a fixation on individual languages and to understand instead how vital linguistic repertoires operate. From Lüpke's point of view, it is crucial to understand that it is not languages in isolation that need preserving, but complex and diverse and self-determined linguistic repertoires that can be revitalized through cooperative work between communities and applied linguists who've learned how to listen.

Conclusions

We have suggested in this chapter that the colonial linguistic project and its applied linguistic offshoot produced a vision of language that had little to do with how people understood languages locally. The notion of language was based on European ideas about languages as artefacts tied to literacy and nationhood. As Cameron (2007) makes clear, assumptions about a close organic link between language and culture have a long and problematic history. The moral force of preservationist arguments "lies in the perception of a natural bond between a community and the mother tongue that uniquely expresses its culture and worldview" (p.280). It has all too often been this version of language that has been deployed in attempts to halt the decline of languages in the world. The development of a version of language that was not so much in the world but based on connections between linguistic signs and external objects meant that languages were seen as representational systems. As Mufwene (2016, p.117) notes, languages from the perspective of many language rights activists (including language ecologists, language revivalists, and so on) are considered to be representational systems rather than communication technologies, to be "repositories of several generations of accumulated knowledge, which the populations associated with them would lose if they died". The concern here is not only that languages were seen as representational systems, but also, as Mignolo (2018) suggests, the very idea of *representing* is a "toxic word in the vocabulary of modernity and modern epistemology" (p.109).

These views also became tied to a particular 'ecological' view of language, suggesting that saving languages was also about saving the world. As Muehlmann (2007, p.31) explains,

> there is no doubt that language obsolescence and environmental degradation are processes deeply implicated in the organization of social inequality. It is the disempowered whose languages 'die' and the marginalized and poor who suffer the effects of environmental degradation most immediately. But from this fact alone we cannot conclude that saving languages or rainforests will reverse the social processes that marginalize some groups in the first place.

As Mufwene (2010, 2016) has long argued, we need to move away from the reification and exoticization of languages, suggesting that to maintain one's L1 is somehow a guarantor of self-esteem, a consistent world view, a useful education and economic advancement. It depends on what different relations of language exist locally and how they relate to economic opportunities, and how all of this may be related to educational and health outcomes, the movement of people in search of livelihoods, and the many restrictions that limit the life possibilities of Indigenous people. To suggest forms of empowerment in relation to language, applied linguists need to get real about social, economic, and political relations.

Among the many problems with what Lüpke (2015, pp.93–4) calls the "global master narrative of endangerment" are the inappropriate mapping of language concerns in North America and Australia (where Indigenous languages are threatened in particular ways by dominant languages, and the precarity of the social and economic position of Indigenous people is tied to a particular colonial and continuing neocolonial history) to African and other contexts. From such assumptions flow the supposition that languages spoken by small numbers of people are inevitably threatened, which is not the case. Tied to this vision is also a focus on individual languages at the expense of multilingual communicative repertoires. At the same time, local activists may also talk in terms of enumerated languages. The ways in which people talk about their everyday language use may appear to fit exactly with some of the ways of talking we have questioned here: As one informant from Ghana described the local language situation, there are "more than sixty. Nigeria has more than two hundred languages ... Africans are crazy. You move only five hundred meters, the language changes" (Pennycook and Otsuji, 2019, p.80). People do of course live in a world in which language labels and enumerations are the common stuff of everyday language talk, but their understanding of what those language labels mean may be both diverse and flexible.

This is a key point for how applied linguists can start to move forward from a Global South perspective: We need to try to grasp language and languages from alternative standpoints that may encompass very different ways of thinking about relations among linguistic, semiotic and material resources. While the Global South is marked by profound differences, it can also present a useful political collective where the lines along which differences need to be considered can be mapped: We can generalize about the domains in which it is particularly important to understand forms of difference. In relation to issues of language vitality (as opposed to endangerment) this would include an understanding of the nature of families and social networks that provide different forms of language support, thus rethinking the normative assumptions of the "graded intergenerational disruption scale" (Fishman, 1991) that have been at the core of many beliefs about language vitality and endangerment. This also entails an appreciation that language repertoires shift over time as people go through schools, enter relationships, foster children, join social groups, work, and so on. Each individual has to some extent a unique repertoire (Johnstone, 1996; Otheguy et al., 2018) reflecting their individual experiences, and the collective sum of such individual repertoires does not add up to form some idealized language or speech community. People do not acquire languages so much as "a complex language ecology consisting of repertoires and registers, and the knowledge of when and with whom to use them" (Lüpke, 2015, p.95).

For applied linguistics to engage with southern multilingualisms, therefore, collaborative work must be able to encompass deep forms of difference and disparity. This by no means implies a necessary direction of collaboration between northern knower and southern informant but rather a collaboration between situated knowers. The point is to seek meeting points between different ways of knowing, between different accounts of language and its relation to family, culture, and land. When the common trope is invoked that a language is 'sleeping' rather than 'dead' (Perley, 2012) – "My tribal heritage language, *myaamia*, was sleeping for a long time" (Leonard, 2017, p.17) – it is important to consider the different ways of thinking that this invokes, the implications for language in relation to landscape and people and use. As Monaghan (2012, p.53) puts it, language and stories are understood as still being "in the land, having been placed there by the ancestors" and to reclaim such sleeping languages may be as much a spiritual process as one involving documentation. In order to change the ways we think about this, and in order to enable language projects that meet community interests to succeed, we need to "decolonise 'language'" (Leonard, 2017, p.32). A key concern is moving beyond a simple pluralization of knowledges – epistemology, Savransky suggests, remains "the ultimate horizon" of postcolonial and decolonial (Mignolo, 2011a, 2018) approaches alike – and to engage instead with issues of ontology. And all this requires ways of listening and researching that change some of the key ways we do research. We return to this question in Chapter 6 after looking at pedagogical implications for an applied linguistics of the Global South.

Note

1 *wangan ngootyoong* is a term meaning 'respect' in the Keerraywoorroong language.

5
DECOLONIZING LANGUAGE IN EDUCATION

Introduction: The decolonial imperative

The focus of this chapter is on decolonizing language in education as part of the broader project to decolonize applied linguistics. There cannot arguably be a discussion of applied linguistics without a focus on language in education, even if one aspect of this larger project is to provincialize the role particularly of English language teaching from the central place it has held in the field for too long (Motha, 2014). At the same time, southern perspectives in applied linguistics cannot be developed without prior, or at least simultaneous, processes of *decolonization*, even if it "is a messy, dynamic, and contradictory process" (Sium et al., 2012, p.11). As we saw in the last chapter, one of the ways to approach the idea of language reclamation is through a process of decolonizing language, of challenging the ways language has been constructed in the Global North, and opening up a space for alternative ways of thinking about language (Leonard, 2017). Looking more broadly at areas of the humanities and social sciences, Maldonado-Torres (2007) suggests that a *decolonial turn* is now under way, a "shift in knowledge production of similar nature and magnitude to the linguistic and pragmatic turns" (p.261). This decolonial turn "involves interventions at the level of power, knowledge, and being through varied actions of decolonization" (p.262).

In its broadest sense, this call to decolonize can be seen as part of a global project to "decolonize Man/Human, to liberate *pluriversal humanity*" (Mignolo, 2018, p.170). Hayman et al. (2018) call for a decolonization of the Anthropocene, arguing that the particular set of discourses that have come to define environmental science overlook alternative ways of understanding relations between people and the world:

Rethinking current models of and approaches to water governance through an Indigenous ontology that privileges relationships, reciprocity, and respect offers a powerful counter-narrative that can inform Euro-American approaches to law and governance—in effect a reversal or decolonizing of the colonial process.

(p.82)

Such challenges call into question a wide range of assumptions about knowledge, science, nature, language, water, and the possibility, for example, of understanding glaciers in alternative ontological terms (see Chapter 6). Walsh (2018) emphasizes the need for *decolonial insurgency* (p.34) that would align with other forms of praxis and pedagogy "*against* the colonial matrix of power in all of its dimensions, and *for* the possibilities of an otherwise" (p.17).

In support of Maldonado-Torres' (2007, 2010) contention that we are witnessing a decolonial turn across many areas, there have been calls for decolonization in economics, philosophy, anthropology, international relations, religious studies, psychology, and the humanities and social sciences more broadly (Wallerstein, 1996), including African literature (Chinweizu et al., 1983), sociology (Bhambra 2007, 2014; Savransky, 2017) and education (Whitinui et al., 2018). Reviewing work such as Steinmetz's (2013) edited book on the entanglements of sociology and Empire, Magubane (2015, p.14) calls for a "decolonizing of the sociological imagination". Connell (2018, p.405) likewise argues for the importance of decolonizing sociology, a project that "requires rethinking the composition of sociology's workforce and changing the conditions in which it produces and circulates knowledge". This is, she reminds us, a process of *redistribution* of both knowledge and resources.

In this chapter, following these decolonial projects elsewhere, we seek to analyse the Eurocentrism or northern perspective that underlies much of applied linguistics, with a particular focus on language in education. Epistemological ethnocentrism deals not so much "with individual assumptions and biases, but those common to scholars in an entire discipline or study" (Reagan, 1996, p.5). Closely linked to the Eurocentric biases that inform much of applied linguistics is the problem of *undone science*,

a systematic occurrence that is embedded within relations of power and influence within and around academia. For every scientific project that is supported and funded, there is another project that was not funded or accorded attention by scholars and those that finance them.

(Richardson, 2018, p.232)

From this perspective, Eurocentrism in the social sciences is not only about "how the focus of academic work tends to be on European societal phenomena, but also how this focus on European social life leaves the social life and thought of other communities and nations understudied, unattended to or, worse, actively suppressed" (Richardson, 2018, p.233).

Language in education in applied linguistics, for example, has focused almost entirely on how language is taught in the Global North. Even when taught in the Global South or to people whose origins might be traced to the Global South, the focus has been on how changes have emerged and developed in the traditions of education of the Global North (Howatt, 1984; Howatt and Widdowson 2004) and extended and applied to the Global South. As critiques of the role of organizations such as the British Council in 'brokering English studies' in India (Rajan, 1992; Thikoo, 2001) have suggested, the tendency to assume that northern knowledge and educational practices are both superior and applicable to contexts in the South has a long and ugly history. The applied linguistics that we envisage is one grounded in the experiences of Chinese, African, Hindu, Muslim, and Meso-American traditions (Reagan, 1996). An awareness of the underlying philosophies of education in these other traditions is helpful to understand how students from such contexts may react to Western education.

Decolonization, Indigenization and the social organization of knowledge

The term decolonization is "both illuminating and limiting" (Zeleza 2017, p.2). It is limiting because it traces its roots to Eurocentric notions and epistemologies about Africa and elsewhere. Decolonization should not be the sole motivating force for change because, inasmuch as there is a desire to decentre Western knowledge, it is necessary to bear in mind that colonialism is not the sum total of African or other histories. Neither Eurocentrism nor projects to unwind Eurocentrism should be allowed to overwhelm the capaciousness of African knowledges. Africa has different libraries of which the Eurocentric is only a part. A project that seeks to liberate African knowledges must begin by understanding the variety, development, and intersections of Afro-Christian, Afro-Islamic, and Griot libraries (Zeleza, 2017, p.3). Nonetheless, we should not underestimate the extent to which northern/Western knowledge has permeated the multiple and different facets of scholarship, and the lives of Africans, migrants, and the vulnerable, both in the Global South and the Global North (Zeleza, 2017).

Decolonization is faced with the challenges of Eurocentrism, not only because it has permeated the humanities and social sciences, but also because it constitutes a structural challenge. Eurocentrism is not only a system of thought but also a "social activity that is not strictly driven by logic and methods, but by the interactions of scientists with each other and with the public" (Richardson, 2018, p.234). If we can identify Eurocentrism as a structural problem, then it is possible to see both how it is perpetuated by individuals, groups, and across time and space, and how and where possible interventions might occur. Similarly, it is possible to integrate Indigenous perspectives critically into the curriculum, but still, paradoxically, "reproduce Eurocentric and non-Indigenous patterns of authority and hierarchies of knowledge in the classroom" (Furo, 2018, p.279). Integrating Indigenous perspectives may not succeed in challenging Eurocentrism if the "patterns of organization" which structurally produce and sustain it – such as patterns of hiring, the official curriculum, or university and classroom hierarchies – are not changed. Eurocentrism in the classroom can only be challenged if decisions are also made beyond classroom walls. Where Indigenous perspectives challenge authority, they may not be welcome, and the goal shifts to co-opt them through the "rhetorics of inclusion" (Furo, 2018, p.282).

Decolonization discussions therefore need to operate at a number of different institutional levels, including staffing, faculty, curriculum, and the nature of learning. Even though curriculum issues are clearly important in a decolonization debate, decolonization should be about much more than curriculum changes, or simply adding scholars and activists from the Global South on the syllabus, or adding new research contexts to existing research agendas. Responses to "Why is my curriculum White?" should not end at adding non-White scholars and writers to the curriculum. What is required is a fundamental rethinking of the curriculum, including how the students will orient to the material used in the course. Bhambra (2007, p.879) suggests that a pluralization of other voices in sociology "can never be enough" to release the transformative potential of decolonial thought, unless their emergence calls into question "the structures of knowledge that have previously occluded them". In the same spirit, we argue here that pluralizing applied linguistic knowledges can never be enough unless their emergence calls into question the metaphysical structures of the imagination that keep the relationship between epistemology and ontology intact.

The objective of revising the curriculum should be to facilitate an enhancement, rather than a limitation, of difference, thus overcoming "monocultural approaches to knowledges" (Icaza and Vazquez, 2018, p.117). A decolonization of the curriculum of applied linguistics should therefore be one that seeks to expose students to multiple types of knowledges about language, and an agenda that includes ways in which applied linguistics is sensitive to political and historical forces. The agenda will be driven not only by student agitation and other internal forces, but also by forces outside the broader sphere of the university that include, but are not restricted to, a focus on generalized colonial violence, racial discrimination in academia, and structures of global knowledge transmission (Icaza and Vazquez, 2018, p.117; Kubota, 2019).

When exporting theory from the Western academy, colonialism brought with it the assumption that theory is the product of Western tradition, and that the aim of the academies outside the West is to apply it. We should not be fooled here by the status of applied linguistics as an "applied" field: Applied linguists have been happy to promote both their theories and practices to the rest of the world as the newest and best. It is this mindset that theories from the Global South seek to challenge by proposing an alternative: for scholars in the Global South to theorize their own reality. This does not mean excluding the Global North, but rather, striking the right balance between different ways of knowing (a topic we return to in Chapter 7). The local production of knowledge unfolds in relation to a complexity of social forces and should take into account society's needs, demands, and aspirations. Decolonization cannot therefore involve only the replacement of one elite knowledge system by another. It involves the incorporation of perspectives from students, staff, administrators, parents, and other interested communities. It should go beyond simply centring Indigenous knowledge in an Indigenous curriculum, and instead seek to integrate contemporary sophisticated technological knowledge of local youth. Integrating "Indigenous perspectives is not identical with decolonizing the curriculum. Both of these endeavours are valuable but are not accomplished through the same means" (Furo, 2018, p.279).

The focus on Indigenous knowledge and Indigenization raises several further points: Indigenization is not the same as decolonization. Indigenization is a process of naturalizing Indigenous knowledge rather than replacing Western knowledge with Indigenous knowledge. Indigenization can be understood as weaving or braiding together two distinct knowledge systems so that learners can come to understand and appreciate both (Wilson, 2004). In the same way that it is important to appreciate that any language revival project will always be as much about the production of new and changed language practices (Chapter 4), it is important too not to emphasize such knowledge as always 'traditional' since it needs to incorporate contemporary modes and practices. Decolonization, by contrast, focuses centrally on challenging colonial ideologies that emphasize the superiority of, and privilege ascribed to, Western/Northern thought and approaches. Another concept closely aligned with decolonization and Indigenization is reconciliation. Reconciliation is about effecting new relationships between Indigenous and non-Indigenous peoples. This means revisiting experiences of trauma that Indigenous peoples may have faced. If reconciliation is an important concept in Indigenization and decolonization, we have to explore the role that trauma plays in a relearning of Indigenous languages and in applied linguistics.

The emphasis particularly on Indigenous thought and practices also puts epistemology under the spotlight. As Savransky (2017) remarks, the focus on epistemological decolonization (challenging northern canons of knowledge) both overlooks the significance of ontological questions and fails to challenge the fundamental distinction between epistemology and ontology. It thus takes for granted what Santos (2014) calls an "abyssal line" between epistemology and ontology, knowledge and reality (Savransky, 2017, p.13). As the discussion in the previous chapter of language ontologies suggested, the issue had to be with what language itself is, rather than just how we think about it. Such ontological questions challenge the idea that language may be a unified underlying principle, and as the discussion in the next chapter suggests in relation to seascapes and alternative water-based ontologies, we need to operate at more than just an epistemological level. We need to be careful that our decolonial critiques do not result in reproducing a metaphysical Eurocentrism. What is required is to mobilize and develop an insurgent sociological imagination, what Santos (2014) calls "postabyssal thought". A "postabyssal" imagination in applied linguistics resists the bifurcation of epistemology and ontology. A 'decolonial imagination' is necessary for the social sciences and humanities to be sensitive to silenced and marginalized realities (Santos, 2014).

Decolonizing language in education

Central to any approach to decolonize applied linguistics – a central theme of this book, and one to which we return again in Chapter 7 – has to be a focus on language in education. Education is a central domain in which language politics are played out: It has been a key site of intervention, from external intervention through missionary schools and development projects, to internal interventions through government and private schools. Education is a realm in which languages are regulated and determined: Whether as a colonial vernacular policy, a government modernization project, or a neo-liberal paradigm of choice, the result in schools is always a particular mode of language governance. The language ideologies, southern multilingualisms, and language reclamation projects discussed in the previous chapters almost always involve educational dimensions: It is through education that many language policies are implemented. A southern applied linguistics, therefore, needs not only to decolonize our thinking about language but also about education.

A focus on language in education brings to the fore the question of the medium of instruction in schools and universities. As outlined in Chapter 2, a major factor in the making of the South – the systematic exploitation and wealth extraction from poorer regions of the world – was the postwar 'development' process. Colonialism itself had inflicted its long and violent incursions on many parts of the world (Walter, 2017) and had left many newly independent countries with a language-in-education dilemma: Local languages had often been used as the medium of instruction in primary education as part of a project to inculcate "habits of industry, obedience, punctuality, order, neatness, cleanliness and general good behaviour" (Collinge, 1894, cited in Pennycook, 2007d); colonial elites meanwhile had gained an education in the major European colonial languages and were often eager to promote these languages to unify new states and provide a common medium of education.

With independence, education became a key site of development aid (or, to be more honest about these processes, ensuring a country aligned politically and economically with the donor, while extracting resources, controlling commodity prices, and positioning postcolonial others as always backward, behind, and undeveloped): As part of the 20th-century discourses of development (Escobar, 1995) considerable attention was paid to education, with the languages of the former colonial powers playing a key role. While these discourses of development have waned in some international contexts, they also continue in more informal ways in many programmes involved in English and other European language education projects. In so-called English-language *voluntourism*, for example, as Jakubiak (2016) notes, assumptions about English and development still greatly influence how such programmes operate and the views the volunteers bring to their education contexts. This promotion of European languages in education projects has been widely critiqued, particularly since the use of European languages deprived students of an adequate education in their mother tongues (Phillipson, 1992; Skutnabb-Kangas, 2000).

As critical appraisals of the promotion of English and other European languages in development projects suggested, language education in former colonial languages had many deleterious effects, including distorting already weak primary education sectors, advantaging urban elites over rural poor, constraining the use of other languages, and diverting resources from other areas, while failing to establish any clear connections between language and social, cultural, and economic change (Appleby et al., 2002; Ferguson, 2013). A first stage of decolonization of language education, therefore, has been the struggle to introduce a much greater role for mother-tongue education (Kamwangamalu, 1997, 2008, 2016). The problem with "the maintenance and use of the colonial languages in education and social intercourse", argues Prah (2018, p.17), is that it "leads to one destination, the terminus of assimilation; estrangement from our African cultural character and moorings; and alienation from precisely what we need to build on". And yet, as we suggested in Chapter 3, the replacement of European languages by their African counterparts may not provide the emancipatory impetus intended, since these so-called mother tongues may all too often be the neocolonial counterpart of their colonial nemesis: The very notion of separate and nameable languages and either–or options between them is also arguably in need of decolonization.

Much of the discussion of education for Torres Straits Islanders, Nakata (2007) argues, starts with the assumption that "oral traditions and the first language of the student are fundamental elements that can have a profound effect on educational achievement" (p.172). Such truisms of educational provision for minority and Indigenous populations will be familiar with many involved in progressive educational programmes. Whether advocating bilingual education, or some other mixture of mother tongue and European language education, the general assumption is that transition from an 'oral culture' in home languages to the literate traditions of schooling in majority languages is best done by an education through the first language. And yet, as Nakata points out, locating students within an 'oral tradition' "narrows down their presence in history to 'something' that is 'not' part of the literate traditions, and as separate and apart from the complex world of negotiating colliding historical trajectories over the past two hundred years" (p.172).

The problem more broadly is that any approach that considers only a predominant community language misses the point of southern multilingualisms. There is a major gap in thinking about educational multilingualism, especially in southern contexts, "a singular failure to engage with the nature of multilingualism in these areas and how multilingualism can be harnessed as a resource, say, in a sector like education" (Mwaniki, 2018, p.36). The problem with "language-specific approaches", Nakata (2007, pp.175–6) points out, is that whether they focus on bilingual education, English as a second language, or local languages, they assume "that all students have a common language". The situation is always more complex, with multiple languages and multiple relations to oral and written modes operating across communities. Oral and literate worlds are not separate but "entwined, inter-textual and continue to evolve as traditions and artefacts of our engagements with each other" (p.176). Likewise, "bilingual advocates fail to explore in more detail the value of complexities in the lifeworld of Islanders in their everyday communications" (p.177). Part of any project to decolonize applied linguistics and language education, therefore, needs to step away from simple assumptions that replacing a former colonial language with an Indigenous one is in itself an emancipatory move. This view still operates from a northern framework that fails to understand the differences that the South brings to the fore. As Makalela (2018b, p.119) notes, the "orthodox language-teaching profession has always regarded literacy from a monolingual perspective and has prohibited multilingual writers from drawing on their antecedent genres for the development of multilingual literacies".

Innovations: Decolonization, transformation, and the multilingual university

One way to understand the decolonization of applied linguistics is to locate it within the broader context of the decolonization of the university. Applied linguistics can be understood as a wide array of different practices (and see further discussion in Chapter 7) but one aspect of the field is that it is a set of courses taught at the tertiary (and often graduate) level. Universities have long been a site both of processes of colonization (this is where northern knowledge enters local knowledge economies) and of struggles over decolonization (this is where struggles over forms of knowledge happen). This longer battle has gained a particular dynamic in recent years:

> The struggle to decolonize university knowledge systems is intimately intertwined with forms of physical and economic colonial violence. These forms of violence, including genocide, interpersonal racism in academia, and global structures of academic knowledge transmission, serve to ensure that the configurations of people, resources, and space that allow for new decolonial knowledges to emerge never come to exist.
>
> *(Richardson, 2018, p.232)*

Even though the process of decolonization is not a novel one, it has recently received intensified global attention in both universities and the media, in Cape Town, Amsterdam, Cambridge, London (SOAS), Leeds, Oslo, Oxford, and Paris, amongst others. That decolonization is also a pertinent issue in North America is particularly apparent in "land-grant" universities, and especially among those universities built on land forcefully taken away from First Nations people on the basis of dubious treaties or crude land grabs. Some of the land-grant universities were originally funded through endowments secured through profits from the slave trade (Georgetown University has been struggling to engage with this history; Working Group, 2016, with students now required to pay into a reparation fund). The accumulation of land is one of the defining features of a competitive, modern research university: "Land as capital and not as campuses is an innovation of land-grant universities. That is, states are able to trade, develop, and sell land to fund the construction of public universities" (La paperson, 2017).

From some perspectives, therefore, decolonization of the university starts with questions of the land since most land-grant universities in the United States are built on occupied Indigenous lands (La paperson, 2017). Following Tuck and Yang's (2012, p.2) position that "decolonization is not a metaphor", that it should stand for the repatriation of Indigenous lands and should address "the real and symbolic violences of settler colonialism", decolonization may focus centrally on the land, buildings, and history of tertiary institutions, and the record of dispossession they may represent. The idea that decolonization should be restricted in its meaning to a repatriation of land, however, may overlook the importance of *decolonizing the mind*, as Ngũgĩ (1986, p.4) put it in his classic book on the languages of African literature: While "imperialism continues to control the economy, politics and cultures of Africa", African people continue to struggle for a "new era of true communal self-regulation and self-determination".

A lot has been written about the decolonization of South African Universities (Antia and van der Merwe, 2018) since the #FeesMustFall movement in 2015–2016. Strikes erupted again at the beginning of the 2019 academic year at a number of universities in South Africa, notably the University of Witwatersrand, and University of KwaZulu-Natal. The students in the protests demanded that their student debt be cleared, they be provided with better accommodation, and that no student should be excluded from an institution of higher learning on financial grounds (Jagmohan and Craig, 2019). The strikes highlighted the failures of South African higher education to transcend the legacies of its colonial and apartheid past (Vorster and Quinn, 2017). Case (2015, p.3) argues that the continuation of colonial and apartheid legacies in post-apartheid South Africa is "one of the under-recognized tragedies of the democratic settlement in South Africa". Since the first democratic elections in South Africa in 1994, even though there has been an increase in the number of Black students who enrol in South African higher education, just under 20 per cent of the Black youth are enrolled. This percentage is substantially lower than that of other racial groups, namely, Indians and Whites. Equally concerning is the higher dropout rate among Black students compared to other population groups, which has been attributed to a number of factors, including the poor preparation for higher education of Black students in secondary school. The position that Blacks are ill-prepared for higher education, however, like all deficit-oriented arguments – whether individual or institutional – may be turned back on itself (Shilliam, 2018a, b): The problem is not so much that the Black students are ill prepared for higher education, but that the South African higher education system is still unable to handle Black students who excel.

According to Mamdani (2018), the origins of the African university can be traced back to the 19th century, the earliest being the Universities of Cape Town (1829), Stellenbosch (1866), and Witwatersrand (1896), which were newly developed, while in the North, the University of North al-Azhari grew out of the Islamic Centre of knowledge. By and large, the African university is still very much what it was originally — a colonial project (Mbembe, 2001; Nyamnjoh, 2012). Instruction in African universities is largely conducted monolingually in French, English, or Portuguese (Alexander, 2002). The African university is typically framed in terms of a European "universalism", from which a majority of the colonized are excluded. This universalism is largely discipline-based, with clear distinctions between administrators, teaching staff, and fee-paying students, organized around departments, committees, and disciplinary formations that have the power to fund, hire, and promote, and that, consequently, wield substantial levers of power (Richardson, 2018).

The nature of decolonization of university knowledge will also vary across the Global South. Decolonization of knowledge presumes the production of knowledges in higher education. In Africa, the dominant knowledge production countries, calculated (not unproblematically) in terms of the number of journal articles and academic books, are Algeria, Egypt, Kenya, Morocco, Nigeria, South Africa, and Tunisia. Other African countries' production of knowledge in higher education is negligible. South Africa produces the largest number of publications in absolute numbers and Tunisia relative to gross domestic product (McGregor, 2016). There are, however, encouraging signs that the situation is changing, as shown in the recent increase in research conducted by local African scholars. From 1996 to 2012, the number of research papers published in scientific journals with more than one African author has more than quadrupled, from about 52,000 to 112,500 or 1.2 per cent to 2.3 per cent. Sub-Saharan Africa more than doubled its research output between 2003 and 2012, though this is taking place against the background of a low base (Schemm, 2013). Other countries such as Ethiopia are also showing dramatic improvements in their knowledge production, recording a dramatic increase of over 28 per cent in a single year.

Nevertheless, the vast majority of the universities in Africa cannot be said, according to Zeleza (2017), to meet the criteria of research or research-intensive universities. Research productivity in its many different forms is a prerequisite to contribute effectively to sustainable development and in global competition for talented students, top faculty, scarce resources, and reputational capital. It is not surprising that most African universities do not feature in international rankings (irrespective of how one views the validity and reliability of such insidious rankings; Zeleza, 2017). It is hard to imagine how decolonization can occur easily in contexts of such limited knowledge production, though perhaps the state of crisis, transition, or disruption that universities now find themselves in will create opportunities for African educators to reinvent higher education in ways more fitting to their own needs (Zeleza, 2017). African institutions are experimenting with innovative approaches to enhance research training and knowledge production, through the creation of institutions such as the Consortium for Advanced Research Training in Africa, which is composed of eight African universities and four African research centres.

Other innovative approaches with which African institutions are experimenting include strategies to enhance African knowledge production through the development of North/South collaboration, such as the Carnegie Fellowships in which African scholars in Canada and the United States collaborate on the same projects in one or more of the following areas: curriculum, graduate training and mentoring, and joint research projects. The relationship between North/South institutions, however, is increasingly complicated by the growing number of campuses established in the Global South by northern universities, echoing previous colonial relationships in which smaller campuses were located in the South, but the major campuses in the North. Improvements of research output will also require that attention be paid not only to innovative North/South initiatives but to important aspects relating to university infrastructures: quality of research environment, funding, research incentives, and availability of time, all of which have a bearing on African research productivity. African universities may facilitate a development of their knowledge base by exploiting the contexts in which they are situated: African islands, for example, have exceptional knowledge of the oceans which they can capitalize on in their knowledge production.

Much of this discussion, however, continues to define success and productivity in terms of established northern norms: Productivity itself is a particular way of thinking about research efficacy, while numbers of research articles, citation indexes, university rankings, and so forth all set up a particular framework for deciding what kinds of knowledge count and in what ways. More profound challenges include questions of how universities operate, what kinds of knowledge count, and what languages they will function in. The first issue concerns ways in which universities constrain the dissemination of knowledge. While many maintain a discourse of "civic engagement" and celebrate, largely for marketing purposes, their "public intellectuals", they also prevent the wider dissemination of knowledge by the policing of their ownership of knowledge and their physical boundaries (lack of access to campuses and libraries without identification, restrictions on auditing classes, and so on; Riemer, 2016a, p.35). The constraints on knowledge dissemination may remain in place, irrespective of whether the knowledge pool had been decolonized. Universities are becoming increasingly regulatory spaces that at times blur the boundaries between education and national restrictions on mobility. Any serious efforts at analysing the lives of students who receive training in applied linguistics have to be sensitive to the extent to which universities are increasingly playing the role of border control enforcement agencies.

If universities therefore need structural changes in order to make knowledge more widely available, questions of what kinds of knowledge count go to the heart of the university enterprise. Processes of "nativization, domestication and creation of intellectual sovereignty in knowledge production" require degrees of autonomy and self-sufficiency for both researchers and institutions (Prah, 2017, p.15): "Intellectual sovereignty means a free, liberated and self-determining agency in knowledge production, which answers first to societal particularities while contributing secondarily and almost inadvertently to universal knowledge" (Prah 2017, p.15). Beyond questions of intellectual sovereignty, however, are further issues around the type of knowledge that counts. As Santos (2018, p.45) argues, southern epistemologies also need to include *artisanal knowledges*, "practical, empirical, popular knowledges, vernacular knowledges that are very diverse" and closely linked to other social practices. If, as Albury (2017, p.37) contends, *folk linguistic research methods* may play an important role in the *decolonization of sociolinguistic theory and method*, other forms of local, folk, and artisanal knowledge may play a similar role, though they present serious challenges for what counts as academic knowledge.

The decolonization of universities draws attention to the relationship between critical theory and decolonial scholarship, an issue that recurs throughout this book. Post-Marxist theory remains strongly embedded in a Western-based discourse on universal human rights which may unfortunately exclude alternative and competing realities from the global South. Post-Marxist theory lays itself open to the criticism that it does not have a successful strategy to incorporate experiences from the Global South and consequently its theorization excludes the experiences of a majority of communities from the Global South. This is the point that Santos (2018) makes with respect to Chomsky's political project: "With Chomsky we learn that there is a South and that we must go South in solidarity with it. But he is equally unhelpful in leading us to learn from the South" (p.221). Savransky (2017) extends the argument and emphasizes that perhaps the left may not fully comprehend that what is at stake in decolonization is much more than a search for cognitive justice or different knowledges, but rather, a search for a different world.

The African university is an imported institution distinct from traditional African institutions. It is operated and managed through committees and rarely sees any experimentation with traditional African governance structures such as *indaba* or *imbizo*. It is feasible, however, for universities to break away from their colonial heritage. As van der Walt (2013) argues, there are many reasons to challenge the assumptions, for example, around English as a default language of higher education in South Africa, and to explore instead the possibilities of multilingualism at many levels. Makalela (2018b) proposes the use of "multilanguaging in mainstream classrooms to transform academic literacy in order to encompass multilingual writers' antecedent genres and to scaffold academic writing" (p.119). A "multilingual, academic literacy approach" is essential, he argues, for students to be able to "make sense of the academic world" (p.133). Makalela's *ubuntu translanguaging pedagogy*, drawing on local South African language practices as well as a broader African epistemology of being (*ubuntu*) aims to "disrupt perceived language boundaries among preservice student teachers and to recreate complex multilingual spaces that reflect the *ubuntu* principles of ecological interdependence" (2017, p.17) and to combine "African worldviews of interdependence and general use of languages without boundaries" (2018c, p.262). As van der Walt (2013), puts it, the "possibilities for multilingual education are limited only by our own fixed ideas about language, learning and the nature of education" (p.180).

Mignolo (2018) cites Unitierra (Universidad de la Tierra) as an example of an institution that was developed in the last decade of the 20th century and that, unlike colonial African universities, was conceptualized not "from, but with Indigenous struggles and postulates of knowledge, in conversation with other forms of critical thought and liberation-based theory and praxis" (Mignolo, 2018, p.73). In Unitierra, one learns without the "necessity of professors, curriculum, students, textbooks, and degrees" (Mignolo, 2018, p.73). To conduct an applied linguistics without professors, curriculum, students, textbooks, and degrees would require a fundamental reconceptualization of applied linguistics, and yet, for an applied field engaged in practice, it opens up immense possibilities. Unitierra might be successful because it is not dependent on validation or funding from mainstream academic and funding institutions; such autonomy is necessary if decolonized institutions are to interact with mainstream universities on an independent footing. If this is currently a step too far for the field, applied linguistics does at least need to learn the lessons of territorial, cognitive, and linguistic decolonization implied by a recognition of the lands on which institutions are built, an appreciation of other forms of knowledge about language, learning, and education, and the possibility of a multilingual and multi-epistemological curriculum.

Challenges: Decolonizing applied linguistics

Looking more specifically at applied linguistics, there are a number of challenges in any decolonial project. Where language and education are concerned, testing, unfortunately, will never be far behind. Modes of assessment will often be perceived from the perspective of students, as repressive and debilitating: They may find that they have restricted room or latitude in their assignments, due to word limits, formatting prescriptions, due dates, and the penalties imposed for late submissions, which may compel students to submit unfinished assignments. In many ways, assessment regimes now mirror "practices of new (public) management" (Darmon, 2015, p.308; in Riemer, 2016a, p.38). In the context of sub-Saharan Africa, Antia (2018, p.2) argues that "the current monolingual and exoglossic practices" (tests are in a European language) in end-of-school examinations "constitute a set of sociolinguistic aberrations" and "structural violence and inequality" with serious negative effects on the students. If students could be tested multi-or translingually, they would get much better results, and the tests themselves would be seen as much fairer and more valid. New ways of testing multilingual repertoires (see Chapter 4) can bring more inclusive practices to the educational domain (Lopez et al., 2017). Schissel et al. (2018, p.2) make a case for a multilingual approach to testing that "would encourage learners to make full(er) use of their language resources within classroom-based language assessments". Language assessment, therefore, stands as a prime domain of applied linguistics in need of decolonization through an understanding both of the roles it plays in maintaining North–South inequalities (as a major gatekeeper of mobility) and of the ways it can be rethought in terms of multilingual repertoires (Shohamy and Pennycook, 2019).

A great deal could be said about second language acquisition (SLA) models and their northern assumptions about learners, languages, resources, and contexts.

Given that most current approaches to SLA scarcely even address social conditions of learning, let alone larger political questions about epistemological Eurocentrism, we shall not concern ourselves with much of this. Some brief comments about the much-trumpeted Douglas Fir Group (DFG, 2016) model will serve to show how most of this work is in desperate need of decolonization. Contrasting the models of language in second language acquisition studies and World Englishes, Ortega (2018, p.65) suggests that we have in applied and sociolinguistic fields a basic choice "between essentialist and non-essentialist ontologies of language". If this perhaps overstates the extent to which World Englishes exemplifies a non-essentialist position (it might be argued instead that it operates only with a pluralized vision of language), it nonetheless suggests a deep concern that this may be the best available option relative to the static, monologic vision of language that is assumed in most work on second language learning. Ortega (2018) goes on to suggest, however, that in the DFG (2016) proposal there are some signs of hope.

The DFG (2016) model aims to incorporate social dimensions to the standard SLA framework through an interdisciplinary approach, a "new, rethought SLA" that can "contribute to the development of innovative and sustainable lifeworld solutions that support language learners in a multilingual world" (2016, p.39). It reiterates the common contemporary tropes outlined in Chapter 3: "The phenomenon of multilingualism is as old as humanity, but multilingualism has been catapulted to a new world order in the 21st century" (DFG, 2016, p.19). The various scholars involved in this project "recognize that our affiliation with institutions in only two parts of the world, the United States and Canada, bound our intellectual views" (p.20). The project is thus open to the critique that by emphasizing interdisciplinarity, and multilingualism as the norm, it still fails to engage with anything beyond its own northern scope. As a result, language educators

> around the world may feel marginalized by a framework that relegates them to the role of "stakeholders" on the side of business leaders, politicians, and other organizations interested in "multilingualism", not as an educational project but as a subject of a neoliberal agenda of "globalization, technologization and mobility".
>
> *(Kramsch and Zhang, 2018, p.132)*

Even though there is arguably some hope in more recent laudable suggestions for "considering multilingualism as the central object of inquiry and embracing social justice as an explicit disciplinary goal" in order to "provide the necessary sustainable support for the kind of transdisciplinary SLA the DFG envisioned" (Ortega, 2019, p.24), the concern continues that interdisciplinarity operates as an internal northern discussion (Pennycook, 2018c), multilingualism is still conceived from a northern perspective, and social justice needs a decolonial and anti-racist politics if it is to engage with "white ignorance" (Mills, 2017, p. 56; Kubota, 2019). For Flores and Rosa (2019, p.146), the idea that "the incorporation of racialized populations into mainstream institutions as 'valued colleagues' will inherently promote more equity" misses again the politics of institutional racism. Ultimately, as Kramsch and Zhang (2018) remark, looking at this model from the perspective of language educators in different parts of the world, there is a "clash between this futuristic (some would say 'utopian') manifesto and the global reality of language instruction" (p.132). So, if this is as far as northern models of second language learning have come, they still have a long way to go before they could be considered any part of a decolonization project.

A further problem is that while there are reasons to acknowledge some progress in SLA research as it has moved slowly beyond a remarkable narrowness of understanding of language diversity and context, the celebrated multilingual turn in SLA (May, 2014; Ortega, 2013) is nevertheless a turn which still retains the acquisition of the same set of languages as targets of acquisition. This is not much of a turn, just a slight expansion that retains its Eurocentric multilingual roots. As Spinner (2010) points out, 84 per cent of the articles in the journal *Second Language Research* over the previous decade dealt with the acquisition of English, German, Dutch, French, Italian, and Spanish, while the remaining 16 per cent covered acquisition of all of the world's other languages. The languages in which multilingualism is written about, furthermore, remain narrow:

> a lot has been written about multilingualism in English; a fair amount has probably been written in Chinese, French, German, Italian, Japanese, Norwegian, Russian, Spanish, and maybe a handful of other languages. However, the vast majority of languages have never even been used to produce academic publications about multilingualism.
>
> *(Piller, 2016b, p.27)*

Liddicoat's (2016) study of citation and research practices in journals on multilingualism, suggests that "English-language monolingualism is a normal research practice in work in multilingualism" (p.11). The problem, as he explains, is that "languages other than English, and their associated epistemologies, are made almost invisible in the research practice of the field and are represented as making only a peripheral contribution to the field and to its theoretical bases" (p.12). Drawing on Santos' (2007a) discussion of an ecology of knowledges (*uma ecologia dos saberes*), Liddicoat points out that this creates "an absence of knowledge and of academic traditions from outside English-speaking academic practice and in so doing represents them as not having a contribution to make when understanding the field" (p.12). This in turn becomes part of the process by which research written up in English is presented as universally applicable while research in other languages takes on a role as being local, particular to a context. There is therefore "a construction of certain epistemologies of multilingualism as being less relevant or as hierarchically inferior or less important for academic work than others" (p.14).

On the one hand, generalizations (the pernicious 'universals' of Eurocentric coloniality) are proposed based on findings across a narrow selection of European languages, while on the other, patterns of acquisition that may be quite different for other languages (such as Bantu languages) are rarely considered (Spinner, 2010).

The issue, then, is not only the lack of other languages studied or the lack of other languages in which multilingualism is described, but also that generalizations are made from a narrow set of European languages (Liddicoat, 2018). There is a dearth of studies not only of different languages but of speakers of those languages learning other languages: second language acquisition (SLA) research may occasionally look at isi Xhosa or Setswana, for example, but almost always in the context of learning English, French, or other European languages, rather than Africans learning other African languages. An interesting exception to this narrow trend is the work of Thomas (forthcoming) looking at the acquisition of Swahili by Ghanaian students in Tanzania. The general understanding of SLA is nonetheless based on a narrow range of contexts, languages, and understandings of language. Alternatives might not just challenge assumptions about phonology or morphosyntax, but rather much wider assumptions about language and learning.

Other areas of applied linguistic work have also been taken to task for their Eurocentric assumptions. The "globalizing discourse of critical discourse analysis (CDA)", for example, has been challenged for employing "western worldviews, values, concepts, models, analytic tools, topics of interest, and so forth, as universal and exclusive standards" (Shi-Xu, 2015, p1). While CDA may produce some useful ideology critiques (though the logocentric bias of this work has also received critique; Thurlow, 2016), it "forms a hegemonic discourse, reproducing old-fashioned colonialist knowledge and excluding alternative visions" (Shi-xu, 2015, p.1). In a call to decolonize CDA in Latin American contexts, Resende (2018, p.9) argues that the first requirement is to acknowledge that "this intellectual endeavor occurs in a settler colonial society, construed by means of the fundamental violence of deterritorialization, political domination, assimilation, exploitation and extermination – and this violence is not over, it is not past: it is today." As we have noted at various other points in this book, there is a recurrent concern with old-school critical work: It operates with universalizing tropes of critical thought and fails to engage with more serious concerns about knowledge production, coloniality, and the need for a decolonizing project not *directed by* the old-guard of CDA but rather *directed at* their modes of analysis and generalization.

Decolonization of applied linguistics should not be reduced to a process of liberal pluralization while resisting the decentring of Western knowledges. Research into new Englishes/World Englishes, for example, may be a welcome advance because it widens the range of varieties of English being studied, yet it is debatable whether new Englishes/World Englishes can be said to seriously contribute to a decolonization of English studies. While Ortega (2018, p.65) usefully contrasts the "non-essentialist understandings" of language that have come about through an exploration of the "deterritoralization of English" with the "essentialist ontology of language that locks research into a monolingual worldview" prevalent in second language acquisition studies, the World Englishes framework nonetheless operates predominantly by a strategy of pluralization without calling into question the linguistic assumptions that strategies of decolonization would require. By maintaining a faith in the norms of standard language ideologies, it argues for a pluralization rather than a questioning of the power and status of the varieties of speech used by the educated elite in the Global North. Pluralization of Englishes leads to a reinforcement of *otherness*. As Rubdy (2015) notes, drawing on the work of Kumaravadivelu (2003), we need to decolonize rather than just pluralize English as part of any emancipatory project. For a decolonization of new/World Englishes to occur, as in other areas of applied linguistics, struggles for social and cognitive justice (Santos, 2007b, 2014) need to be combined with alternative ways of thinking about language that focus less on some putative variety of English and more on how English resources may be part of multilingual repertoires.

While much more could be said about specific domains of applied linguistics (and we return to a more general discussion of decolonizing the field in Chapter 7), we shall close with a brief consideration of language education. Efforts to decolonize the teaching of national languages through translanguaging (Garcia and Li Wei, 2014), translingual practices, and multilingual pedagogies, may at least have the potential to weaken the connection between standard languages and national cultures, thereby creating spaces for foreign language education to be influenced by other language varieties and alternative and competing cultures. In the rush to talk of translanguaging, it is often overlooked that, at least for García (2014), this was always a decolonizing project drawing on Mignolo's decolonial option (2011a; see Chapter 3). Nonetheless, Jaspers (2018, p.2) warns, as translanguaging is widely taken up, it may in fact "be less transformative and critical than is often suggested". The emancipatory potential of translanguaging, as with all critical projects, needs to be treated with circumspection, not least because a proposition that translanguaging frees the linguistically repressed subject may overlook ways in which named languages operate socially and politically both as part of a state apparatus and as a focus of emancipatory projects (see Chapter 4).

Attempts to react to the needs of learners in a global economy potentially instrumentalize foreign languages, enhancing the commodification of both education and language. Decolonizing the teaching of foreign languages – decoupling languages from their national and colonial boundaries and racist pasts – may be reinscribed within a neo-liberal order in which languages end up being treated as mere resources, important only for their exchange value rather than cultural significance (Kramsch, 2019). According to Tochon's (2019) approach to the decolonization of language education, drawing on the work of Freire (1994, 1995), it is important to critically explore the role that language teachers play as advocates of a simplistic, structuralist image of language as a reified object measured in standardized tests used for bureaucratic purposes. "Bureaucracy is part of a dehumanizing agenda that treats humans like robots that respond to well-specified goals. Bureaucracy hinders forms of emancipatory learning that could focus on proficiency and cross-cultural understanding" (Tochon, 2019, p.264).

As Jakubiak (2016) notes in his critique of *volontourist* English language programmes, one aspect of the discourses of development that inhabit these programmes is a view that teaching methods in the South are outmoded. As he notes, this not only overlooks questions of contextual appropriacy and the locus of the northern gaze (see next chapter for further discussion) but also fails to recognize that such old-fashioned methods are also equally common in the Global South back home (in poorer schools in districts where these volunteer teachers have never been). A major challenge for a decolonized applied linguistics, then, is to decolonize teaching methods and our understanding of them (Pennycook, 1989). Amongst other things, this implies engaging with the many other traditions of language education (and without inscribing them into the reductively 'traditional' of Methods discourse), in African, Meso-American, Chinese, Hindu, Buddhist, and Islamic educational thought and practice (Reagan, 1996, 2018). Phan (2017) makes a similar point in her critique of the development of mediocre English-medium education, as Western institutions sell their educational packages wholesale to regions of Asia. Comprehending what language in education means in these other traditions may help the Global North to become more sensitive to alternative and contrary viewpoints within applied linguistics in the Global North itself, and may heighten sensitivity about assumptions that the Global North makes about what constitutes education.

Drawing on the work of Mignolo (2010) and others, Kumaravadivelu, (2016) stresses the importance of *delinking* from Eurocentric categories of thought, in order to *unfreeze* the subaltern's potential for *thinking otherwise*. Kumaravadivelu (2016) calls for a *grammar of decoloniality* that would include on the one hand a discontinuation of those patronizing studies that seek to show that the non-native subaltern teacher can teach as well as their native speaker counterparts, and on the other hand the designing of "context-specific instructional strategies that take into account the local historical, political, social, cultural, and educational exigencies" (p.81), as well as various other projects to ensure that materials and practices draw on local forms of knowledge, culture, and expertise (Kumaravadivelu, 2012). If teaching methodologies can engage with such decolonizing practices, there is no reason why other domains of applied linguistics cannot do likewise. Ending on a cautionary note, however, Kumaravadivelu (2016) affirms that while the *decolonial option* is the only meaningful way to address these concerns, it demands action. "Without action", he insists (2016, p.82), "the discourse is reduced to banality". We know the subaltern can speak and write, he points out, but "Can the subaltern act?".

Kumaravadivelu's (2016) argument takes us to an important juncture in this discussion. It is evident that although some areas of applied linguistics have been subject to a decolonial critique – teaching methods is one example, and some areas of language policy discussed in the previous chapter might be another – there is a very long way to go. It is also very clear that decolonization is a complex and contested category, and that different versions of decolonization vary widely in their goals. It is also important that these discussions do not remain only textual deliberations but also include action. As Connell (2018) notes with respect to sociology, this is about the redistribution of knowledge and resources, and unless the field of applied linguistics *acts* to bring about epistemological, ontological, and material change, a decolonization project will end only in talk. While we have only skimmed domains of applied linguistics in desperate need of decolonization, it is also crucial that we move beyond talk and into fields of action.

Conclusion: Towards a decolonial imagination in applied linguistics

Language and education are highly significant domains in any decolonizing project, both because they have colonial pasts that in themselves need decolonization, and because they may play a key role in decolonization processes themselves. We are acutely aware that under the broad umbrella of decolonization, there are many potential paradoxes, disagreements, diverse images of decolonial futures, and possible strategies of arriving at these different futures. Crucial too are questions of whether decolonization projects overlap with, are reducible to, or are incommensurable with other social justice projects. Thus, any effort to address decolonization has to confront the many ways of understanding what this may entail (Stein and Andreotti, 2016). The decolonization that we are proposing here may be aligned with, but is also different from the Freirean-based approaches in Tochon's (2019) or Macedo's (2019) calls for a decolonization of foreign language education: "Whereas in Paulo Freire the major objective is the educational project, in the epistemologies of the South it is the ecologies of knowledges, from which the possibility of strengthening the social struggles against domination may emerge" (Santos, 2018, p.261).

The distinction is an important one. While the significance of Paulo Freire's legacy is not in question, his work on the one hand was centrally concerned with the oppressions caused by capitalism as well as a lack of political freedom, while from an epistemologies of the South perspective, "domination has three pillars: capitalism, colonialism, and patriarchy" (Santos, 2018, p.259). On the other hand, Freire's work was centrally concerned with literacy and pedagogy, while a global South perspective is concerned more broadly with forms of knowledge. From an applied linguistic point of view, one might assume that it is precisely the Freirean interest in critical literacy for the oppressed that should be our focus in any project to decolonize language education. Our argument, however, following the work of Grosfoguel (2011, 2013), Mbembe (2001), Mignolo (2018), Walsh (2018) Santos (2014, 2018), and others who work in decolonial politics and southern epistemologies, is that while we continue to align with much of Freire's work, we are trying to make a case for the bigger picture here, one where decolonizing applied linguistics is not just an issue for critical educational projects but a much wider set of concerns about knowledge and research.

There is limited scholarship on how applied linguistics as a discipline has handled decolonization issues and the impact of such processes on applied linguistics in subfields such as language policy and planning, language rights, language endangerment, and language teaching. To become exposed to the deeply transformative potential of non-Eurocentric thinking, applied linguistics, like disciplines such as sociology, has to cultivate a "decolonial imagination" that may render it feasible to move beyond epistemology, and to "recognize that there is no social and cognitive justice without existential justice, no politics of knowledge without a politics of reality" (Savransky, 2017, p.11). These are serious challenges for applied linguistics, but challenges that it needs to take on if it is to remain credible in the context of the "decolonial turn" (Maldonado-Torres, 2007). Exposure to other traditions of applied linguistics, decolonial thought, and "artisanal knowledge" (Santos, 2018, p.261) should not only transform how applied linguistic knowledge in the Global North is produced, but also what we understand applied linguistics to be and what counts as applied linguistics. We shall try to pull these arguments together into a more specific decolonial agenda for applied linguistics in Chapter 7. First, however, we will discuss in greater depth in the next chapter questions of research and Indigeneity.

6
CHALLENGING THE NORTHERN RESEARCH GAZE

Introduction: Epistemic racism

One of the primary objectives of this chapter is to provide an investigation into the challenges that the Global South poses to applied linguistics as we seek to develop "epistemologies of the South". We construe epistemologies of the South to be a set of "enquiries into the construction and validation of knowledge born in struggle, of ways of knowing developed by social groups as part of their resistance against the systematic injustices and oppressions caused by capitalism and patriarchy" (Santos, 2014, p.x). The ultimate objective of epistemologies of the South for applied linguistics should, therefore, be not so much to construct alternative ways of thinking or alternative approaches, but rather, "alternative thinking of alternatives"; and not theories of revolution, but strategies to "revolutionize theory" and produce "alternative forms of political praxis" (Bhambra et al., 2018, p.2). A revolutionized applied linguistics theory would comprise "ecologies of knowledges", (Santos, 2018, p.13) which might at times be incompatible and incommensurable, but whose coherence is facilitated through "intercultural translation" (Santos, 2018, p.18). In this chapter, which looks in particular at research, and draws on Indigenous scholarship, we outline how Indigenous "conceptual worlds" (Wagner, 2015), or "non-Eurocentric 'cosmovisions'" (Santos, 2014, p.29) and Indigenous practices, can constitute alternatives to Eurocentrism and an innovative agenda for applied linguistics. We conclude the chapter by discussing the challenges that incorporating Indigenous cosmovisions pose for the field.

One of the defining properties of applied linguistics in the Global North is the exclusion of research conducted in the Global South. As already discussed in Chapter 1, for example, Levon's (2017) critique of Coupland's (2016) edited volume on sociolinguistics points to the omission of the dynamic traditions of sociolinguistic research in the Global South (see Chapters 3–4). The exclusion and invisibility of research from the Global South in applied linguistics is by no means restricted to sociolinguistics, but is also true for other areas of applied linguistics, from language development to language policy and planning, from critical discourse analysis to second language acquisition (see Chapter 5). It is possible indeed to suggest a regressive trend in regard to the "emergences" and "absences" of socio-political contexts from the Global South in applied linguistics from an analysis of language policy and planning handbooks published between 1974 and 2018 (Severo and Makoni, forthcoming).

The thrust of the research trajectory of language policy and planning research, when viewed across many different handbooks, is characterized by movements that are more towards a narrowing than an expansion of research contexts and agendas. An historical orientation to the field is made by the classic *Advances in Language Planning* (Fishman et al., 1974), which provides an exploration of the nature of the relationship between language policy and newly independent African states. In addition, the 2012 *Cambridge Handbook of Language Policy* (Spolsky, 2012) contains a chapter on the relationship between language policy, imperialism, and colonialism, in which Makoni et al. concentrate on colonial and postcolonial language policies. The recent *Oxford Handbook of Language Policy and Planning* (Tollefson and Perez-Millans, 2018), however, does not have explicit reference to colonial or postcolonial contexts, even though a majority of the world's population lives in such contexts.

If the impetus for the greater inclusion of language policy in newly independent states in the 1970s was clear (language policy questions were very much to the fore in the context of decolonization and independence), there is equally in the current epoch every reason for a much more inclusive view of language in the world. It is exactly at this historical juncture, when applied linguistics, in its trajectory as a maturing discipline, should be more open to experiences from southern contexts. That it has become blind to this knowledge, thus failing to appreciate the degree to which the Western-centric basis for knowing the world is deeply challenged by the vastness of the majority world (Santos, 2014), is a sad indictment on a field that should be more politically aware. The exclusion and invisibility of contexts outside Euro-America may be a consequence of the failure of applied linguistics to "make sense of the world at large other than through general theories and universal ideas" (Santos, 2014, p.19), reinforced by a proclivity in applied linguistics to conceive of the Eurocentric epistemological North as the only source of valid knowledge. "By the same token, the South, that is, whatever lies on the other side of the line, is the realm of ignorance" (Santos, 2014, p.6).

The problem of excluding contexts in the Global South, however, is not simply resolved by incorporating these contexts into existing theoretical frameworks. The real task, by contrast, is to change the predominant terms and assumptions, and to revisit principles upon which the new contexts are included (Mignolo, 2018, p.149). A major challenge to epistemologies of the Global North in applied linguistics is posed by *epistemological racism* (Kubota, 2019), or what Scheurich (1997) refers to as *civilizational racism*. Epistemological or civilizational racism is deeply embedded in academic knowledge systems in the Global North and by extension can be found in applied linguistics. It privileges 'White' epistemological assumptions about knowledge, regarding them as norms against which other forms of knowledge have to be measured. The concept of epistemological racism is reminiscent of Fanon's (1967, p.192) "cultural imposition" (l'imposition culturelle). Cultural imposition or epistemological racism produce a view of 'whiteness' as the norm, both physically and in terms of social, cultural, and linguistic practices, leading to a tendency for southern scholars to view themselves through others' eyes—a form of 'double consciousness' (du Bois,1970/1903). Double consciousness describes the psychological tension suffered by dominated groups in politically, economically, and socially oppressive societies. The term originally referred to the challenges of looking at one's self through the perspectives of racist white society (as does Fanon's cultural imposition).

Closely linked to epistemological racism is what Battiste (1998) defines as a culturalist approach to epistemology, an academic and pedagogical posture and orientation inherited from colonialism, and based on the assumption that mainstream (i.e. Western, colonial, Eurocentric) culture and knowledge are a global and universal norm, from which Indigenous knowledge deviates. A culturalist perspective homogenizes both Western and Indigenous cultures. According to Deloria (1997), "white lies" represent epistemological dominance as the foundation of colonialism and ideas of cultural supremacy, justifying the accumulation of wealth that was founded on the genocide of Indigenous peoples in the Americas and around the world.

Epistemic racism constitutes the cornerstone of the knowledge structures of the Westernized university. Its epistemic privileging of the social and historical experiences of a few men from four countries in Western Europe (Italy, France, England, and Germany) and the United States is the result of four genocides/epistemicides in the 16th century against Jewish- and Muslim-origin populations in the conquest of Al-Andalus; against Indigenous people in the conquest of the Americas; against Africans who were kidnapped and enslaved in the United States; and against women accused of being witches who were burned alive in Europe (Grosfoguel, 2013). Genocide, Indigeneity, settler colonialism, and research need to be understood as closely intertwined. Both Indigeneity and genocide are paradoxically rooted in otherness:

> The category of indigeneity reveals a basic paradox: The colonizer and indigenous other are separate from, but simultaneously dependent upon, one another. Likewise, with genocide, the perpetrator and othered victim are separate but are at the same time dependent on each other. Genocide and indigeneity are [so] conceptually related that one can consider them different sides of the same phenomenon.
>
> *(Chalmers, 2016, p.177)*

It is feasible to conceptualize the relationship between Indigeneity and genocide as a two-stage process of erasure in settler colonies, with imposition of the category of Indigeneity as a preliminary that precedes a formal act of genocide (Chalmers, 2016). The cornerstone of the epistemic foundations of the Western university have to be understood against this background of genocide: They are both racist and sexist and, of course, colonialist.

Epistemological racism has an impact on knowledge production in applied linguistics, as it leads to a marginalization and erasure of knowledge by scholars in the Global South, female scholars of colour, and other minoritized groups. In contemporary neo-liberal cultures of competition and excessive consumption in the Global North, scholars of colour may, however, find themselves not resisting, but rather, being complicit with white Euro-American hegemonic knowledge through their academic practices and professional activities. These practices and activities may inadvertently perpetuate the hegemony of White Eurocentric knowledge, consequently marginalizing women scholars of colour (Kubota, 2019). To challenge applied linguistic research in the North, epistemologies of the South in applied linguistics need to turn attention not only to an analysis of narratives about masters/colonizers, but also towards an analysis of how our applied linguistic practices, teaching, learning, supervision, and grant-seeking practices may further entrench North/South asymmetry. When extended to applied linguistics – a discipline so often concerned with White theories about White languages, with White language tests to exclude people of colour, and with White language practices extended to the rest of the world (see Chapter 5) – an understanding of epistemological racism points to the ways in which applied linguistics in the Global North is construed as a norm against which applied linguistics from other regions has to be measured. We suggested in Chapter 5 that such underlying assumptions about language and education can be challenged through a project of decolonization in applied linguistics. In this chapter we take this argument further through an exploration of alternative cosmovisions.

Researching communities to death

One of the central concerns for those who have suffered at the hands of academic colonialism is that linguistic and anthropological research has been carried out on these communities as one arm of coloniality and epistemic racism. "There has been a long- standing view among research subjects, especially indigenous peoples", Gomes (2013, p.13) notes, "that the anthropological project is essentially irrelevant and at worst, exploitative". For Smith (2012, p.102), "being researched is synonymous with being colonised". Martin and Mirraboopa (2003) suggest that "the quantity of research conducted in Aboriginal lands and on Aboriginal people since British invasion in the late 1770s is so immense that it makes us one of the most researched groups of people of earth" (p.203). Indigenous people, Sarkar (2018, p.494) suggests, have been "researched to death" (Brant Castellano, 2004). Smith makes a similar point, suggesting that from the

> vantage point of the colonized, a position from which I write, and choose to privilege, the term "research" is inextricably linked to European imperialism and colonialism. The word itself, "research", is probably one of the dirtiest words in the indigenous world's vocabulary.
>
> *(2012, p.1)*

At a time when there is already a growing tide of scepticism towards knowledge, research, and academic institutions (fanned by 'climate change sceptics', conservative commentators, 'alternative facts', 'post-truth' positions, and a popular view that since 'everyone has a right to their opinion', then every point of view is equally valid, and that every fact is open to at least a two-sided debate; see Block, 2019), it is important to understand that this Indigenous challenge is very different from such populist scepticism. To think of research as a dirty word, as one of the dirtiest words in one's vocabulary, urges us to understand the painful implications of a history of research done to and on you. While we should also be cautious here not to dismiss an entire body of knowledge in an overgeneralized critique of anthropology or linguistics (Gomes, 2013) – many linguists and anthropologists have worked with Indigenous communities and been strong advocates for those people and their rights in larger political as well as academic forums – we should recognize the pain, mistrust, and exploitation that has so often been a result of research from the outside, as well as the problem that however well-meaning those researchers may have been, they may all too rarely have had the adequate intellectual and empathetic tools to engage with the languages, cultures, and epistemologies that confronted them.

> To recuperate anthropology with a heart, we will need to put our minds to retrieving the discipline's spirit of compassion by standing *with* indigenous peoples and other marginalised communities, and not on the sidelines, in their struggles against structural violence.
>
> *(Gomes, 2013, p.14)*

In the wider field of social scientific research, it has been acknowledged that research "needs emancipation from hearing only the voices of Western Europe, emancipation from generations of silence, and emancipation from seeing the world in one colour" (Guba and Lincoln, 2005, p.212). As Chilisa (2011, p.1) puts it, "current academic research traditions are founded on the culture, history, and philosophies of Euro-Western thought" and "exclude from knowledge production the knowledge systems of formerly colonized, historically marginalized, and oppressed groups". Central to many of these critiques is the idea of *decolonization* of research methodologies (Smith, 2012) and the development of alternative approaches to research (and see Chapter 5 for a more extended discussion of decolonization). We are arguing for the centrality of Indigenous cosmovisions in our epistemologies of the South in applied linguistics. Grosfoguel (2016) identifies five questions or challenges that have to be considered in such an enterprise: (1) Can we produce a radical anti-systemic politics beyond identity politics? (2) Is it possible to articulate a critical cosmopolitanism beyond nationalism and colonialism? (3) Can we produce knowledge beyond Third World and Eurocentric fundamentalisms? (4) Can we overcome the traditional dichotomy between political economy and cultural studies? and, (5) How can we overcome Eurocentric modernity, without throwing away the best of modernity as many Third World fundamentalists do? We have sought to develop such a perspective in this book, through what we tentatively term an *ubuntu-nepantla* way of thinking and doing (see Chapter 7).

Grosfoguel (2016) cautions us against the danger of throwing out the baby with the bathwater when we challenge core ideas of modernity, a position that has been taken up in a number of ways, including Chakrabarty's (2000) argument for *provincializing* European modes of thought (see Chapter 2). To develop an epistemology of the South that is not restricted to applied linguistics in the Global North or South, we need to develop an epistemic perspective from the subaltern side of colonial difference. Expressed differently, we need to develop a critique of Western-centric applied linguistics through "border thinking". Border thinking (Mignolo, 2018; Santos, 2018) is a response to both hegemonic and marginal fundamentalisms, and has been variously understood as researching from the periphery, as an outsider, or from a point of disadvantage. Border thinking draws on the work of Anzaldúa (1987, 2002) on borders/fronteras, and what it means to inhabit the physical and discursive borderlands between Mexico and the USA, between hegemonic accounts of normativity and Chicanx minoritized lives. It is from her work that we draw the term *nepantla*, a Nahuatl word meaning *tierra entre medio* (an unstable, unpredictable, precarious in-between space; Anzaldúa, 2002, p. 1).

Gaundry and Lorenz (2018) identify three educational responses to Indigeneity: Indigenous inclusion, Indigenous reconciliation, and decolonial Indigenization. Post-secondary institutions in Canada have focused far more on Indigenous inclusion than on any sense of decolonial Indigenization. It is crucial, however, for epistemologies of the South in applied linguistics to move beyond inclusionary positions to embrace decolonial epistemologies implied by a mobilization of Indigenous cosmovisions. Such epistemic perspectives, as Dussel (2013) emphasizes, have a relative exteriority from Eurocentric modernity. Indigenous cosmovisions were affected but not destroyed by genocide/epistemicide and, thus, can be harnessed to leave open the possibility that there are opportunities for a "world where many worlds are possible", a Zapatista slogan (Grosfoguel, 2013, p.87). Issues related to Indigenous cosmovisions are complicated not only by the challenges of "intercultural translatability", but also by the plurality of meanings of what Indigeneity means and who meets the criteria of Indigenous: Indigenous identities are emergent and what Indigeneity means may vary significantly, intersecting with issues of race and marginality (Gomes, 2013). Indigenous forms of knowledge nonetheless provide a range of possible means of epistemic renewal in the social sciences more broadly, and applied linguistics more particularly, and it is to these that we now turn.

Innovations: Applied linguistics and Indigenous cosmovisions

An applied linguistics undergirded by epistemologies of the South has to be grounded in concepts that expand the repertoires of social emancipation that can constitute alternatives to neo-liberalism through different Indigenous cosmovisions. There are a number of *emancipatory scripts* (Santos, 2018), or newly reinvented ancestral concepts, that are part of Indigenous cosmovisions and world practices. We are aware of the seeming paradox in calling these terms both traditional and reinvented, yet we want to draw attention to the ways they are simultaneously traditional – they have always been in circulation – but also reinvented – they are being used to serve new purposes in contemporary times. Among many currently emerging terms, *pachamama, ahimsa (ahinsa), ubuntu, chachawarmi,* and *sumac kawasay* are of particular interest. The term *pachamama* is conventionally translated from Aymara and Quechua as Mother Earth but also as World Mother (Dransart, 1992; Hill, 2008) The term a*himsa*, also spelled a*hinsa*, originates from the Sanskrit root *hims* and means non-violence. Mahatma Gandhi is well known for promoting the principles of *ahimsa* and *satya* (truth) (Ramchiary, 2013), applying it to different aspects of his life (Chapple, 1993; Gandhi, 2002). These newly reinvented ancestral scripts, derived from Indigenous peoples of the Americas, Africa, South Asia, and Oceania, who were victims of colonialism and suffered severe epistemicide, have expanded the repertoires of social emancipation and political liberation, leading us to believe, optimistically, that the formation of other worlds is feasible. "This rich experience will be wasted unless it is grasped and valorized by an epistemological turn capable of grounding an adequate politics of knowledge" (Santos, 2018, p.9). The newly reinvented ancestral concepts render it intellectually plausible for us to move beyond the limitations of Western-centric politics and knowledge that is central to applied linguistics in the Global North.

The quest and search for epistemological diversity of the world demands that these expanded repertoires of human dignity and social liberation be conceived as being relevant beyond the ethnic groups and geographical region in which they originated. The concept of *ubuntu* (I am what I am because of who we all are) (Kamwangamalu, 1999; Makalela, 2018a, b; Makoni and Severo, 2017), for example, which originates among the Bantu in Southern Africa, is linked to different ways of understanding the human: *umzimba* (body, form, flesh), *umoya* (breath, air, life), *umphefumela* (shadow, spirit, sound), *inhliziyo* (heart, centre of emotions), *umqondo* (head, brain, intellect), *ulwini* (language, speaking), (Venter, 2004). It can be seen as having far wider applications beyond Southern Africa. Brazil has inherited various African practices, communication styles, customs, and variations of *ubuntu*, that reflect the Africanity of Brazilian social practices, even in the spoken Portuguese of Brazil (Makoni and Severo, 2017, p.73). By combining the mutual dependence implied by *ubuntu* (languages only exist because others do) and the precarious borderland thinking of *nepantla* (languages are an unstable inbetweenness rather than firmly bordered entities), we can envisage an intra-Southern conceptual field that addresses more clearly the ways of thinking we want to open up here.

The Qeuchua idea of *chachawarmi* is a key concept in the liberation struggles of Indigenous women in Latin American countries, and beyond. It dispenses with a duality typical of Western-centric feminisms. Such non-Eurocentric renditions of European concepts may expand our understanding and comprehension of key concepts for applied linguistics. *Vivir bien* (Bolivia) or *buen vivir* (Ecuador) are Spanish terms (living well, plentiful life, to know how to live, harmonious life) that emerged in the late 20th century to refer to the practices and visions – Aymara *sumaq qamana*; Quecha *sumac kawasay* – of Indigenous peoples of the Andean region of South America (Solón, 2017). These concepts became popular as people sought alternatives to neo-liberalism, and other forms of political and economic oppression (Gonzalez and Vasquez, 2013; Gudynas, 2011, 2016). They have also been incorporated into the Bolivian and Ecuadorian constitutions (Pietari, 2016; Tanasecu 2013), leading to the development of "Earth Jurisprudence." The concept of the rights of nature (as established in the Constitution of Ecuador) combines Western and non-Western cultural elements. According to Indigenous cosmovisions or philosophies, it makes no sense to attribute rights to nature, for nature is the source of all rights. Ecuador, however, "is the first country in history to guarantee rights to nature, in its constitution" (Tanasescu, 2013, p.846). Bolivia followed suit in 2009. Granting rights to nature is a "new approach to environmental law that conceptualizes the natural, non-human world as something worthy of protection for its own sake, and not as something to be used for the benefit of people" (Pietari, 2016, p.38). The notion that nature has rights is a major conceptual development in the protection of the Earth. Before the Ecuadorian constitution, which granted rights to the Earth (Nature or *Pachamama*), an environmental lawsuit could be filed only if a personal injury was demonstrated in connection with the environment, but under the Ecuadorian Constitution, people can now sue on behalf of the environment even if they experienced no personal injury (Herold, 2017).

The idea of *Pachamama* encapsulates the complex interconnection between space and time with the cosmos as being in a state of constantly becoming. The cosmos, from this perspective, is always emergent and, we can add, inchoate. In this Indigenous cosmovision, the past, present, and future coexist and relate to each other dynamically. From *Buen Vivir*, time is understood cyclically rather than linearly, a vision that is incompatible with northern notions of growth and development. This vision questions the very idea of "development" as an idea that runs in various guises through many applied linguistics models (most obviously language development and its tendency towards linear sequencing of morpheme acquisition), which presuppose movement towards a higher point and learning towards a normative end. While complexity theory (Larsen-Freeman and Cameron, 2008) or the Douglas Fir Group (2016) have sought to bring greater complexity to the reductive models of linear accretion, they do so in an additive, agglutinative mode (the circles and boxes of the Douglas Fir Group model), rather than seeking an alternative, more parsimonious, more appealing cosmovision.

Vivir Bien is relevant to epistemologies of the South in applied linguistics because it envisions a continual struggle. The Spanish conquest of over 500 years initiated a new cycle that did not come to an end with the attainment of independence by the republics in the 19th century. The cycle continues under new guises, reinforced by economic, cultural, and linguistic structures. Indigenous cosmovisions, when integrated into epistemologies of the South, may lead us to a decentring of humanity. In Indigenous cosmovisions and world practices, human communication and musical abilities are not unique to humans; rather, they are shared by other species as well. Humans are not exceptional in folklore, as the ability to talk is seen in animals and plants. Indigenous cosmovisions open possibilities of a much broader applied linguistics, in which interaction and communication with non-humans are also an important part of the discipline (Appleby and Pennycook, 2017).

The inclusion of these 'other' contexts in applied linguistics requires us to revisit some common assumptions about language and the relationship between humans and non-humans. Human groups and members of collectives as far apart as Athapaskan peoples in the Canadian Northwest Territories (Smith, 2002) and Amazonian groups such as the Archur (Taylor, 1993) or the Runa (Kohn, 2013) frequently enter complex communicative relationships with numerous non-humans, often by using special linguistic forms. In the Southwestern United States, as reported by Basso (1990), the land itself speaks to the Western Apache through the names that certain places bear, underscoring the degree to which communication with different kinds of non-humans permeates our universe (Deacon, 1997). Carter (2005) comments on how place names are indicators of human interaction with the environment among the Māori. In Māori genealogies, a list of names shows an order of descent from an eponymous ancestor. Absolutely everything that makes up the human, spiritual, and natural worlds – every person, tree, stone, mountain, fish, plant, the earth, and the stars – has a *whakapapa*. When Māori view the landscape, they see *whakapapa* and kinship relations that they can interact with through place names. As discussed in Chapter 4, the ontological questions posed by such different ways of thinking about language, people, and place pose major challenges to our linguistic epistemologies.

A "terracentric" bias nonetheless inhabits some of these assumptions about people, language, and the land. As Hayman et al. (2018) suggest, there is a tendency to overlook the importance of people and water. The traditional oral narratives, toponyms, and cultural practices of the Tlingit and Tagish (First Nation people of the circumpolar North) suggest an "alternative ontological water (ice) consciousness" that can "inform and potentially reimagine contemporary international debates concerning water ethics, water law, water governance, and water management" (p.77). Ingersoll's (2016) *seascape epistemology* likewise illustrates how Indigenous identity emerges and is tied not only to the land but also to the oceans. Indigenous Hawaiian identities, she argues, emerge when they enter the water; "I become a historical being riding waves, running as a liquid mass, pulled from the deep and thrown forward with a deafening roar. I disappear with fish and strands of seaweed as I course through veins of ocean currents" (2016, p.1). In the ocean, Indigenous Hawaiian communities are able to reconnect with their Kanaka heritage. For Ingersoll (2016), the goal here is to "decenter the conversation toward independent and alternative ways of knowing and producing knowledge that allow for empowerment and self-determination within a multisited world" (Ingersoll, 2016, p.3).

In seascape epistemology, it is the ocean, not the land, that is central. The ocean and the wind are not treated as 'things', but rather as aspects of an interconnected system, providing an orientation to life. This orientation is both theoretical and practical, providing a template for how to move through the ocean and how to approach life, For Hayman et al. (2018), Tlingit perspectives on glaciers offer "an alternative ontological awareness of glaciers as well as a nuanced Indigenous empirical scientific knowledge that moves away from the Eurocentric models of categorizing and understanding the natural world" (p.77). From this point of view, their relation to glaciers ("the future rivers of the Anthropocene") offers an alternative to Western climate science, and alternative ways of understanding: "Thinking with glaciers as powerful actors in the forging of human and more-than-human identities can be viewed as an effort to re-imagine relationships with water and ice and depart from terracentric histories, and futures" (p.87). Moving beyond terracentric views can change the ways we understand islands, from 'islands in a far sea', pointing to the size and remoteness of islands in the Pacific, to a 'sea of islands', implying a holistic perspective important for connecting rather than dividing Māori and Pasifika peoples (Pennycook, 2015; Shilliam, 2015).

Part of this project is therefore a repopulating of the social sciences with non-human beings and shifting the focus away from internal analysis of social conventions and institutions and towards interactions of humans with (and between) animals, plants, physical processes, artefacts, images, and other forms of being. This kind of southern applied linguistics, therefore, seeks to side-step anthropological dualisms such as nature and society, individual and collective, body and mind, while retaining the democratic idea that the world is neither the exclusive terrain of one's racial nor ethnic group, but rather, the terrain of all different types and forms of life (Descola, 2014; Mbembe, 2016). This is where southern epistemologies and Indigenous cosmovisions meet post-humanist concerns about humanist traditions (Pennycook, 2018a), where the dangers of yet another northern co-opting of southern epistemologies can come to share a more equitable understanding that humans share the universe with non-humans. Indigenous cosmovisions and world practices require that we develop metaphors that are consistent with the communities that we are describing. For example, in a robust critique of metaphors of language death and their impact on speakers of these languages, Perley (2012) proposes the use of the metaphors of languages "sleeping" and "awakening", instead of the highly emotive metaphors of language death and endangerment (see Chapters 3 and 4 for a fuller exposition of this topic in this book). The metaphor of language sleeping and awakening helps to bring insights into issues of agency and spirituality, both of which are relevant to Indigenous cosmovisions (Lüpke and Storch, 2013, p.358). From such a perspective, not only can languages have agency, or an existence that is neither wholly separate from nor wholly dependent on humans, but it can be seen as sharing a life with other objects.

Objects can retain agency even when they are not used. Buganda drums, some of which are kept where kings are buried, retain high levels of agency and are still sacred even where they may disintegrate. One of the best-known drums able to represent the power and superiority of the king among the Baganda is *Mujaguzo*. Drums in African traditions constitute a power that drives a performance. Drumming, music, and dance are almost always an accompaniment for any type of ceremony: birth, marriages, work, and funerals. Most communities have diverse uses of drums (Amegago, 2013 Drums may be used to communicate information and send messages, a practice popularly referred to as 'talking drums', which imitates speech. Ganda drum music is deeply tied to Luganda language (Mabingo, 2015; Nannyonga-Tamusuza, 2005). Each drumming is associated with a specific preexisting text and message, and the drum is considered the custodian of the language among the Buganda people. Music is not merely entertainment but, rather, is ultimately bound to visual and dramatic arts as well as the larger fabric of life. Many African languages are both tonal (that is, meaning can depend on variations in pitch) and rhythmic (that is, accents may be durational), giving speech a musical quality that may be imitated by drums and other instruments. Drums are used for many purposes, the sound of drums being first heard when a child is born, and accompanying each individual through their life at all major events until death (birth, name giving, puberty, courtship dances, weddings, seasonal festivities, during work, family gatherings, or for spiritual reasons; Nannyonga-Tamusuza, 2005).

If drums are used as a prism to expand the analytical repertoires we adopt in applied linguistics, we will have to frame language intersemiotically or transmodally, emphasizing how the co-presence and engagement of different verbal and non-verbal elements in Indigenous perspectives, as well as particular dynamics of affect between people, animals, plants, and spirits, requires a broader understanding of what constitutes language (Dias, 2019; and see Chapter 4). Professionals such as religious experts, blacksmiths, and healers, have the capacity to shift agency from one medium to another. For Mbembe (2016), it is not only agency that can be extended to non-humans, but power, as well. From this perspective, languages are not systems that, if not used by humans, become extinct, but rather complex parts of an interwoven range of people, place, and things. Humans are part of a very long and deep history, over which they neither have complete control, nor a monopoly. They share this history with other entities, so the dualistic partitions of minds from bodies, meaning, and matter or nature, cannot be conceptually sustained. Matter has morphogenetic capacities of its own and does not need to be commanded into generating form. It is not an inert receptacle for forms that come from outside, imposed by an exterior agency. To be a subject is no longer to act autonomously in front of an objective background, but to share agency with other subjects that have lost their autonomy. Further, we have to shift away from dreams of mastery.

In other words, a new understanding of ontology, epistemology, ethics, and politics has to be achieved. It can only be achieved by overcoming anthropocentricism and humanism, the split between nature and culture (Mbembe, 2016). To say a language is sleeping is not just optimism; it is a different cosmovision.

An important characteristic of Indigenous cosmovisions, world views, and philosophies is the extensive use of rich and dense metaphors that produce fresh descriptions of entities, and not simply representations of entities "out there". They also serve to institute new narratives. The use of metaphors in Indigenous cosmovisions is not the opposite of conceptuality, but rather, serves to illuminate the constitutive features of lived reality. Some Indigenous cosmovision discourses, such as Afro-Caribbean philosophy, have a plethora of root metaphors such as *anancy, caliban*, creolization, cross-culturality, fragments, hybridity, *mestizaje*, scar/wound/schizophrenia, submarine, and twilight (Headley, 2011). *Anancy* (or Anansi) has become the collective memory of the Caribbean experience, representing Africans' struggle for survival and resistance within the colonized world (Meder and Illes, 2010, p.20) The African trickster figure, either animal or human, is central to most island folktales in the Caribbean (Marshall, 2012). Anancy stories are the product of resistance which reveal nontraditional subversion that "guarantees hope in a hopeless system" (Araya, 2014, p.43). Language is important in Anancy and other stories because "it was in language that the slave was perhaps most successfully imprisoned by his master, and it was in his misuse of it that he most effectively rebelled" (Braithwaite, 1971, p.237 in Headley, 2011, p.505). If, in applied linguistics of the Global South, we are to view language through an anancy lens, language use will be expected to be vague, ambiguous, indeterminate, multivocal, and used for subversive purposes consistent with the social objectives which the trickster aims to accomplish when seeking to survive or subvert existing power hierarchies.

In many Indigenous cultures, stories are a common repository of knowledge and facilitate the process of knowing (Ranjan, 2017). Māori academics (indigenous to Aotearoa/New Zealand), have developed approaches to key principles of Māori research, oral traditions, and narrative enquiry to articulate Māori experiences. The application of *whakapapa* ("genealogical descent of all living things from the gods to the present time"; Barlow, 1994, p.173) provides identifying personal *korero* stories and integrates them within layers of interrelated *kaupapa* (a way of doing things from a Māori world view) about their *whanau* (family) and Māori culture and society, providing a framework that links research to Māori beliefs and practices (Smith, 2012; Ranjan, 2017). Indigenous cosmovisions can also have pedagogical relevance. They can be used to facilitate students' engagement and contribution to community development and sustainability. The objective of Indigenous cosmovisions is the development of students who are equipped with a *critical Indigenous consciousness*. Ober (2017, p.10) also emphasizes the importance of storytelling from a *kapati* (cup of tea) perspective: In Australian Aboriginal societies, storytelling or 'yarning', "is a natural part of life; it is used to inform past histories, kinship structures, beliefs, values, morals, expected behavior and attitudes". By setting up a context in which research participants feel comfortable (with a cup of tea or other food and drink), and by getting people to tell stories, Ober suggests Aboriginal and Torres Strait Islander people "can bring our ways of making meaning and making sense into the research space" (2017, p.14). As this example suggests, an Indigenous research perspective does not have to insist on cultural purism but can take a contemporary practice – talking over tea – as a way into a deeper set of cultural practices to inform research.

In an era concerned with the survival of Indigenous languages, language as a general phenomenon needs to be thought of as being thoroughly connected to one's world view (see Chapter 4). This is not a question of world views based on particular languages but on views of language based in particular world views. Mika (2016, p.165) proposes a way of thinking about language in terms of "the worlding of things". Drawing on the Māori understanding of *whakapapa*, Mika argues that Māori "identify language as a sort of gathering of entities rather than an instrument for singling out one thing as thoroughly and separably evident" (2016, p.165). We do not mean to suggest that language in use is not indexical, performative, or historical, but that language is not exhausted by these linguistic or anthropological categories. We need to be open to possibilities that it might not be possible in all contexts to determine what language is, and that we need to broaden the epistemological repertoires of our understanding of language, as not all communicative phenomena can be understood as instances of a general phenomenon called language. There are different varieties and genres of something called language, and these differences in what language may be are the multiple natures of language. The inclusion of non-humans that is commonly part of such alternative cosmovisions, as apparent in the Anansi stories or the use of drums, potentially purges applied linguistics of its anthropocentric orientation. An epistemology of the South in applied linguistics has to question underlying assumptions about language. Epistemologies of the South should at least facilitate other ways of framing language, so that instead of thinking about language death and endangerment, metaphors such as language sleep might be more appropriate.

Challenges: Research and shared ontologies

Opening up such perspectives clearly poses a range of challenges for applied linguistics and ways of doing and thinking about research. Key concerns here are the difficulty of reconciling local and more generalizable approaches, the rapid co-opting of new terms, and the dangers of new forms of essentialization. Chilisa's (2011) *postcolonial Indigenous research paradigm* is a "framework of belief systems that emanate from the lived experiences, values, and history of those belittled and marginalized by Euro-Western research paradigms" (p.19). An issue we need to address here, however, is what kind of paradigm such a framework can entail: While this emphasizes the lives of the globally marginalized, there is a difficulty when a commonality is assumed. For Martin and Mirraboopa (2003, p.205), developing an Indigenist research perspective includes recognition of particular world views, knowledges, and realities as distinctive and vital to existence and survival; honouring the social mores of communities as essential processes through which they live, learn, and situate themselves as Aboriginal people in their own lands and when in the lands of other Aboriginal people; an emphasis on social, historical, and political contexts which shape experiences, lives, positions, and futures; and privileging the voices, experiences, and lives of Aboriginal people and Aboriginal lands. More specifically, Martin and Mirraboopa (2003) develop a *Quandamooka ontology* – Quandamooka is the land, waterways, skies, spiritual, and law systems of the Quandamooka people of Queensland, Australia – based around ways of knowing, being, and doing that are deeply based in an understanding of the interconnectedness of people, place, animals, and things.

Chilisa's postcolonial Indigenous research paradigm has a wide scope, including "shared aspects of ontology, epistemology, axiology, and research methodologies of the colonized Other" in former colonized societies in Africa, Asia, and Latin America, as well as "among indigenous people in Australia, Canada, the United States, and other parts of the world", and also "among the disempowered, historically marginalized social groups that encounter the colonizing effect of Eurocentric research paradigms" (p.20). This ties in closely with the discussion of southern research epistemologies as politically rather than geographically focused, reflecting a wide scope that includes not only southern and poorer regions but also the marginalised within the North (cf. Santos, 2018). A focus primarily on Indigenous concerns takes the discussion away from geographical southern orientations, since there is a desperate commonality of Indigenous dispossession across the world. Issues of commonality, however, raise other concerns. While we can accept the notion of a Eurocentric research paradigm that has developed through the disciplinary mechanisms of academic work – consolidating, rejecting, writing handbooks, reifying methodologies, setting the terms of the debate (qualitative or quantitative?) – the idea of a rival paradigm, a 'shared' framework, based on a vast disparity of people and places, is harder to grasp.

There are good reasons to talk in terms of commonalities of Indigenous or southern perspectives, yet attempts to reground research and epistemology in local contexts and practices clearly opens up issues of greater diversity. On the one hand, then, we have localized ontologies based in particular places (and place matters fundamentally here) and practices. On the other hand, there is also the possibility of looking at commonalities across these world views and experiences. If the critique of northern research is of both its universalizing assumptions and its "extractivist methodologies" (Santos, 2018, p.130) – extracting knowledge like a raw material – the question that follows is how the varied epistemologies of the South form anything beyond a loose collection of varied ideas and goals. What kinds of abstraction can be made from such local ontologies towards a wider set of common views, yet views that always stress locality, place, and relations with others? This is a challenge that needs careful consideration if a southern perspective can offer more than just a massive plurality of competing epistemologies and research approaches.

A discussion of research ethics can show how local practices can inform more general principles. For Chilisa (2011), "an ethics theory built on relationships and responsibilities to the researched informs every aspect of the postcolonial and Indigenous research process, from choice of topic and data collection instruments to data analysis and dissemination of findings" (p.171). Indigenous research agendas, Smith (2012) argues, are characterized particularly by "key words such as healing, decolonization, spiritual, recovery" (p.122), terms and concepts that clearly emerge from the colonial history and current concerns of Indigenous peoples. Of particular interest here is the discussion that ethics in research needs to be locally formulated

> Indigenous groups argue that legal definitions of ethics are framed in ways which contain the Western sense of the individual and of individualized property – for example, the right of an individual to give his or her own knowledge, or the right to give informed consent.
>
> *(p.123)*

By contrast, drawing on ethical responsibilities within Māori communities suggests different concerns, such as *Aroha ki te tangata* (a respect for people); *Kanohi kitea* (the seen face, that is present yourself to people face to face); *Titiro, whakarongo … korero* (look, listen … speak); *Manaaki e takahia te mana o te tangata* (share and host people; be generous); *Kaua e mahaki* (don't flaunt your knowledge) (2012, p.124).

These are clearly a rather different set of ethical principles from those generally proposed in research proposals, forms, and research methodology guidelines. On reflection, however, they would surely be useful for all researchers to consider. These really should be our norms. And yet, while the adoption of these and other terms of research engagement beyond their countries or regions of origin should be welcome, it is equally important to caution against universalizing their applicability. This would create a similar problem to the one that we are guarding against in terms of scholarship in the Global North (Mignolo, 2018), as we seek to challenge applied linguistics from research in the Global South. The newly reinvented ancestral concepts – from *Ubuntu* to *Buen Vivir* or *Quandamooka ontology* – invoke practices and ideas that are alien to Western-centric politics and knowledge, and are expressed in their languages of origin. In other cases, they constitute hybrid, non-Eurocentric renditions of concepts, such as law, state, or democracy, and are accordingly expressed in other languages, usually qualified in European languages by an adjective (communitarian democracy, plurinational state).

The concept of *ubuntu* (Makoni and Severo, 2017; Makalela, 2018a) is founded on an ontology whose origins can be traced to Southern Africa. It had a decisive influence in the Truth and Reconciliation Commission that addressed the crimes committed during the apartheid era. *Ubuntu* appears in the epilogue of the South African Constitution Act 200, 1993: "There is need for understanding but not vengeance, reparations but not retaliation, Ubuntu but not victimization", and, has also been deployed in sociolinguistics (Kamwangamalu 1999), and as a basis for approaches to multilingualism, with an orientation more towards being human than being language-centred (Makalela, 2018c). From an ubuntu sociolinguistic perspective, personhood and language and being human are strongly related and are mutually reinforcing and interlocking. Language practices and language use are ways of performing one's humanity. And yet there is also a danger that such ideas become rapidly co-opted. *Ubuntu* has already become commodified and used extensively in the service of South African capitalism (McDonald, 2010). This use undercuts some of its original multiple meanings, including personhood, interpersonal relationships, and mutual responsibilities. This is also the concern that Todd (2016) draws to our attention: The use of such terms and their cosmologies all too quickly become unacknowledged aspects of the northern episteme. We therefore tread very warily when we suggest that *ubuntu-nepantla* thinking offers ways forward, for in doing so, it is already potentially in the process of being co-opted.

The valorization of different cosmovisions may risk new forms of fundamentalism and unwarranted group essentializations of knowledge, such as Afro-centrism, Asia-centrism, and Native American-centrism. This essentialization may homogenize groups, and be unable to capture subtle differences within groups that may have a substantial impact on epistemologies, and may create a false impression that positions that are articulated by the powerful few are necessarily germane and represent the interests of entire groups, thus obscuring the interests of the marginalized within the marginalized. Even if marginalization is incorporated into southern epistemologies, it is necessary to bear in mind that marginalization is multidimensional and multilayered, and in many situations, women, through the intersection of patriarchy, colonization, sexism, and racism find themselves oppressed along multiple lines (Smith, 2002). Even though we are arguing for the importance of Indigenous cosmovisions in applied linguistics, it is important to bear in mind that, historically, in contexts of indirect rule as well as in traditional and Indigenous law, non-Western colonial knowledge was used to facilitate and legitimize colonial domination (Pennycook, 1998; Santos, 2018).

If Indigenous cosmovisions are locally based, inherently heterogeneous, inchoate, pluri- and multi-epistemic, and potentially emergent, it becomes difficult to determine which variety and whose brand of epistemology should be recognized in any given context. This complicates how cosmovisions can be incorporated into applied linguistics and evaluated in normative educational contexts. The mobilization of Indigenous cosmovisions as a platform in applied linguistics, and a strategy in decolonization, is also complicated by the fact that decolonization has many meanings. Decolonization is neither new nor uncontested. Fanon (1967) was critical of calls for decolonization if construed as equivalent to Africanization and he was deeply sceptical of the role of the African "national bourgeoisie" in regard to Africanization as "retrogression" (Mbembe, 2016; and see Chapter 2). Ngũgĩ wa Thiong'o (1986) adopted a more positive attitude towards decolonization, viewing Africanization not as undergirded by a politics of "racketeering and looting", but as driven by a re-centring of African languages in a politics of language. As we have suggested in the previous chapter on education, the role of African languages, and how we think about them in educational contexts, is also a domain in need of its own decolonization. The various proposals for decolonial thinking and southern epistemologies, particularly when they engage seriously with Indigenous modes of thought, present a range of challenges for how alternative ways of thinking can be taken up without becoming decontextualized, appropriated, or essentialized.

Conclusion: Decolonization, white ignorance, and critical Indigenous consciousness

The introduction of Indigenous cosmovisions should be interpreted as one of the strategies for a decolonization of applied linguistics. Because most courses in applied linguistics are taught at universities, the introduction of Indigenous cosmovisions is thus ultimately designed to contribute to a decolonization of, and a rethinking of, the university (see Chapter 5), in both the Global South and the Global North. It is reasonable to concentrate on the university as a significant site of decolonization, due to the role that the colonial university played in the development of, and bolstering of, colonial theories of racism, as well as operating as a conduit for colonial ideologies more broadly. The call for decolonizing is by no means restricted to the Global South, but also includes the Global North, as is evident in #feesmustfall in Universities in South Africa, and more recent attempts, including that of Georgetown University, Washington, DC, to atone for its past ties with slavery (Working group, 2016), and the UK campaign "Why is my curriculum White?" (Bhambra et al., 2018).

There are many possible areas of decolonization, including access to the university, university careers for faculty, institutional structure and governance, relations between the university and society, and research and teaching content. The epistemologies of the South that underpin the applied linguistics that we are seeking to develop address not only structural and ideological inequalities between North and South but also draw attention to coloniality as an integral part of capitalist and heteropatriarchal domination in contemporary societies. Santos (2018) suggests the distinction between colonialism and coloniality – first proposed by Quijano (1991) and subsequently taken up by the *grupo modernidad/colonialidad* (Maldonado-Torres, 2007; Mignolo and Walsh, 2018) – is unnecessary: "instead of distinguishing colonialism from coloniality, we should rather characterize the different forms that colonialism and decolonization assume over the course of time" (Santos, 2018, p.110). We find both approaches useful: The colonialism/coloniality distinction draws attention to the continuing modes of colonialism in academic and many other domains, while the prospect of characterizing different forms of colonialism and decolonization offers great potential for a more fine-grained understanding of what is at stake in different domains.

It is time, we have been suggesting, for applied linguists to ask similar questions: What complicities does applied linguistics need to face (Kubota, 2016)? Why is the applied linguistic curriculum so White? This is akin to Lin's (2013) proposal for "the global South as method" (p.229). Drawing on Chen's (2010) 'Asia as method', which contends that we have long used the 'west as method' (uncritically using theories and methods from the global North), Lin (2013, p.230) urges us to "look to other places in southern Asia, Africa, South America (the global South), and so on to discover new categories, new epistemologies, new concepts about language and education practices" not as a simple reversal of the Global North as method, but as a range of diverse and grounded strategies for renewal. It is this process of renewal that we have tried to make central through much of the discussion in this and other chapters: This is a project aimed at finding new ways of doing applied linguistics.

Processes of decolonization and renewal remain crucial because as Santos (2014, p.3) makes clear, "genuine radicalism" no longer seems possible in the Global North. Most who claim a radical position are subject to one "of the tricks that Western modernity plays on intellectuals": one is destined "to produce revolutionary ideas in reactionary institutions". Meanwhile, those who indeed act radically are not heard or are actively silenced. Our call for an applied linguistics that seeks to address social and political struggles should not be construed to mean there is no scholarship in applied linguistics that has sought to confront issues related to colonial, social, economic, racial, heteropatriarchal, or linguistic discrimination. There are many such strands of applied linguistics. Phillipson's (1992) linguistic imperialism "takes place within an overarching structure of asymmetrical North/South relations, where language interlocks with other dimensions, cultural (particularly in education, science, and media), economic, and political" (Phillipson, 1997, p.239). Studies of discrimination within languages (Cameron, 1995; Lindemann, 2005) draw attention to the ways in which speakers of varieties of African or Indian English may be discriminated against in job-seeking contexts (Dovchin, 2019; Dixon and Angelo, 2014; Poynting and Noble, 2004), or students of Asian background may be ridiculed for their "broken English" (Mahboob and Szenes, 2010). Language-based discrimination becomes institutionalized in language tests, particularly when these become part of state-based immigration regimes (McNamara, 2012; Shohamy and Menken, 2015). Piller (2016a), emphasizes that language is an important factor in entrenching disadvantage, inequality, and discrimination, and thus is central in any project aimed at social justice.

While such calls for social justice in sociolinguistics are crucial, a southern applied linguistics pushes us further, since, following Santos (2014, p.133), there cannot be "global social justice without global cognitive justice". Ideologies of political contestation, Santos (2018, p.viii) notes, "have largely been coopted by neo-liberalism" and are not anchored in the experiences of local communities' struggles with oppression, discrimination, and heteropatriarchy. We again draw attention to intersectionality as an analytic tool that insists that discrimination based on race, class, gender, language, and, we add, physical ability, do not operate independently of one another but, rather, as interlocking systems (Crenshaw, 1988, 1991). We construe struggles in a very broad sense to include "silent struggles", "active and confrontational struggles", and "possible and nonconfrontational struggles" (Mignolo, 2018, p.67). It is this perspective on struggle that is so often lacking, even in critical applied linguistic work that seeks to address issues that centre on discrimination and promote social justice. And when we consider questions of 'social justice', we also, as Mills (2017) insists, have to deal with "*white ignorance* as a cognitive phenomenon" (p.56) that has played a major role in the development of *racial liberalism* – the ways in which northern liberalism has been shaped by racial ideologies. Ideas of *social justice* need to account for *racial injustice* (Mills, 2017, p.34). Emerging *raciolinguistic* frameworks, (Alim et al., 2016; Rosa and Flores, 2017; Rosa, 2018) provide one important avenue of research here, showing how "processes of racial and linguistic co-naturalization" rearticulate "colonial distinctions between populations and modes of communication that come to be positioned as more or less normatively European" (Rosa, 2018, p.5)

We need to consider the implications of what happens when epistemologies of the North in applied linguistics are used in the Global South and confront concerns of how to address, mitigate, and possibly reverse the social inequality, discrimination, economic and political oppression, and heteropatriarchy encountered by peoples of the Global South, whether in the geographical North or geographical South. Both critical Eurocentric and conservative epistemologies of the North in applied linguistics may reinforce social and linguistic discrimination. Both critical and conservative Eurocentric thinking are representations of different versions of epistemologies of the North. We are therefore seeking to go beyond critical Eurocentric thinking, which rather than successfully transforming the world as once expected, has created situations in which dreams turned into nightmares, revolutions were betrayed, and positive expectations were turned into negative outcomes (Santos, 2018, p.vii–viii). While critical theory has often been highly critical of the North, and urged us to consider the global disparities with the South, it has all too often, as Santos (2018) reminds us, failed to show how and why we must learn from the South. Critical Eurocentric analysis has run out of steam, unable to engage with alternative modes of thinking.

We are therefore arguing for the importance and urgency of going beyond Global North thinking in applied linguistics, because we live in an epoch in which the most morally repugnant forms of social and economic inequality and social discrimination are not consistently and robustly challenged, and thus increasingly achieve levels of political acceptability. We need to mobilize social and political forces so that we may change this unacceptable state of affairs both in the Global South and Global North. How these forces can be mobilized in applied linguistics is one of the challenges we are addressing in this book, drawing on a number of analytical strategies. Research, we have been suggesting, is a cornerstone of this kind of reimagining of applied linguistics, who it is for and what it tries to do. Epistemological translations across "abyssal lines" are difficult, so "strategic concessions" (Kovach, 2010), which acknowledge the role of epistemology, categorizations, ontologies, and technologies, such as alphabetic writing and other digital scripts, have to be used. Special attention needs to be paid to how even teaching in square rooms affects and transforms representations and interpretations across contexts and epistemologies. Learning to navigate different epistemologies and ontologies has important social value, serving as a useful strategy for the emergence of better relationships and for addressing material and cultural inequalities.

A *critical Indigenous consciousness*, referring to the embodiment of perspectives beyond individualistic goals, placing the significance of education in community well-being, and enabling students to display an inward gaze and self-reflexivity (enabling them to discern how we might be complicit with hegemonic, oppressive, and assimilationist forces, under which colonialism and neo-liberalism have placed us; Lee, 2017), suggests some ways forward here. The term *liminal* has been used in anthropology to capture the lives and experiences of groups of people on the margins. Researching from the margins may lead to researchers being marginalized themselves in their workplace or career. The issue for us, therefore, is how research from the margins, or research from the Global South, can be mobilized to advance mainstream applied linguistics research in the Global North, and not lead to a further marginalization of these researchers. We recommend that researchers actively choose the margins, choose to study people marginalized by society, and perceive themselves as scholars who will work for, with, and alongside communities who occupy the margins of society. Intercultural translation (Santos, 2018) plays an important role as a mediator between potentially incommensurable epistemological discourses and cultures in the Global North and Global South, or different types of knowledge, even within the Global North itself (Grosfoguel, 2013). What these educational, epistemological, and research challenges mean for a renewed and decolonized applied linguistics from the South will be the focus of the next and final chapter.

7

APPLIED LINGUISTICS FROM A SOUTHERN PERSPECTIVE

Introduction: South–North entanglements

As we have tried to make clear throughout this book, the idea of the Global South is by no means an easy or uncontested concept. It is not an idea without its own challenges and contradictions, though it is no less important as a result. Although we can unpick various difficulties, tensions, and complications around the idea, it remains a useful way of drawing our attention to global inequalities and the need for renewal. The Global South refers to the people, places, and ideas that continue to be occluded from the narratives of whose languages, ideas, and cultures count in the modern world. It combines a focus on both those regions of the world that have been systematically deprived of wealth, status, and freedom – many of which are indeed in the geographical South – with a broader focus on other histories of exclusion and disenfranchisement (Indigenous communities in many parts of the world are an obvious example). The idea of the Global South can refer equally to the urban poor in cities in the northern hemisphere and the rural poor in the southern hemisphere, to those struggling against racial, homophobic, and sexist forms of prejudice to those in precarious employment in different parts of the world (or those unable to meet high tuition costs in universities in either the Global North or the Global South). If this inclusivity perhaps makes the idea of the Global South too broad to make any claims of coherence, it is also important to understand that many of these conditions of inequality indeed map onto particular people and places that are often, as Santos (2018) remarks, in the physical South.

Perhaps too the notion of southern epistemologies tries to do too much, and to be inclusive of too many forms of knowledge born in too many kinds of struggle (the struggles of precarious workers and the unemployed, of documented and undocumented migrants and refugees, of victims of sexism, homophobia, and racism, of ethnic and religious minorities). The 'southern' label is sometimes being asked to stretch too far, to make global inequalities salient, to draw our attention to regions of the world that are often overlooked, to focus on political struggles as people strive to overcome patriarchal, environmental, racial, territorial, economic, discriminatory, and other injustices, and to bring to the fore alternative ways of thinking and other ways of knowing. If the Global South's applied linguistics perspectives are to thrive, the obligation will be on the advocates of such applied linguistics perspectives not only to argue for the importance of the alternative frameworks but also to provide nuanced descriptions of the frameworks from the Global North to which they are seeking to constitute alternatives.

The decolonial counterpart of the southern epistemologies perspectives also perhaps tries to go too far in its total delinking from all Western thinking since the Enlightenment, its attempt to do away with Western knowledge and decommission Western institutions. Both nonetheless present challenges to applied linguistics that cannot be circumvented. How can we deal with the inequalities in global knowledge production, the lack of inclusion from scholars from outside the dominant regions, the imposition of inappropriate frameworks to address language and education outside the central regions and institutions? A southern view of applied linguistics takes up recent critiques of the lack of diversity in applied linguistics – that "knowledge in applied linguistics may be shaped by social and contextual factors such as race, given that scientific enterprise has historically been shaped by dominant communities, especially white males" (Bhattacharya et al., 2019, p.2) – and takes it into a wider domain of knowledge production. It opens up for discussion ways in which applied linguistics needs to engage in much more profound ways with colonial histories, institutional racism, global inequalities of knowledge production, the exclusion of scholars and contexts from many parts of the world, the need for grounded understandings of language and learning rather than inappropriately universalized claims to knowledge.

Global South perspectives are encapsulated in struggles for basic, economic, political, and social transformation, struggles that are relevant to applied linguistics because they are intellectual and political contestations "*over* language, *about* language, *in* language and *for* language which enables and promotes the consciousness and organization upon which such transformation depends" (Jones, 2018, p.3). Southern epistemologies are arguably coming of age (as the subtitle of Santos' 2018 book suggests), or at least there is a clear upsurge in scholarship that engages with the Global South, with institutions being created with the mandate to study the Global South. There has also been a proliferation of journals specifically addressing issues from the Global South, including the *Bandung Journal of the Global South* (published by Brill as of January 1, 2019), the *Journal of Global South Studies* (University of Florida Press), and *Project MUSE—The Global South* (Indiana University Press). Ironically, of course, the institutionalization of the Global South seems to be occurring more widely in the Global North than in the Global South.

Without the benefit of historical hindsight, it is not easy to determine what is causing this recent upsurge in interest in the Global South. As we made clear in Chapter 2, it is not as if this has not been on the table for at least a century, or possibly five. Perhaps it is a growing disillusionment with the failing politics of the wealthy nations, an increased disenchantment with the xenophobic policies that have been the response to increased migration, a developing awareness through different media of another world that has been ignored, a concern that for all the trumpeting of its own successes, the West really does not have answers to, or even an adequately moral position on, concerns about climate change, the Anthropocene, racism, and inequality. The trend towards the South is well captured in the subtitle of Comaroff and Comaroff's (2011) book *Theory from the South: Or, How Euro-America is Evolving Toward Africa*, and this movement is clear across the humanities and social sciences. Applied and sociolinguistics is also witnessing an upsurge in related work, such as Kerfoot and Hyltenstam's (2017) edited book *Entangled Discourses: South–North Orders of Visibility*; Heugh and Stroud's (2018) special issue of *Current Issues in Language Planning*; Heugh et al.'s (in press) edited *A Sociolinguistics of the South*; Makalela's (2018) edited *Shifting Lenses: Multilanguaging, Decolonisation and Education in the Global South*, and Deumert et al.'s (2019) edited *Colonial and Decolonial Linguistics: Knowledges and epistemes*.

However complex and messy Southern Theory may be – and we've drawn attention to some of the difficulties of using geographical nomenclature for a much wider politics – it is also clear that there are major issues here and they need to be addressed. The sociology of global disparities and absences in scholarship demand that a southern applied linguistics develop a relentless critique of the skewed nature of contemporary scholarship while also trying to engage with all that is missing. We have also drawn attention to the fact that there is a longer history of critique here than is sometimes acknowledged in the upsurge of critical southern work, a long lineage of critical work, from dependency and centre–periphery theories to Third World and postcolonial studies. While there are also differences across these critical frameworks, southern applied linguistics should not be understood as suddenly emerging from South African or Brazilian scholarship in the 21st century. There are many precedents, and part of the concern here is precisely this history of at best forgetting, and at worst ignoring, studies such as Khubchandani's (1997) work on a *plurilingual* ethos in India, or Dasgupta (1993), or Dua (1994), or Krishnaswamy and Burde (1998) on English in India, or Parakrama (1995) on English in Sri Lanka, all of which have far more interesting things to say – both politically and epistemologically – than the over-cited northern canon and its reproduction of colonial linguistics through concepts such as linguistic imperialism and World Englishes.

Sey's (1973) exploratory study of Ghanaian English predates many accounts of the nature and status of English in Ghana by capturing empirically the ambivalent status of English in the lives of educated Ghanaian speakers. One aspect of Ghanaian use of English with wider relevance beyond Ghana is the role and status of a locally acquired foreign accent (LAFA), a speech style also called "slurring" in Ghana: "Slurring is an African approximation of American speech in which LAFA speakers bid for membership of an imagined global community" (Shoba et al., 2013). Other work from Ghana opens up new perspectives on pidgins, Dako and

Bonnie (2014), for example, tracing the development of a Ghanaian Pidgin widely used by male students in Ghanaian universities and by students in prestigious secondary schools in the Cape Coast in the late 1960s to early 1970s. This pidgin differs from another pidgin used by young males in Accra, thus showing that both class and gender differences can be significant across regional pidgin use (Dako and Bonnie, 2014; Shoba et al., 2013). Such developments vary greatly across regions of Africa, with South African students not having access to a pidgin in the same way that their Ghanaian peers do.

Even though some of the features of the Ghanaian contexts reported in such research may be found in other contexts in the Global South, what is striking about Global South scholarship is that there is rarely any systematic cross-referencing of material across different locations in the Global South (though see Severo and Makoni, 2014, for work on Angola and Brazil). There are journals that publish articles in applied linguistics in Ghana, South Africa, Brazil, and other countries, but rarely does one find systematic cross-referencing of material or multisite theory building, or theory building grounded in different locations (Harrison, 2016). Another disturbing aspect of Global South applied linguistics is the tendency for regional exclusivity. Rarely does one find articles about other regions of Africa in the journal *Southern African Linguistics and Applied Language Studies*; and rarely does one find material about other regions of Africa in Ghanaian journals, or on regions other than India in the *Indian Journal of Applied Linguistics*. What is required is greater intellectual interaction in applied linguistics among Africa, Asia, and South America as a means to escape what Satya Mohanty calls the "long intellectual shadow of the Age of European Empire" (Bhatnagar and Kaur, 2012, p.18).

We take the position that a Global South applied linguistics perspective should involve neither a total delinking from Western epistemologies nor a scholarship in which there is only interaction in the Global South. We thus propose a way of thinking where Global South and Global North applied linguists talk to each other in a way similar to Harrison's (2016, pp.162–3) depiction of how anthropological texts have enabled Wittgenstein to be in conversation with Das (1998, 2006); Foucault and Agamben to talk to Mbembe (Comaroff and Comaroff, 2011) or to vernacular philosophers on the frontlines of war and shadow economies in the Global South (Nordstrom, 2009); Mbembe's (2017) genealogy of Blackness from the Atlantic slave trade to contemporary times to be in conversation with Caribbean theorists (Thomas, 2011); and, we might add, Latour, Deleuze, and others to converse with Amerindian philosophies in the work of Viveiros de Castro (2014).

Conversations such as these are among the trends contributing to current theoretical and discursive changes. Applied linguists need to work out how these productive relations can occur within our own field. We want to avoid thinking about this in terms of a rather insipid notion of dialogue, or an equally problematic dialectic, or a hapless hybridity. Nor, despite Anzaldúa's (1987) linking of *fronteras* and *mestiza* ways of thinking, do we propose a *mestiza/mestiça* framework (cf. Heugh, 2017): As Milani and Lazar (2017, p.313) observe, it is potentially "problematic to brush over the colonial and racial loading of the term 'mestizo' in an attempt to theorise the pluriversality of southern positionalities". On these grounds we have suggested (tentatively and with caveats and more as a way of thinking about thinking than as a proposed solution) an *ubuntu-nepantla* way of thinking and doing that brings together both Southern African understandings of interdependence and Central American considerations of borderlands so that we can simultaneously see the entangled relations between North and South as well as the possibility of their dissolution and our inbetweenness.

We have tried to show throughout this book – and in line with this book series – both the innovations and the challenges such a perspective raises. The two ideas – innovations and challenges – are not always easily separable: Innovations in thinking present challenges to the field, and challenges can suggest innovatory directions. In short, however, we want to argue that a southern applied linguistics presents profound possibilities for renewal. What is being proposed here is far more than a critique of northern assumptions about language, literacy, learning, and education: This is also an argument that if the field can open up, it will be addressing not just questions of appropriacy (making more appropriate suggestions for language education programmes in the Global South, for example) but also changing the possibility for how we think about language programmes. But this raises many challenges to the ways we think about language and what kinds of knowledge we take to be important. And there are other concerns that the breadth of ideas within southern perspectives may simply open the field to any project that claims a southern orientation. We conclude with a brief outline of the tasks ahead for southern applied linguistics.

Innovations: An indisciplinary applied linguistics

For applied linguistics to operate – ethically, responsibly, accountably – in an inequitable world – a world made inequitable by particular political economic policies and practices – it needs to engage with the unequal divide in knowledge production and skewed knowledge circulation. The lopsided nature of knowledge distribution means, as we suggested above, that ideas and connections across the South are frequently mediated through the Global North, rather than enabled through South–South connections: "The links between Asia and Africa and South America have always been present but in our times they have been made invisible by the fact that Europe is still the central mediator of Afro-Asian-Latino discourse" (Ngũgĩ wa Thiong'o, 2012a, np). The tendency for both those in the Global North to keep their eyes firmly on the North, and those in the Global South to likewise look to the Global North leads many to overlook connections between different regions of the Global South, and to remain in the intellectual shadow of the Global North and its empires (Mohanty in Bhatnagar and Kaur, 2012).

Certain people from certain places (the Global North) in certain languages (overwhelmingly English) produce the vast amount of knowledge about language, second language learning, education, language policy, and so on, and make universal claims to the applicability of that knowledge to the rest of the world. This is not just vaguely inappropriate knowledge, but rather knowledge that seeks to colonize. To oppose this requires several kinds of action that can bring a strong element of renewal to a discipline that all too often speaks only to itself, and largely in English. A central part of this is a process of decolonization of knowledge and practices, of language and theories of second language acquisition, of language policies, and language in education. As Shi-xu (2016, p.6) puts it, we need to "systematically and thoroughly deconstruct cultural hegemony in our own discipline and beyond" and "enlist more and more scholars from especially developing Third World societies to participate in the construction or re-invention of various cultural frameworks of research" including both "aboriginal, native cultural and intellectual resource" and "local specific conditions, needs and aspirations".

Decolonizing applied linguistics suggests first of all the need to decolonize 'language' – or the way that language is framed in linguistics and applied linguistics – as part of any reclamation project (Leonard, 2017). We can identify several key northern ideas about language that are at best inappropriate when applied to southern contexts and at worst are downright harmful. These include a legacy of considering languages in terms of cognitive, literate systems rather than embodied and embedded cultural processes; a tendency to reify languages as if they exist outside of human relations; and a set of assumptions about languages as repositories of knowledge that once lost, lead simultaneously to the loss of shared forms of culture and knowledge. Language *reclamation* itself can be understood as a process of *decolonization* both in terms of giving new life to a language that has been cast aside by processes of coloniality and modernity, and in terms of changing the ways in which language is understood (resisting the colonial archives of linguistic modernity). Decolonization from this point of view involves community needs and goals rather than top-down assumptions about grammatical fluency (Leonard, 2017), and above all, community ontologies of language.

For some sociolinguists, the answers to issues of language policy and language education in the South are to promote multilingualism (while denouncing a monolingual outlook), mother-tongue education (critiquing education in European languages), and language-rights-based policies (decrying the loss of languages and world views). A decolonial/southern epistemologies position, however, suggests this is at best inadequate and at worst detrimental, since it does not capture what multilingualism can mean from a southern perspective. Promoting northern multilingualism in the South, assuming that it makes sense to talk of mother tongues, or viewing multilingualism as a desired outcome of education rather than its starting point, fail to engage with a plurality of multilingualisms. Yet pluralizing multilingualism (multilingualisms) as if this overcomes the critique that northern multilingualism is a pluralization of monolingualisms, may also fall short unless it engages with ontological difference. Ideas such as *multilingual repertoires* (Lüpke and Storch, 2013), *multilingua francas* (Makoni and Pennycook, 2012), *multilanguaging*, or *ubuntu translanguaging* (Makalela (2017, 2018b, c) provide potential ways forward here, though not an answer: All such ideas have to be subject to critical scrutiny even if their stated objectives are to address inequalities that arise from "epistemological apartheid" (Mafeje, 1998). Proposals that claim southernness must be open to critical examination, particularly in the ways in which they formulate theory and the nature of the relationship between theory, social context, and praxis. Ngũgĩ wa Thiong'o (2012b) cautions against what he calls "poor theory", by which he means the tendency to conflate verbosity and density of words with deep thoughts and insights. Connell (2007, p.207) argues for what she refers to as "dirty theory" to refer to theories in their social contexts.

We need to decolonize language pedagogy (Macedo, 2019) and multilingualism (Phipps, 2019), and especially the teaching of "colonial languages that over-celebrate Eurocentric values while sacrificing ways of being and speaking of people who do not fit the white, middle-class mold and are always excluded from this mold no matter how hard they try to fit in" (Macedo, 2019, p.12). How can we decolonize the field of foreign language education, Macedo (2019, p.14) asks, and challenge its "vast whiteness as reflected in classrooms, teacher preparation programs, and national and international language teaching organizations?" We should be wary too of new empires and new languages, cautious not to suggest that the rise of China presents in itself a decolonial option, since the massive expansion of the teaching of Chinese in Africa and elsewhere – sponsored by the Chinese government, coordinated by Confucian Institutes – may offer an alternative to European languages but not necessarily an alternative to Empire (Wheeler, 2014; Makoni et al., 2012).

And perhaps above all we need to decolonize TESOL, particularly with respect to the ongoing discrimination against TESOL's subalterns, the so-called non-native speaker of English, and their struggle against the "insidious structure of inequality in their chosen profession" (Kumaravadivelu, 2016, p.82). Decolonizing TESOL, Rubdy (2015, p.53) suggests, requires "both a redistribution of power in communication and significant shifts in the entire manner in which we approach the teaching of English". Given the lack of progress in the long history of struggle to unravel assumptions about native and non-native speakers in language education, we need to turn to decolonial theory to enable the "*unfreezing* of the subaltern's potential for thinking *otherwise*" (Kumaravadivelu, 2016, p.79). López-Gopar (2016, p.1) calls for the decolonization of primary English language teaching in Mexico by challenging the association of "English with 'progress' and neo-liberal practices – that regard the world as a global market where everything can be sold and purchased, including the English language with its assumed benefits" while Indigenous and minoritized languages are simultaneously denigrated, stigmatized, and minoritized. A project to decolonize primary English language teaching needs to be historically grounded, to help students, teachers, parents, and others to collaboratively reflect on "how the discourses of coloniality and colonial difference impact their own lives" and how Indigenous language practices and ideologies are "rooted in coloniality" while English is bound up with discourses of modernity. It is the multilingual life worlds of Indigenous children that need to drive the curriculum (López-Gopar, 2016, pp.195–200). As we saw in Chapter 5, such decolonization processes could usefully extend to language testing, (critical) discourse analysis (Resende, 2018; Shi-xu et al., 2016), or sociolinguistic theory and method by applying alternative ontologies and epistemologies of language than those that currently dominate the field (Albury, 2017).

If Viveiros de Castro's (2014, p.48) project is one of turning anthropology into "a permanent exercise in the decolonisation of thought", our proposal for applied linguistics is that it too should become an ongoing project in the decolonization of ideas about language, education, language policy, translation, and more. The point here is not just to decolonize thinking within applied linguistics, but to take up applied linguistics as one of the drivers of contemporary linguistic thought. Linguistics, in a way that applied linguistics has fortunately been largely able to avoid (aside from some of the ugly skirmishes around second language acquisition; see Seidlhofer, 2003), presents itself as a field of competing frameworks, with students being interpellated into different ideological frameworks on the basis of assertions of "scientific" authority for a favoured theory, even in the absence of disciplinary consensus. This means, for example, that students taught by Chomskyans will be taught the correctness of generativism and the folly of cognitive grammar; systemic functionalists assert their own correctness, decrying Chomskyan analysis and ignoring all others; cognitive linguists assert the authority of their analysis, drawing on the tradition of science for their own analytical practices; and on it goes (Riemer, 2016b). The academic competition between different models in linguistics is about far more than minor intellectual battles: It is about careers, institutional power, and the injunction for students "to fight for their corner" by deploying "the full ideological power of claims of scientificity, reason, empirical responsibility, etc to do so". And at the same time it is about making a claim that this ideological battle is the one that matters; we don't have to look elsewhere – towards the South, for example – for disciplinary renewal.

It is more than an idle claim to suggest that applied linguistics is in a position to become a driver of change in this battlefield. It is the work of applied sociolinguists such as García (2009; and Li Wei, 2014), drawing on her long experience working with high schools in New York, or of Kusters and her colleagues (De Meulder et al., 2019; Kusters and Sahasrabudhe, 2018) pushing the boundaries of how we understand sign languages, gesture, and sensory inequality, that are making the urgent case for renewal in sociolinguistics. Indeed, the remarkable growth in sociolinguistics over the last decade from obscure variationism to diverse engagement has been driven by this applied sociolinguistic push. Similarly, the fact that it is applied linguists that are asking ontological questions about language – what is this thing called English that we are dealing with (Hall and Wicaksono, 2019)? – suggests both a failure by many linguists to delve into essential ontological questions in relation to language, and a coming of age of applied linguistics as it takes on theoretical questions. This needs to be an applied linguistics, however, that does not revel in its new status as a domain to be reckoned with, but rather an applied linguistics that strives to challenge the ways we rethink language, learning, and education. The applied linguistics of the Global South we are proposing is not only one that questions the ideological and colonial basis of some aspects of language, but which takes the issue further by exploring ways in which our ontological and epistemological assumptions about language may feed into a particular type of politics. Many of the ontological and epistemological assumptions about language in linguistics, including "individualism", "rationalism", and "uniformity", reinforce a model of personhood – a model of what people are like – particularly compatible with the requirements of contemporary globalized economies. Just like the other human sciences (see Riemer, 2016b), linguistics contributes to one of universities' central contemporary roles: ideologically converting, or, to use Riemer's word, "formatting" students into "atomized, normalized, and rationalistic subjects to match market norms" (Riemer, 2016b).

Applied linguistics from a southern perspective seeks not so much to add further details to the disciplinary archive but rather to develop an applied linguistic *anarchive* by addressing the *darker side of applied linguistics* (cf. Mignolo, 2011a): The profound ties of colonial and neo-colonial projects to language teaching; the exoticization of differences that reinforces the construction of racialized and ethnicized Others; and the normative assumptions about gendered and sexual relations that obscure the politics of sexuality. In order to redress these deep-seated concerns, we need not merely to encourage a more inclusive applied linguistics that opens the doors to southern voices and encourages more research on southern contexts; we need to open up to a much wider range of ways of thinking, to see the South as method (Lin, 2013) rather than object. The challenge, therefore, is about more than an agenda of southern inclusion but rather about expanding epistemological repertoires, of opening up to the obligation to understand that inquiries into applied linguistic concerns elsewhere in the world must also be inquiries into other ways of thinking that offer possibilities of disciplinary renewal.

Moita-Lopes' (2006) case for *indisciplinary* applied linguistics gives us a much more useful way forward than other discussions about trans- or interdisciplinary work. Mignolo (2018 p.105) talks of the importance of an "undisciplinary stance", which he links to Walsh et al.'s (2002) *Indisciplinar las Ciencias Sociales* or his own "epistemic disobedience" (Mignolo, 2009). This is "decolonial thinking and doing" that aims to "desprenderse del patrón colonial de poder" in Quijano's terms – delink from the colonial matrix of power – to engage in *epistemic reconstitution* (Mignolo, 2018 p.120). Rather than *undisciplinary*, however, we prefer to use Moita-Lopes' *indisciplinary* (if we must use English terms) since it suggests a more active sense of opposition and hovers somewhere between the Spanish, Portuguese, French, and English terms. However we translate the term, it is clearly very different from the bland interdisciplinary or transdisciplinary tropes that now circulate. It is about a more active process of non-conformity, of resisting the straitjacket of normativity that prevails within disciplines. For Moita-Lopes (2006) such an indisciplinary applied linguistics is both ideological and hybrid (*mestiça*), a call, following Santos' (2004b, 2005, 2007) for "outras vozes e outros conhecimentos" (other voices and other knowledges) (Moita-Lopes, 2006, p.85) in applied linguistics, a field of work that responds to contemporary issues of inequality and injustice, engaged with questions of class, race, gender, and sexuality – a *queer* applied linguistics (cf. Thurlow, 2016) – overcoming the theory/practice divide, engaged with multiple and fluid subjectivities, taking power and ethics as central to its agenda.

At the very least, it is clear that it is not only applied linguistics as a discipline that needs to be challenged but also the disciplinary formation of knowledge in general (whether disciplinary, interdisciplinary, or transdisciplinary). Another aspect of the innovative implications of southern applied linguistics therefore is the revisioning of the field in indisciplinary terms, as a coming together of different language-oriented projects, epistemes, and matters of concern, opening up applied linguistics to an ethical engagement with alternative ways of thinking about language and context from the Global South, so that renewal of applied linguistics comes not via other disciplines but rather through alternative forms of knowledge (Pennycook, 2018c). Moita-Lopes' (2006) *lingüística aplicada indisciplinar* provides one way of thinking about the field as *queer, diverse, politically engaged*, and reformed through an engagement with southern epistemologies. Applied linguistics at least needs to learn the lessons of territorial, cognitive, and linguistic decolonization implied by a recognition of the lands on which institutions are built, an appreciation of other forms of knowledge about language, learning, and education, and the possibilities of engaging with other language ontologies.

A point that has repeatedly been made is that applied linguists, like many other social scientists, hear only themselves when they talk of language and education programmes. This is the problem that a sociolinguistics of the South may be *about* the South but not *with* the South. Rather than attempting to think *about* difference, the ontological turn discussed in Chapters 4 and 6 seeks to think *with* the difference that thinking from the South itself entails (Savransky, 2017). One of the issues here is to get beyond simply pluralizing knowledges: For much of decolonial theory, the central focus is an epistemological one, whereas to take difference seriously must entail ontological questions as well (Savransky, 2017). In a manner akin to Butler's (1993) point that to see gender as a 'social construct' assumes that its biological counterpart 'sex' is an objective natural given – as recent challenges to categories of both sex and gender by LGBTQI movements have shown, a biological two-way division of sex, against which a social category of gender can be contrasted, does not hold – taking up ontological questions in relation to language pushes us to consider along similar lines that language may have multiple natures: The noncountable language (langage) may after all be countable (Hauck and Heurich, 2018; Course, 2018).

Southern applied linguistics presents a great potential for renewal in applied linguistics. The discipline (if it is usefully seen as one) has become stuck in its internal debates and modelling, adding complexity to accounts of second language acquisition (DFG, 2016) but failing to consider that it is not looking elsewhere for alternative modes of understanding. Following Savransky's (2017) discussion of transforming sociology, we have been arguing that "exposure to the difference that decolonial thought makes" can not only transform how applied linguistic knowledge is produced, but also what we consider applied linguistics to be (p.12). For

Savransky (2017), this demands the possibility of imagining a different relationship between knowledge and reality, and thus a different role for how we go about our research, writing, and teaching of applied linguistics. As we emphasized in the previous chapter, the implications are not just adding some extra knowledge but about a very different, more respectful, more open way of doing applied linguistics, and resisting the "enclosure of knowledge" (Riemer, 2016a, p.33).

Deconstructing this cultural hegemony is one thing; disseminating the results of that deconstruction is another. This raises the question of whether the existing format of journals, conferences, and ways in which editorial boards are constituted are the most effective means and channels for the dissemination of the results of the deconstructed fruits of academia in the world of applied linguistics. While the notion of the decolonial turn as a greater intellectual challenge than its linguistic, discursive, sensory, or pragmatic precursors is important for our understanding of southern perspectives on applied linguistics, as Connell (2018) and Kumaravadivelu (2016) remind us, a decolonial project has to involve at least as much construction as deconstruction, as much action as talk. Innovation in applied linguistics may come from renewed ideas, from alternative ways of thinking, from different knowledge and different kinds of knowledge, but it will also depend on rethinking journal structures, changing editorial boards, reorganizing conference finances, changing the ways things are done. As Connell (2018) reminds us too, for all the broad claims and politics of decolonial approaches, this may also just involve seeking out and making available texts from elsewhere. Above all, however, the point here is that this is far more than a process only of critique: The importance of a southern applied linguistics lies in its potential to renew the discipline. For Savransky, it is not only a question of the development of epistemologies of the South and an ecology of knowledges but also the cultivation of a *decolonial imagination* (2017, p.13). And from there we can start to think otherwise, and work for the possibilities of an otherwise (Walsh, 2018).

Challenges: *Ch'ixinakax utxiwa*

The ideas outlined in this book present many challenges on different levels. On the one hand they challenge orthodox ideas in applied linguistics; on the other hand, they also raise challenges themselves in how we take up ideas of decolonization and southern epistemologies. The project to decolonize language, for example, has to engage with the long-entwined history of linguistics and colonialism (Errington, 2008; Rajagopalan, 2020), as well as the many other social forces that brought about linguistics as we now know it. This itself is a major task of unwinding a long history of knowledge production, from colonial linguistic ideologies to Cold War funding in the US of work that separated language from society (and particularly any work critical of capitalism and the inequalities it produces) in favour of language as a technical tool (Heller and McElhinny, 2017). And once all that has been unravelled, once we understand that the ways we think about language are not the result of an ever-closer encounter with a natural object but the result of specific social, cultural, political, and economic forces, we have to then learn to listen, to think otherwise, to ask about multiple language ontologies not just multiple languages.

The question of where we need to look for a decolonization and renewal of applied linguistics also presents challenges. We should be wary of simply 'looking South', of assuming that ideas from the geopolitical South – from Freire, Gandhi, or Mandela – hold the necessary answers. We need to seek out and cite more southern scholars (Todd, 2016) while also being cautious not to assume the possibility of some 'authentic voice' from the South. As Santos (2018) reminds us, the South is a political concept, and is centrally about struggle. Although the history of globalization and colonialism means that there is a strong overlap between the political and geographical, it is also important to look at possibilities in the geographical North, from Indigenous people to other struggles. At the same time, however, we need to think carefully about our own location and locus of enunciation. It matters from where we talk and what the local conditions of our work and lives present to us in their daily existence. Sceptical of the various discourses of decolonization, Cusicanqui (2012, p.104) suggests that the work of the decolonial theorists, ensconced in their northern universities, "neutralizes the practices of decolonization by enthroning within the academy a limited and illusory discussion regarding modernity and decolonization". Too much of this work, she argues, co-opts and appropriates the work of Indigenous intellectuals.

There is, in her view, nonetheless a possibility of decolonization that affirms local culture, knowledge, and bilingualism – multicoloured and *ch'ixi* (*Ch'ixinakax utxiwa* is an Aymara understanding of the parallel coexistence of difference) – and, particularly through South–South connections that can escape

> the baseless pyramids of the politics and academies of the North and that will enable us to make our own science, in a dialogue among ourselves and with the sciences from our neighboring countries, by affirming our bonds with theoretical currents of Asia and Africa—that is, to confront the hegemonic projects of the North with the renewed strength of our ancestral convictions.
>
> *(2012, p.107)*

Understanding and facilitating these South–South connections is another important challenge: What can a renewed applied linguistics look like that deals not only with North–South relations but also South–South interrelatedness? As Todd (2016) suggests, there is often a double bind in the politics of knowledge, on the one hand that the significance of Indigenous and southern thought for posthuman and ontological discussions is overlooked, and that on the other hand, when not overlooked, it is appropriated in a way that distorts many important aspects of Indigenous thinking. The same point can be made about either the development of translinguistic paradigms that draw, whether consciously or not, on southern visions of the world (Heugh and Stroud, 2018) as well as more overt take-up of ideas such as "ubuntu translanguaging" (Makalela, 2018a, b, c). As Todd (2016) reminds us, the people who created and maintain the languages, knowledges, and cultures that northern linguists, anthropologists, and philosophers have been studying so long, and which have placed such a major role in reinvigorating moribund disciplines, are all too often effaced again in the global politics of knowledge.

We need to be cautious about rushing headlong into everything South, or taking up the decolonial turn in the same ways that other turns (linguistic, discursive, ontological, somatic, performative, sensory, etc) have been taken up and discarded. One of the problems of engagement with Southern Theory is that it is open to many interpretations: Southern Theory becomes a movement against positivism in the social sciences, a programme about relations with the land, a proposal for fluid multilingualism, a project to ensure more scholars in the geographical South gain access to northern academic privileges, and so on. The breadth of ideas now covered by southern and decolonial theory runs the danger of making it anything that critical scholars want it to be. Southern applied linguistics therefore needs to avoid becoming a space for everyone's pet project: Language maintenance for the Global South, understanding the relation between language and place from a southern feeling of emplacement, linguistic landscapes as expressions of southern difference, and so on. There is a danger that the breadth of Southern Theory can lead it to become an easy contemporary add-on to show global relevance.

Caution is needed lest supposedly southern perspectives become once again projects of projection rather than listening: What is considered to be progressive in the North is projected onto the Global South as what scholars there are (or perhaps should be) interested in. And relatedly, projects that do not fit this progressive mould – forms of southern positivism, for example, or demands for access to European languages (De Souza, 2017) – are likely to be rejected as northern capitulation rather than southern creation (the old false consciousness framework mapped onto North and South). It is useful to recall Milani's (2017, p.174) cautionary warning that the main problem with the idea of the South is that "the very act of using this spatial, sociocultural, political, and historical position" creates a problematic binary (that poststructuralism had at least helped us think our ways out of) between North and South, suggesting necessary conditions in the one and not the other, and excluding certain forms of analysis. On some levels, although the North–South distinction draws attention to some key concerns, it can also be a clumsy dichotomy that might be better reconceptualized by ideas such as marginalization (Milani, 2017).

If, as Mignolo (2018) has insisted, a decolonial project needs to delink from the entirety of Enlightenment thought, we may overlook how intertwined southern and northern thinking is, and how anticolonial resistance – such as Gandhi's – was centred around Indian concepts of *satyagraha*, but also drew on the thinking of Thoreau and Tolstoy. It is important to see how modes of thought, particularly those developed within the West but in opposition to it, have an important role here (Chakrabarty, 2000). If we take Enrique Dussel, for example, who is seen as an important figure in the development of South American *liberation philosophy* (Dussel, 1977), we have to understand both the originality of his critique of Western thinking about modernity and the way his thinking reworks that Western thought (Flores Osorio, 2009). Both the overarching critics of modernity, such as Foucault, or those, such as Habermas, who still suggested salvageable elements in the modernist project, Dussel argues, wrongly see modernity's origins in the Enlightenment rather than the colonization of the Americas. Emphasizing the 'invention of the Americas' (1995), Dussel draws on and reworks many sources, including Fanon, Marx, and Ricoeur, but a major early influence was the philosopher Emmanuel Levinas (1969), himself reacting against the horrors of the Holocaust (as a Lithuanian Jew, Levinas was rethinking his relationship to Heidegger's philosophy). One might, of course, just argue that the dominance of northern thought (as well as the ways academic and publishing institutions work) make an engagement with the major figures of this tradition inevitable, but an alternative argument suggests a more complex intertwining of ideas, so that we cannot simply reject bodies of thought in their entirety. Thus, we cannot proceed with a southern project without acknowledging the deep connections across ways of thinking. And we should always remind ourselves too that many of those northern philosophies – like Western art – were already full of southern appropriations that were not deemed worthy of naming.

We must also ensure that Southern Theory doesn't become an easy critique of everything else. Amongst current superficial trends is a critique of the various 'post' positions (postmodernism, poststructuralism, postcolonialism) on the basis that they were interested only in questions of diversity, lacking ways of dealing with real social and economic inequality, and even, from some points of view, buying in to neoliberal agendas (which supposedly also support diversity). More recently, posthumanism has come in for critique on the grounds that, like postmodernism, which apparently claimed that "all of us, 'we', are living in *postmodern times*" (emphasis in original), posthumanism claims a universality that suggests that "all on the planet is posthuman" (Mignolo, 2018 p.119). There seem no good grounds, however, to accuse either postmodernist or posthumanist thought of such universalist assertions: Such metanarratives were anathema to postmodern thinking, and to suggest that posthumanism posits a global condition is surely a strange reading of posthumanist politics. Posthumanist thought raises many similar questions about how southern epistemologies can challenge the centrality of European concepts of humanity. We have no interest here in defending posthumanism or postmodernism, and we are also very aware of the northern lineages of thinking that underpin many of these ideas, and the internal northern dialogues in which they participate, but it is nevertheless important not to let southern or decolonial theory become a tool to dismiss everything else as northern, Western, universal, and so on. This ends up looking too much like what is being critiqued: Yet another attempt to establish a new and different intellectual paradigm better than all those that have gone before.

Conclusion: Southern applied linguistics

So where, finally, do we end up? We have tried to show in this book that the constellation of ideas gathering around southern epistemologies and the decolonial option need to be taken seriously. They offer multiple forms of renewal for applied linguistics. Southern perspectives draw our attention to the unequal forms of knowledge distribution between North and South: Most of what is seen as knowledge about the world emanates from a limited number of sources, in a limited number of languages, yet all too often claims universality. There are different ways of thinking about universality, however, from the universalism that assumes that northern experiences relate to everyone by dint of a shared humanity, to a more inclusive position that suggests that knowledge could be "universally pooled … a universal fund, which, tools permitting, is accessible to all. These tools prominently include relevant languages and metalanguages and also acquired procedural skills or methodologies for accessing the specific epistemology" (Prah, 2017, p.12).

Southern perspectives demand of northern applied linguists to take a step back, to pause, to ask what possibilities are being excluded as new ideas are put forward. Sociolinguists and applied linguists, for example, have trumpeted their discovery of multilingualism as the global norm, and decried the monolingual mindsets that fail to grasp the benefits of bilingualism, without pausing to consider in more depth the particular nature of this multilingualism, and all that it is still missing. And this is not, as Savransky (2017) reminds us, merely a question of pluralizing knowledge, but rather of asking what ontological questions are also raised when we open up to different ways of thinking. This in turn can bring us to question the universalist belief that some underlying language capacity underpins all the different language instantiations, and to ask instead whether we may need to deal with diverse language ontologies.

For applied linguistics, it is important to recognize the complicity between ways of knowing embedded in the field and a history of colonialism, discrimination, and unequal knowledge distribution. The ways these forms of knowledge are tied both to a colonial history and a colonial present link them to violence and privilege. All of us then need to work towards a redistributive project of knowledge and resources, an acknowledgement that new forms of knowledge can reinvigorate the field, but this will not happen without a struggle, without deliberate action, without work to allow other knowledge to be taken up. As we take up new forms of knowledge (different kinds of knowledge as well as new knowledge), caution is then needed about how it is used, acknowledged, redistributed. Research, above all, needs to work from a more respectful place. In times of neo-liberal economic policies, xenophobic nationalism, and environmental degradation, the realities of the Global South are very different from those of the North, and unless applied linguists can learn to see from the South, the frameworks for understanding will never be bridged.

So, a southern applied linguistics is one that is aware of the global currents of knowledge production and seeks to disrupt and change the way knowledge happens. It is open to new and alternative kinds of knowledge and seeks ways that they can play a role in the field. It is conscious of the history of disciplinary formation and how that cannot be separated from social, economic, and political forces. It is capable of reflecting on the ways it thinks about language, language policy, translation, language education, language in the workplace, second language acquisition, language assessment, discourse analysis, and more, and prepared to rethink the ways these terms have been developed and used. It understands its broader political and ethical responsibilities in an inequitable world, and that as an applied field of work, it must develop relations of respect for other kinds of knowledge and other ontologies. It acknowledges that disciplines themselves are problematic and is ready to move away from hierarchical forms of knowledge construction towards more equitable indisciplinary forms of knowledge. This is a more exciting applied linguistics than the one we have inherited from the institutions of the North, an applied linguistics that can start to transform our understandings of language in the world.

REFERENCES

Abdelhay, A., Severo, C. & Makoni, S. (forthcoming) *Colonial Linguistics and the Invention of Language: The case of Sudan and Brazil*.

Abrams, D. & Strogatz, S. (2003) 'Modelling the dynamics of language death'. *Nature* 424, 900.

Adejunmobi, M. (2004) *Vernacular Palaver: Imaginations of the local and non-native languages in West Africa*. Clevedon: Multilingual Matters.

Ahmed, S. (2012) *On being Included: Racism and diversity in institutional life*. Durham, NC: Duke University Press.

Aikhenvald, A. (2002) *Language Contact in Amazonia*. Oxford: Oxford University Press.

Alatas, S. H. (1977) *The Myth of the Lazy Native*. London: Frank Cass.

Albury, N. J. (2016) 'Defining Māori language revitalisation: A project in folk linguistics'. *Journal of Sociolinguistics* 20, 287–311. doi:10.1111/josl.12183.

Albury, N. J. (2017) 'How folk linguistic methods can support critical sociolinguistics'. *Lingua* 199, 36–49.

Alexander, N. (2002) *An Ordinary Country: Issues in the transition from apartheid to democracy in South Africa*. Scottsville, South Africa: University of Natal Press.

Alim, S., Ibrahim, A. & Pennycook, A. (Eds.) (2009) *Global Linguistic Flows: Hip hop cultures, youth identities and the politics of language*. New York: Routledge.

Alim, S., Rickford, J. & Ball, A. (Eds.) (2016) *Raciolinguistics: How language shapes our ideas about race*. Oxford: Oxford University Press.

Altbach, P. G. (1981) 'The university as center and periphery'. *Teachers College Record* 82(4), 601–622.

Amegago, M. (2013) *African Drumming: The history and continuity of African drumming traditions*. Trenton, NJ: Africa World Press.

Antia, B. E. (2018) 'Multilingual examinations: Towards a schema of politicization of language in end of high school examinations in sub-Saharan Africa'. *International Journal of Bilingual Education and Bilingualism*. doi:10.1080/13670050.2018.1450354.

Antia, B. & van der Merwe, C. (2018) 'Speaking with a forked tongue about multilingualism in the language policy of a South African university'. *Language Policy*. doi:10.1007/s10993-018-9493-3.

Anzaldúa, G. (1987) *Borderlands/La Frontera. The New Mestiza*. San Francisco: Aunt Lute Books.
Anzaldúa, G. (2002) '(Un)natural bridges, (un)safe spaces'. In G. Anzaldúa & A. L. Keating (Eds.) *This Bridge We Call Home: Radical visions for transformation*, pp. 1–5. New York: Routledge.
Appleby, R., Copley, K., Sithirajvongsa, S. & Pennycook, A. (2002) 'Language in development constrained: Three contexts'. *TESOL Quarterly* 36(3), 323–346.
Appleby, R. & Pennycook, A. (2017) 'Swimming with sharks, ecological feminism and posthuman language politics'. *Critical Inquiry in Language Studies*. doi:10.1080/15427587.2017.1279545.
Araya, K. (2014) 'Anancy stories beyond the moralistic approach of Western philosophy'. *Boletin de Literatura Oral* 4, 43–52.
Archer, K. (2013) *The City: The basics*. London: Routledge.
Arendt, H. (1968) *The Origins of Totalitarianism*. New edition (original 1951). Orlando: Harcourt Press.
Australian Bureau of Statistics (2018) www.abs.gov.au/ausstats/abs@.nsf/Lookup/by%20Subject/2071.0~2016~Main%20Features~Aboriginal%20and%20Torres%20Strait%20Islander%20Population%20Data%20Summary~10.
Ayobolu, S. (2017) A tiger's tigritude. http://thenationonlineng.net/a-tigers-tigritude/.
Banda, F. (2009) 'Critical perspectives on language planning and policy in Africa: Accounting for the notion of multilingualism'. *Stellenbosch Papers in Linguistics* 38, 1–11.
Barlow, C. (1994) *Tikanga Whakaairo: Key concepts in Maori culture*. Auckland, New Zealand: Oxford University Press.
Basso, K. (1990) *Western Apache Language and Culture: Essays in linguistic anthropology*. Tucson: University of Arizona Press.
Battiste, M. (1998) 'Enabling the autumn seed: Toward a decolonized approach to Aboriginal knowledge, language and education'. *Canadian Journal of Native Education* 22(1), 16–26.
Beck, R. (2018) 'Language as apparatus: Entanglements of language, culture and territory and the invention of nation and ethnicity'. *Postcolonial Studies* 21(2), 231–253.
Becker, A. L. (1995) *Beyond Translation: Essays in modern philology*. Ann Arbor: The University of Michigan Press.
Bernabé, J., Chamoiseau, P. & Confiant, R. (1993) *Éloge de la Créolité*. Paris: Gallimard.
Bessire, L. & Bond, D. (2014) 'Ontological anthropology and the deferral of critique'. *American Ethnologist* 41, 440–456.
Bhambra, G. K. (2007) *Rethinking Modernity: Postcolonialism and the sociological imagination*. Basingstoke: Palgrave Macmillan.
Bhambra, G. K. (2014) *Connected Sociologies*. London: Bloomsbury Academic.
Bhambra, G., Gebriel, D. & Nisancioglu, K. (2018) 'Introduction: Decolonising the university'. In G. Bhambra, D. Gebriel & K. Nisancioglu (Eds.) *Decolonizing the University*, pp. 1–19. London: Pluto Press.
Bhatnagar, R. & Kaur, R. (April 2012) Literature to combat cultural chauvinism. From Indian literature to world literature: In conversation with Satya Mohanty. Interview. *Frontline* 29(6). 5–9.
Bhattacharya, U., Jiang, L. & Canagarajah, S. (2019) 'Race, Representation, and Diversity in the American Association for Applied Linguistics'. *Applied Linguistics*. doi:10.1093/applin/amz003.
Blaut, J. M. (1993) *The Colonizer's Model of the World: Geographical diffusionism and Eurocentric history*. New York: The Guilford Press.
Block, D. (2008) On the appropriateness of the metaphor of LOSS. In K.W. Tan & R. Rubdy (Eds.) *Language as Commodity: Global structures, local marketplaces*, pp. 187–203. London: Continuum.

Block, D. (2018) *Political Economy and Sociolinguistics: Neoliberalism, inequality and social class*. London: Bloomsbury.
Block, D. (2019) *Post-truth and Political Discourse*. Cham: Palgrave Macmillan.
Blommaert, J. (2005) *Discourse*. Cambridge: Cambridge University Press.
Blommaert, J. (2008) 'Artefactual ideologies of textual production of African languages'. *Language and Communication* 28(4), 291–307.
Blommaert, J. (2010) *The Sociolinguistics of Globalization*. Cambridge: Cambridge University Press.
Bonfiglio, T. (2010) *Mother Tongues and Nations: The invention of the native speaker*. New York: Mouton de Gruyter.
Branson, J. & Miller, D. (2007) 'Beyond "language": Linguistic imperialism, sign languages and linguistic anthropology'. In S. Makoni & A. Pennycook (Eds.) *Disinvention and Reconstituting Languages*, pp. 90–116. Clevedon: Multilingual Matters.
Brant Castellano, M. (2004) 'Ethics of Aboriginal research'. *Journal of Aboriginal Health* 1(1), 98–114.
Bruthiaux, P. (2003) 'Squaring the circles: Issues in modeling English worldwide'. *International Journal of Applied Linguistics* 13(2), 159–177.
Busch, B. (2012) *Das sprachlige Repertoire oder Niemand ist Einsprachig. Vorlesung zum Antritt der Berta-Karlik-Professur an der Universität Wien*. Klagenfurt: Drava.
Business Ghana, 9th February 2018.
Butler, J. (1993) *Bodies That Matter: On the discursive limits of 'sex'*. London: Routledge.
Cameron, D. (1995) *Verbal Hygiene*. London and New York: Routledge.
Cameron, D. (2007) 'Language endangerment and verbal hygiene: History, morality and politics'. In A. Duchêne & M. Heller (Eds.) *Discourses of Endangerment: Ideology and interest in the defence of languages*. pp. 268–285. London: Continuum.
Canagarajah, A. S. (1999) *Resisting Linguistic Imperialism in English Language Teaching*. Oxford: Oxford University Press.
Canagarajah, S. (2013) *Translingual Practice: Global Englishes and cosmopolitan relations*. New York: Routledge.
Canut, C. (2011) 'La langue Romani: Une fiction historique'. *Langage et Société*. 136, 55–80.
Carnoy, M. (1974) *Education as Cultural Imperialism*. New York: David McKay.
Carter, L. (2005) 'Naming to own place names as indicators of human interaction with the environment'. *AlterNative: An International Journal of Indigenous peoples* 1(1), 6–24.
Case, J. (2015) Reimagining the curriculum in a postcolonial space: Emerging the public good purposes of higher education in South Africa. Keynote Address. HELTASA, North West University, Potchefstroom, South Africa, November 17–20.
Castells, M. (2000) *The Information Age: Economy, society and culture. End of millennium. Vol. III* (2nd ed.). Oxford: Blackwell.
Césaire, A. (1955) *Discours sur le Colonialisme*. Paris: Présence Africaine.
Chakrabarty, D. (2000) *Provincializing Europe: Postcolonial thought and historical difference*. Princeton, NJ: Princeton University Press.
Chalmers, J. (2016) 'A genocide that precedes genocide: Reconciling "genocide" and indigeneity with a paradox of otherness'. *AlterNative: An International Journal of Indigenous Peoples* 12, 177–189.
Chapple, C. (1993) *Nonviolence to Animals, Earth and Self in Asian Traditions*. Albany: State University of New York Press.
Chen, K-H. (2010) *Asia as Method: Toward deimperialization*. Durham, NC: Duke University Press.
Chew, P. G. L. (2010) 'From chaos to order: Language change, lingua francas and world Englishes'. In M. Saxena & T. Omoniyi (Eds.) *Contending with Globalization in World Englishes*, pp. 45–71. Bristol: Multilingual Matters.

Chilisa, B. (2011) *Indigenous Research Methodologies*. New York: Sage.
Chinweizu, Onwuchekwu Jemie & Ihechukwu Madubuike (1983) *Toward the Decolonization of African Literature* (Vol 1). Washington, DC: Howard University Press.
Ciaffa, J. (2008) 'Tradition and modernity in postcolonial African philosophy'. *Humanitas* 21 (1–2), 121–145.
Clyne, M. (2005) *Australia's Language Potential*. Sydney: UNSW Press.
Cohn, B. (1996) *Colonialism and its Forms of Knowledge: The British in India*. Princeton, NJ: Princeton University Press.
Comaroff, J. & Comaroff, J. L. (2011) *Theory from the South: Or, how Euro-America is evolving toward Africa*. New York: Routledge.
Comaroff, J. & Comaroff, J. L. (2012) 'Theory from the South: Or, how Euro-American is evolving toward Africa', *Anthropological Forum* 22(2), 113–131.
Connell, R. (2007) *Southern Theory: The global dynamics of knowledge in social science*. Crows Nest, NSW: Allen & Unwin.
Connell, R. (2014) 'Rethinking gender from the South'. *Feminist Studies* 40(3), 518–539.
Connell, R. (2018) 'Decolonizing sociology'. *Contemporary Sociology* 47(4), 399–407.
Costa, J., De Korne, H. & Lane, P. (2018) 'Standardising minority languages: Reinventing peripheral languages in the 21st Century'. In P. Lane, J. Costa & H. De Korne (Eds.) *Standardizing Minority Languages: Competing ideologies of authority and authenticity in the global periphery*, pp. 1–23. New York: Routledge.
Coupland, N. (Ed.) (2016) *Sociolinguistics: Theoretical debates*. Cambridge: Cambridge University Press.
Course, M. (2018) 'Words beyond meaning in Mapuche language ideology'. *Language & Communication*. https://doi.org/10.1016/j.langcom.2018.03.007.
Couzens, V. & Eira, C. (2014) 'Meeting point: Parameters for the study of revival languages'. In P. Austin & J. Sallabank (Eds.) *Endangered Languages: Beliefs and ideologies in language documentation and revitalisation*, pp. 313–333. Oxford: Oxford University Press.
Crenshaw, K. (1988) 'Demarginalizing the intersection of race and sex: A Black feminist critique of antidiscrimination doctrine. feminist theory and antiracist politics'. *University of Chicago Legal Forum* 1, 139–167.
Crenshaw, K. (1991) Mapping the margins: Intersectionality, identity politics, and violence against women of color. *Stanford Law Review* 43(6), 1241–1299.
Crowley, T. (1999) 'Linguistic diversity in the Pacific'. *Journal of Sociolinguistics* 3(1), 81–103.
Cushman, E. (2016) 'Translingual and decolonial approaches to meaning making'. *College English* 78(3), 234–242.
Cusicanqui, S. R. (2012) 'Ch'ixinakax utxiwa: A reflection on the practices and discourses of decolonization'. *The South Atlantic Quarterly* 111(1), 95–109.
Dako, K. & Bonnie, R. J. (2014) 'I go SS I go Vas 97: Student Pidgin-A Ghanaian Youth Language of Secondary and Tertiary Institutions'. www.researchgate.net/scientific-con tributions/ (accessed 12/24/2018).
Das, V. (1998) 'Wittgenstein and anthropology'. *Annual Review of Anthropology* 27, 171–195.
Das, V. (2006) *Life and Worlds: Violence and the descent into the ordinary*. Berkeley: University of California Press.
Dasgupta, P. (1993) *The Otherness of English: India's auntie tongue syndrome*. New Delhi: Sage Publications.
Dasgupta, P. (1997) 'Foreword'. In L. Khubchandani, *Revisioning Boundaries: A plurilingual ethos*, pp. 11–29. New Delhi: Sage.
Davidson, D. (1986) 'A nice derangement of epitaphs'. In E. Lepore (Ed.) *Truth and Interpretation Perspectives on the Philosophy of Donald Davidson*, pp. 433–446. Oxford: Blackwell.

Davies, A. (1996) 'Review article: Ironising the myth of linguicism'. *Journal of Multilingual and Multicultural Development* 17(6), 485–496.

de Graffe, M. (2019) 'Foreword. Against apartheid in education and linguistics. The case of Haitian Creole in neo-colonial Haiti'. In D. Macedo *Decolonizing Foreign Language Education. The misteaching of English and other imperial languages*, pp. x–xxxii. London: Routledge.

De Korne, H. (2017) '"A treasure" and "A legacy": Individual and communal (re)valuing of Isthmus Zapotec in multilingual Mexico. In M.-C. Flubacher and A. Del Percio (Eds.) *Language, Education and Neoliberalism: Critical studies in sociolinguistics*, pp. 37–61. Bristol: Multilingual Matters.

De Korne, H. & Leonard, W. (2017) 'Reclaiming languages: Contesting and decolonising 'language endangerment' from the ground up'. In W. Y. Leonard & H. De Korne (Eds.) *Language Documentation and Description* Vol. 14, pp. 5–14. London: EL Publishing.

De Meulder, M., Kusters, A., Moriarty, E. & Murray, J. (2019) 'Describe, don't prescribe. The practice and politics of translanguaging in the context of deaf signers'. *Journal of Multilingual and Multicultural Development.* doi:10.1080/01434632.2019.1592181.

De Souza, L. M. (2017) 'Epistemic diversity, lazy reason, and ethical translation in post-colonial contexts. The case of Indigenous educational policy in Brazil'. In C. Kerfoot & K. Hyltenstam (Eds.) *Entangled Discourses: South-North orders of visibility*, pp. 189–208. New York: Routledge.

De Souza, L. M. & Andreotti, V. (2009) 'Culturalism, difference and pedagogy: Lessons from Indigenous education in Brazil'. In J. Lavia & M. Moore (Eds.) *Cross-Cultural Perspectives on Policy and Practice: Decolonizing community contexts*. London: Routledge.

Deacon, T. (1997) *The Symbolic Species: The co-evolution of language and the brain*. New York: Norton and Company Press.

Deloria, V. (1997) *Red Earth, White Lies: Native Americans and the myth of scientific fact*. Golden, Colorado: Fulcrum Publishing.

Descola, P. (2014) *Beyond Nature and Culture*. Chicago: The University of Chicago Press.

Deumert, A. & N. Mabandla (2018) 'Beyond colonial linguistics: The dialectic of control and resistance in the standardization of isiXhosa'. In P. Lane, J. Costa, & H. De Korne (Eds.) *Standardizing Minority Languages: Competing ideologies of authority and authenticity in the global periphery*, pp. 200–221. New York: Routledge.

Deumert, A., Storch, A. & Shepherd, M. (2019) (Eds.) *Colonial and Decolonial Linguistics: Knowledges and epistemes*. Oxford: Oxford University Press.

Development Initiatives (2018) *2018 Global Nutrition Report: Shining a light to spur action on nutrition*. Bristol: Development Initiatives.

Di Carlo, P. (2016) 'Multilingualism, affiliation and spiritual insecurity. From phenomena to process in language documentation'. In M. Seyfeddinipur (Ed.) *African Language Documentation: New data, methods and approaches*, pp. 71–104. Honolulu: University of Hawai'i Press.

Di Carlo, P. (2018) 'Towards an understanding of African endogenous multilingualism: Ethnography, language ideologies, and the supernatural' *International Journal of Sociology of Language* 254, 139–163.

Di Carlo, P. Good, J. & Ojong, R. (2019). Multilingualism in rural Africa. In *Oxford Research Encyclopedia of Linguistics*. Oxford: Oxford University Press.

Dias, J. (2019) 'Reshuffling conceptual cards: What counts as language in lowland indigenous South America'. In L. M. de Souza, M. Guilherme & M. de Souza (Eds.) *Local Languages and Critical Language Awareness: The South answers back*. London: Routledge.

Diaz, J. (2016) 'Radical hope'. *New Yorker*. November 21.

Dixon, S. & Angelo, D. (2014) 'Dodgy data, language invisibility and the implications for social inclusion'. *Australian Review of Applied Linguistics* 37(3), 213–233.

Dong, J. (2010) 'The enregisterment of Putonghua in practice'. *Language and Communication* 30, 265–275.
Douglas Fir Group (DFG). (2016) 'A transdisciplinary framework for SLA in a multilingual world'. *Modern Language Journal* 100, 19–47.
Douzinas, C. (2000) *The End of Human Rights: Critical legal thought at the turn of the century.* Oxford: Hart.
Dovchin, S. (2019) 'The politics of injustice in translingualism: Linguistic discrimination'. In T. Barrett & S. Dovchin (Eds.) *Critical Inquiries in the Sociolinguistics of Globalization*, pp. 84–101. Clevedon: Multilingual Matters.
Dransart, P. (1992) 'Pachamama: The Inka mother of the long sweeping garment'. In R. Barnes, & J. Eicher (Eds.) *Dress and Gender: Making and meaning*, pp. 145–163. New York & Oxford: Berg.
Dua, H. (1994) *Hegemony of English*. Mysore: Yashoda Publications.
du Bois, W. E. B. (1970/1903) *The Souls of Black Folk: Essays and sketches*. Cambridge: Cambridge University Press.
Duchêne, A. (2008) *Ideologies Across Nations: The construction of linguistic minorities at the United Nations*. Berlin: Mouton de Gruyter.
Dussel, E. (1977) *Filosoía de Liberación*. México: Edicol.
Dussel, E. (1995) *The Invention of the Americas*. New York: Continuum.
Dussel, E. (2008) 'A new age in the history of philosophy: The world dialogue between philosophical traditions.' *Prajñā Vihāra: Journal of Philosophy and Religion* 9(1), 1–21.
Dussel, E. (2013) *Ethics of Liberation: In the age of globalization and exclusion*. Durham, NC: Duke University Press.
Eades, D. (2016) 'Theorising language in sociolinguistics and the law: (How) can sociolinguistics have an impact on inequality in the criminal justice process?' In N. Coupland (Ed.) *Sociolinguistics: Theoretical debates*, pp. 367–388. Cambridge: Cambridge University Press.
Ebongue, A. & Hurst, E. (Eds.) (2017) *Sociolinguistics in African Contexts: Perspectives and challenges*. Cham: Springer.
Errington, J. (2001) 'Colonial linguistics'. *Annual Review of Anthropology* 30, 19–39.
Errington, J. (2008) *Linguistics in a Colonial World: A story of language, meaning and power*. Oxford: Blackwell.
Escobar, A. (1985) 'Discourse and power in development: Michel Foucault and the relevance of his work to the third world'. *Alternatives* 10, 377–400.
Escobar, A. (1995) *Encountering Development: The Making and unmaking of the Third World*. Princeton, NJ: Princeton University Press.
Escobar, A. (2011) Sustainability: Design for the pluriverse. *Development* 54(2), 137–140.
Fabian, J. (1983) *Time and the Other: How anthropology makes its object*. New York: Columbia University Press.
Fabian, J. (1986) *Language and Colonial Power*. Cambridge: Cambridge University Press.
Fanon, F. (1952) *Peau Noire, Masques Blancs*. Paris: Éditions du Seuil.
Fanon, F. (1967) *Toward the African Revolution*. (Trans. Haakon Chevalier). New York: Grove Press.
Fardon, R. & Furniss, G. (1984) *African Languages, Development and the State*. London: Routledge.
Ferguson, G. (2013) 'English, development and education: Charting the tensions'. In E. Erling & P. Seargeant (Eds.) *English and Development: Policy, pedagogy and globalization*, pp. 21–44. Bristol: Multilingual Matters.
Finnegan, R. (2015) *Where Is Language? An Anthropologist's Questions on Language, Literature and Performance*. London: Bloomsbury.
Fishman, J. A. (1991) *Reversing Language Shift*. Clevedon: Multilingual Matters.

Fishman, J., Ferguson, C. & Dasgupta, J. (1974) *Advances in Language Planning*. The Hague: Mouton.

Flores, N. (2013) 'The unexamined relationship between neoliberalism and plurilingualism: A cautionary tale'. *TESOL Quarterly* 47, 500–520.

Flores, N. & Rosa, J. (2015) 'Undoing appropriateness: Raciolinguistic ideologies and language diversity in education'. *Harvard Educational Review* 85(2), 149–171.

Flores, N. & Rosa, J. (2019) 'Bringing race into second language acquisition'. *The Modern Language Journal* 103, 145–151.

Flores Osorio, J. M. (2009) 'Praxis and liberation in the context of Latin American Theory', In M. Montero & C. Sonn (Eds.) *Psychology of Liberation: Theory and applications*. New York: Springer.

Francois, A. (2012) 'The dynamics of linguistic diversity: Egalitarian multilingualism and power imbalance among northern Vanuatu languages'. *International Journal for the Sociology of Language* 214, 85–110.

Frank, A. G. (1966) 'The development of underdevelopment'. *Monthly Review* September, 17–30.

Frank, A. G. (1975) *On Capitalist Underdevelopment*. Bombay: Oxford University Press.

Freire, P. (1994) *Pedagogy of the Oppressed*. (Trans. R. R. Barr). New York: Continuum.

Freire, P. (1995) *Pedagogy of Hope: Reviving pedagogy of the oppressed*. (Trans. R. R. Barr). New York: Continuum.

Furo, A. (2018) *Decolonizing the Classroom Curriculum: Indigenous knowledges, colonialism, logics and ethical spaces*. Ottawa, Canada: University of Ottawa.

Gal, S. (2018) 'Visions and revisions of minority languages: Standardization and Its dilemmas'. In P. Lane, J. Costa, & H. De Korne (Eds.) *Standardizing Minority Languages: Competing ideologies of authority and authenticity in the global periphery*, pp. 222–242. New York: Routledge.

Gal, S. & Irvine, J. T. (2019) *Signs of Difference: Language and ideology in social life*. Cambridge: Cambridge University Press.

Galtung, J. (1971) 'A structural theory of imperialism'. *Journal of Peace Research* 8(2), 81–117.

Gandhi, M. (2002) *The Essential Gandhi: An anthology of his writings on his life, work, and ideas*. Random House Digital, Inc.

García, O. (2014) 'Countering the dual: Transglossia, dynamic bilingualism and translanguaging in education'. In R. S. Rubdy & L. Alsagoff (Eds.) *The Global-Local Interface and Hybridity: Exploring language and identity*, pp. 100–118. Bristol: Multilingual Matters.

García, O. & Li, W. (2014) *Translanguaging: Language, bilingualism and education*. Palgrave Macmillan.

Garroutte, E. M. (2003) *Real Indians: Identity and the survival of Native America*. Berkeley: University of California Press.

Gaundry, A. & Lorenz, D. (2018) 'Indigenization as inclusion, reconciliation, and decolonization navigating the different visions for indigenizing the Canadian academy'. *AlterNative, An International Journal of Indigenous Peoples* 14(3), 218–227.

Gibbons, A. (1985) *Information, Ideology and Communication: The new nations' perspectives on an intellectual revolution*. Lanham, MD: University Press of America.

Gilley, B. (2017) 'The case for colonialism'. *Third World Quarterly*. doi:10.1080/01436597.2017.1369037.

Glissant, É. (1981) *Le Discours Antillais*. Paris: Éditions du Seuil.

Gogolin, I. (1994) *Der monolinguale "habitus" der multilingualen Schule*. Münster: Waxman-Verlag.

Gogolin, I. (2002) 'Linguistic and cultural diversity in Europe: A challenge for educational research and practice'. *European Educational Research Journal*, 1(1), 123–138.

Gomes, A. (2013) 'Anthropology and the politics of indigeneity'. *Anthropological Forum* 23 (1), 5–15.

Gonzalez, P. & Vazquez, A. M. (2013) 'An ontological turn in the debate on Buen Vivirsumal kawsay in Ecuador: Ideology, knowledge, and the commons'. *Journal of Latin American and Caribbean Ethnic Studies* 10, 315–334.

Grace, G. (n.d.) The assumption that language consists of languages. Available online at www.ling.hawaii.edu/faculty/grace/langue.html (accessed May 2019).

Graeber, D. (2015) 'Radical alterity is just another way of saying "reality"'. *HAU: Journal of Ethnographic Theory* 5, 1–41.

Gramling, D. (2016) *The Invention of Monolingualism*. New York: Bloomsbury Publishing USA.

Grierson, G. (1907) Languages. In W. W. Hunter (Ed.) *The Imperial Gazetteer of India, vol. 1: The Indian Empire - Descriptive* (new ed.), pp. 349–401. Oxford: Clarendon Press.

Grosfoguel, R. (2011) 'Decolonizing, post-colonial studies and paradigms of political economy: Transmodernity, decolonial thinking, and global coloniality'. *Transmodernity: Journal of Peripheral Cultural Production of the Luso-Hispanic World* 1(1) (np).

Grosfoguel, R. (2013) 'The structure of knowledge in westernized universities: Epistemic racism/sexism and the four genocides in the long 16th century'. *Human Architecture: Journal of the Sociology of Self-Knowledge* 11(1), 73–90.

Grosfoguel, R. (2016) 'What is racism?' *Journal of World Systems Research* 22(1), 1–38.

Guba, E. & Lincoln, Y. (2005) 'Paradigmatic controversies, contradictions, and emerging confluences'. In N. K. Denzin & Y. Lincoln (Eds.) *Handbook of Qualitative Research*, pp. 191–215. Thousand Oaks, CA: Sage.

Gudynas, E. (2011) 'Buen Vivir. Today's tomorrow'. *Development* 54(4), 441–447.

Gudynas, E. (2016) 'Beyond varieties of development: Disputes and alternatives'. *Third World Quarterly* 37(4), 721–732.

Hall, C. J. & Wicaksono, R. (Eds.) (2019) *Ontologies of English. Reconceptualising the language for learning, teaching, and assessment*. Cambridge: Cambridge University Press.

Hardt, M. & Negri, A. (2000). *Empire*. Cambridge, MA: Harvard University Press.

Harpham, G. (2002) *Language Alone: The critical fetish of modernity*. London: Routledge.

Harris, R. (1980) *The Language-Makers*. Ithaca, NY: Cornell University Press.

Harris, R. (1981) *The Language Myth in Western Culture*. London: Duckworth.

Harris, R. (1990) 'On redefining linguistics'. In H. Davis & T. Taylor (Eds.) *Redefining Linguistics*, pp. 18–52. London: Routledge.

Harris, R. (1998) *Introduction to Integrational Linguistics*. Oxford: Pergamon.

Harris, R. (2009) 'Implicit and explicit language teaching'. In M. Toolan (Ed.) *Language Teaching: Integrational linguistic approaches*, pp. 24–47. London: Routledge Press.

Harris, R. & Taylor, T. (Eds.) (1997) *Landmarks in Linguistic Thought 1: The Western tradition from Socrates to Saussure*, 2nd edn. London: Routledge.

Harrison, F. V. (2016) 'Theorizing in ex-centric sites'. *Anthropological Theory* 16(2–3), 160–176.

Haslanger, S. (2012) *Resisting Reality: Social construction and social critique*. Oxford: Oxford University Press.

Hauck, J. D. & Heurich, G. O. (2018) 'Language in the Amerindian imagination: An inquiry into linguistic natures'. *Language & Communication* 63, 1–8. https://doi.org/10.1016/j.langcom.2018.03.005.

Haugen, E. (1972) *The Ecology of Language*. Stanford, CA: Stanford University Press.

Hayman, E. with James, C. & Wedge, J. (2018) 'Future rivers of the Anthropocene or whose Anthropcene is it? Decolonising the Anthopocene'. *Decolonization: Indigeneity, Education & Society* 6(2), 77–92.

Headley, C. (2011) 'Afro-Caribbean philosophy'. In W. Edleglass & J. Garfield (Eds.) *The Oxford Handbook of World Philosophy*. Oxford: Oxford University Press.
Heiss, A. (2003) *Dhuuluu-Yala: To talk straight*. Canberra: Aboriginal Studies Press.
Heiss, A. (2012) *Am I Black Enough For You?* Sydney: Bantam.
Heller, M. (2007) 'Bilingualism as ideology and practice'. In M. Heller (Ed.) *Bilingualism: A social approach*, pp. 1–22. London: Macmillan.
Heller, M. & Duchêne, A. (2007) 'Discourses of endangerment: Sociolinguistics, globalization and social order'. In A. Duchêne & M. Heller (Eds.) *Discourses of Endangerment: Ideology and interest in the defense of languages*, pp. 1–13. London: Continuum.
Heller, M. & McElhinny, B. (2017) *Language, Capitalism, Colonialism: Toward a critical history*. Toronto: University of Toronto Press.
Henrich, J., Heine, S. & Norenzayan, A. (2010) 'The weirdest people in the world?' *Behavioral and Brain Sciences* 33, 61–135.
Herold, K. (2017) 'The rights of nature: Indigenous philosophies reframing law'. Deep Green Resistance. News Service. https://intercontinentalcry.org/rights-nature-indigenous-philosophies-reframing law (accessed 2/18/2019).
Heryanto, A. (1990) 'The making of language: Developmentalism in Indonesia'. *Prisma* 50, 40–53.
Heryanto, A. (2007) 'Then There Were Languages: Bahasa Indonesia was one among many'. In S. Makoni & A. Pennycook (Eds.) *Disinventing and Reconstituting Languages*, pp. 42–61. Clevedon: Multilingual Matters.
Heugh, K. (2017) 'Re-placing and re-centring southern multilingualisms: A de-colonial project'. In C. Kerfoot & K. Hyltenstam (Eds.) *Entangled Discourses: South-North orders of visibility*, pp. 209–229. New York: Routledge.
Heugh, K. & Stroud, C. (2018). 'Diversities, affinities and diasporas: A southern lens and methodology for understanding multilingualisms'. *Current Issues in Language Planning*. doi:10.1080/14664208.2018.1507543.
Heugh, K., Stroud, C., Taylor-Leech, K. & De Costa, P. (Eds.) (In press) *A Sociolinguistics of the South*. London: Routledge.
Hill, M. (2008) 'Inca of the blood, Inca of the soul'. *Journal of the American Academy of Religion* 76(2), 251–279.
Holbraad, M. & Pedersen, M. A. (2017) *The Ontological Turn: An anthropological exposition*. Cambridge: Cambridge University Press.
Hopper, P. (1998) 'Emergent grammar'. In M. Tomasello (Ed.) *The New Psychology of Language*, pp. 155–175. Mahwah, NJ: Lawrence Erlbaum.
Hountondji, P. (2009) *African Philosophy: Myth & reality* (2nd edition). London: Hutchinson & Co.
Howatt, A. P. R. (1984) *A History of English Language Teaching*. Oxford: Oxford University Press.
Howatt, A. P. R. & Widdowson, H. G. (2004) *A History of English Language Teaching* (2nd edition). Oxford: Oxford University Press.
Icaza, R. & Vazquez, R. (2018) 'Diversity or decolonization? Researching diversity at the University of Amsterdam'. In G. Bhambra, D. Gebrial & K. Nisancioglu (Eds.) *Decolonizing the University*. pp. 108-128. London: Pluto Press.
Illich, I. & Sander, B. (1988) *ABC; The Alphabetization of the Popular Mind*, London: Marion Boyars.
Ingersoll, K. A. (2016) *Waves of Knowing: A seascape epistemology*. Durham, CT: Duke University Press.
Inkeles, A. & Smith, D. H. (1974) *Becoming Modern*. London: Heinemann.
Irvine, J. (2009) 'Subjected words: African linguistics and the colonial encounter', *Language and Communication* 28(4): 291–408.

Irvine, J. & Gal, S. (2000) 'Language ideology and linguistic differentiation'. In P. V. Kroskrity (Ed.) *Regimes of Language: Ideologies polities and identities*, pp. 35–83. Santa Fe, NM: School of American Research Press.

Jagmohan, K. & Craig, N. (2019) 'More varsity protests expected as minister, students in deadlock'. *Sunday Tribune News*, 10 February 2019.

Jakubiak, C. (2016) 'Ambiguous aims: English-language voluntourism as development'. *Journal of Language, Identity & Education* 15(4), 245–258.

Jaspers, J. (2011) Talking like a 'zerolingual': Ambiguous linguistic caricatures at an urban secondary school. *Journal of Pragmatics* 43, 1264–1278.

Jaspers, J. (2018) 'The transformative limits of translanguaging'. *Language & Communication* 58, 1–10.

Jeater, D. (2002) 'Speaking like a native'. *Journal of African History* 43, 449–468.

Jensen, S. (2016) *The Making of International Human Rights: The 1960s, decolonization, and the reconstruction of global values*. Cambridge: Cambridge University Press.

Johnstone, B. (1996) *The Linguistic Individual: Self-expression in language and linguistics*. New York & Oxford: Oxford University Press.

Jones, P. (2018) 'Karl Marx and the language sciences – critical encounters: Introduction to the special issue'. *Language Sciences* 70, 1–15.

Jørgensen, J. N. (2008) 'Polylingal languaging around and among children and adolescents'. *International Journal of Multilingualism* 5(3): 161–176.

Joseph, J. (2006) *Language and Politics*. Edinburgh: Edinburgh University Press.

Kachru, B. (2009) 'World Englishes and culture wars'. In B. Kachru, Y. Kachru & C. Nelson (Eds.) *The Handbook of World Englishes*, pp. 446–468. Malden, MA: Wiley.

Kamwangamalu, N. M. (1997) 'The colonial legacy and language planning in Sub-Saharan Africa: The case of Zaire'. *Applied Linguistics* 18, 69–85.

Kamwangamalu, N. (1999) 'Ubuntu in South Africa: A sociolinguistic perspective to a pan-African concept'. *Critical Arts: North-South Cultural Media Studies* 13(2), 131–143.

Kamwangamalu, N. M. (2008) 'Education and language economics in postcolonial Africa'. In P. Tan & R. Rubdy (Eds.) *Language as commodity: Global structures, local marketplaces*, pp. 171–185. New York: Continuum.

Kamwangamalu, N. M. (2016) *Language Policy and Economics: The language question in Africa*. London: Palgrave.

Kerfoot, C. & Hyltenstam, K. (2017) 'Introduction: Entanglement and orders of visibility'. In C. Kerfoot & K. Hyltenstam (Eds.) *Entangled Discourses: South-North orders of visibility*, pp. 1–15. New York: Routledge.

Kesteloot, L. (1991) *Black Writers in French: A literary history of negritude*. Washington, DC: Howard University Press.

Khubchandani, L. (1997) *Revisioning Boundaries: A plurilingual ethos*. New Delhi: Sage.

Khubchandani, L. (2003) 'Defining mother tongue education in plurilingual contexts'. *Language Policy* 2: 239–254.

Kohn, E. (2013) *How Forests Think: Toward an anthropology beyond the human*. Berkeley, Los Angeles & London: University of California Press.

Kothari, R. (1987) 'On humane governance'. *Alternatives* 12, 277–290.

Kovach, M. (2010) *Indigenous Methodologies: Characteristics, conversations, and contexts*. Toronto: University of Toronto Press.

Kramsch, C. (2019) 'Between globalization and decolonization. Foreign languages in the cross-fire'. In D. Macedo (Ed.) *Decolonizing Foreign Language Education. The misteaching of English and other imperial languages*, pp. 50–72. London: Routledge.

Kramsch, C. & Zhang, L. (2018) *The Multilingual Instructor*. Oxford: Oxford University Press.

Kress, G. (2003) *Literacy in the New Media*. London: Routledge.
Kress, G. & van Leeuwen, T. (2001) *Reading Images: The grammar of visual design*. London: Routledge.
Krishnaswamy, N. & Burde, A. (1998) *The Politics of Indians' English: Linguistic colonialism and the expanding English empire*. Delhi: Oxford University Press.
Kroskrity, P. V. (2000) 'Regimenting languages: Language ideological perspectives', in P. V. Kroskrity (Ed.) *Regimes of Language: Ideologies, politics and identities*, pp. 1–34. Santa Fe, NM: School of American Research Press.
Kubota, R. (2016) 'The Multi/plural turn, postcolonial theory, and neoliberal multiculturalism: Complicities and implications for applied linguistics'. *Applied Linguistics* 37(4), 474–494.
Kubota, R. (2019) 'Confronting epistemological racism, decolonizing scholarly knowledge: Race and gender in applied linguistics'. *Applied Linguistics*. doi:10.1093/applin/amz033.
Kumaravadivelu, B. (2003) *Beyond Methods: Macrostrategies for language teaching*. New Haven, CT: Yale University Press.
Kumaravadivelu, B. (2012) 'Individual identity, cultural globalization and teaching English as an international language: The case for an epistemic break'. In L. Alsagoff, S. McKay, G. Hu & W. Renandya (Eds.) *Teaching English as an International Language: Principles and practices*, pp. 9–27. New York: Routledge.
Kumaravadivelu, B. (2016) 'The decolonial option in English teaching: Can the subaltern act?' *TESOL Quarterly*, 50(1), 66–85. doi:10.1002/tesq.202.
Kusters, A. & Sahasrabudhe, S. (2018) 'Language ideologies on the difference between gesture and sign'. *Language & Communication* 60, 44–63.
La paperson (2017) *A Third University is Possible*. Minneapolis and Saint Paul, MH: University of Minnesota Press.
Lane, P. & Makihara, M. (2017) 'Indigenous peoples and their languages'. In O. García, N. Flores & M. Spotti (Eds.) *The Oxford Handbook of Language and Society*, pp. 299–319. Oxford: Oxford University Press.
Larsen, S. & Johnson, J. (2016) The agency of place: Toward a more-than-human geographical self. *GeoHumanities* 2(1), 149–166.
Larsen-Freeman, D. & Cameron, L. (2008) *Complex Systems and Applied Linguistics*. Oxford: Oxford University Press.
Le Page, R. & Tabouret-Keller, A. (1985) *Acts of Identity*. Cambridge: Cambridge University Press.
Le Point. (2018) Le décolonialisme, une stratégie hégémonique: l'appel de 80 intellectuels. www.lepoint.fr/politique/le-decolonialisme-une-strategie-hegemonique-l-appel-de-80-intellectuels-28-11-2018-2275104_20.php?fbclid=IwAR0Z25xonmzP141LWmpmIOhNBQCh6h9BqJKseqB8OZUhGmfpXdX0ZP8Audg.
Lee, T. (2017) 'Native American studies: A place of community'. *AlterNative: An International Journal of Indigenous Peoples* 13(1), 18–25.
Legal Text of the Ecuadorian Constitution of 2008. Available online.pdba.georgetown.edu/Constitutions/Ecuador/English.08html (accessed 2/18/2019).
Leonard, W. (2017) 'Producing language reclamation by decolonising 'language''. In W. Leonard & H. De Korne (Eds.) *Language Documentation and Description*, Vol. 14, pp. 15–36. London: EL Publishing.
Levinas, E. (1969) *Totality and Infinity: An essay on exteriority*. Pittsburgh: Duquesne University Press.
Levon, E. (2017) 'Situating sociolinguistics: Coupland – theoretical debates'. *Journal of Sociolinguistics* 21(2), 272–288. doi:10.1111/josl.12233.

Liddicoat, T. (2016) 'Multilingualism research in anglophone contexts as a discursive construction of multilingual practice'. *Journal of Multicultural Discourse* 11(1), 9–24.

Liddicoat, T. (2018) 'Language teaching and learning as a transdisciplinary endeavour: Multilingualism and epistemological diversity'. *AILA Review* 31, 14–28.

Lin, A. M. Y. (2013) 'Breaking the hegemonic knowledge claims in language policy and education: "The Global South as method"'. In J. A. Shoba and F. Chimbutane (Eds.) *Bilingual Education and Language Policy in the Global South*, pp. 223–231. London: Routledge.

Lindemann, S. (2005) 'Who speaks 'broken English'? US undergraduates' perceptions of non-native English'. *International Journal of Applied Linguistics* 15(2), 187–212.

Lopez, A., Turkan, S. & Guzman-Orth, D. (2017) 'Assessing multilingual competence'. In E. Shohamy, I. G. Or, & S. May (Eds.) *Language Testing and Assessment, Vol. 7. The Encyclopedia of Language and Education* (3rd ed), pp 91–102. Cham: Springer.

López-Gopar, M. E. (2016) *Decolonizing Primary English Language Teaching*. Bristol: Multilingual Matters.

Love, N. (2009) 'Science, language and linguistic culture'. *Language and Communication* 29, 26–46.

Love, N. (2017) 'On languaging and languages'. *Language Sciences* 61, 113–147.

Love, N. and Anslado, U. (2010) 'The native speaker and the mother tongue'. *Language Sciences* 32, 589–593.

Lüpke, F. (2015) 'Ideologies and typologies of language endangerment in Africa'. In J. Essegbey, B. Henderson & F. McLaughlin (Eds.) *Language Documentation and Endangerment in Africa*, pp. 59–105. Amsterdam: John Benjamins.

Lüpke, F. (2016) 'Uncovering small-scale multilingualisms'. *Critical Multilingualism Studies* 4, 36–74.

Lüpke, F. (2019) 'Language endangerment and language documentation in Africa'. In H. E. Wolff (Ed.) *The Cambridge Handbook of African Linguistics*, pp. 468–490. Cambridge: Cambridge University Press.

Lüpke, F. & Storch, A. (2013) *Repertoires and Choices in African languages*. De Gruyter: Mouton.

Mabingo, A. (2015) 'Decolonizing dance pedagogy: Application of pedagogies of Ugandan traditional dances'. *Journal of Dance Education* 15(4), 131–141.

Macedo, D. (2019) 'Rupturing the yoke of colonialism in foreign language education'. In D. Macedo (Ed.) *Decolonzing Foreign Language Education. The misteaching of English and other imperial languages*, pp. 1–49. London: Routledge Press.

Mafeje, A. (1998) 'Anthropology and independent Africans: Suicide or an end of an era?' *African Sociological Review* 2(1), 1–43.

Magubane, Z. (2015) 'Beyond the nation state and the comparative method? Decolonizing the sociological imagination'. *Contemporary Sociology* 44(1), 14–17.

Mahboob, A. & Szenes, E. (2010) 'Linguicism and racism in assessment practices in higher education'. *Linguistics and Human Sciences* 3, 325–354.

Makalela, L. (2017) 'Translanguaging practices in a South African institution of higher learning: A case of *Ubuntu* multilingual return'. In C. Mazak & K. Carroll (Eds.) *Translanguaging in Higher Education: Beyond monolingual ideologies*, pp. 11–28. Bristol: Multilingual Matters.

Makalela, L. (2018a) 'Introduction: Shifting lenses'. In L. Makalela (Ed.) *Shifting Lenses: Multilanguaging, decolonisation and education in the Global South*, pp. 1–8. Cape Town: CASAS.

Makalela, L. (2018b) 'Multilanguaging engagements in higher education: A case of an applied language postgraduate course'. In L. Makalela (Ed.) *ShiftingLenses: Multilanguaging, decolonisation and education in the Global South*, pp. 119–135. Cape Town: CASAS.

Makalela, L. (2018c) 'Teaching African languages the *Ubuntu* way: The effects of translanguaging among pre-service teachers in South Africa'. In P. Van Avermaet, S. Slembrouck, K. van Gorp, S. Sierens & K. Maryns (Eds.) *The Multilingual Edge of Education*, pp. 261–282. London: Palgrave Macmillan.

Makoni, S. (1998) 'African languages as European scripts: The shaping of communal memory'. In S. Nuttall & C. Coetzee (Eds.) *Negotiating the Past. The making of memory in South Africa*, pp. 157–164. Oxford: Oxford University Press.

Makoni, S. B. (2012) 'Language and human rights discourses in Africa: Lessons from the African experience'. *Journal of Multicultural Discourses* 7(1) 1–20.

Makoni, S. B., Brutt-Griffler, J. & Mashiri, P. (2007) 'The use of 'indigenous' and urban vernaculars in Zimbabwe'. *Language in Society* 36(1), 25–49.

Makoni, S. & Makoni, B. (2009) 'Multilingual discourses on wheels and public English: A case for Vague Linguistique'. In J. Maybin & J. Swann (Eds.) *The Routledge Companion to English Language Studies*, pp. 258–271. London & New York: Routledge Press.

Makoni, S., Makoni, B., Abdelhay, A. & Mashiri, P. (2012) 'Colonial and postcolonial language policies in Africa: Historical and emerging landscapes'. In Spolsky, B. (Ed.) *The Cambridge Handbook of Language Policy*, pp. 501–523. Cambridge: Cambridge University Press.

Makoni, S., Makoni, B. & Pennycook, A. (2010) On speaking multilanguages: Urban lingos and fluid multilingual practices. In P. Cuvelier, M. Meeuwis, R. Vanderkerhove & V. Webb (Eds.) *Multilingualism from Below: Studies in language policy from South Africa*, pp. 147–165. Pretoria: Van Schaik Publishers.

Makoni, S. & Meinhof, U. (2003) 'Introducing applied linguistics in Africa'. *AILA Review*, 16, 1–12.

Makoni, S. & Pennycook, A. (Eds.) (2007) *Disinventing and Reconstituting Languages*. Clevedon: Multilingual Matters.

Makoni, S. & Pennycook, A. (2012) 'Disinventing multilingualism: From monological multilingualism to multilingual francas'. In M. Martin-Jones & A. Blackledge (Eds.) *The Routledge Handbook of Multilingualism*, pp. 439–453. London: Routledge.

Makoni, S. & Severo, C. (2017) 'An integrationist perspective on African philosophy'. In A. Pablé (Ed.) *Critical Humanist Perspectives: The integrational turn in philosophy of language and communication*. New York: Routledge.

Makoni, S. & Trudell, B. (2006) 'Complementary and conflicting discourses of linguistic diversity: Implications for language planning'. *Per Linguam* 22(2), 14–28.

Maldonado-Torres, N. (2007) 'On the coloniality of being: Contributions to the development of a concept'. *Cultural Studies* 21(2–3), 240–270.

Maldonado-Torres, N. (2010) 'On the coloniality of being: Contributions to the development of a concept'. In W. Mignolo & A. Escobar (Eds.) *Globalization and the Decolonial Option*, pp. 94–124. New York: Routledge.

Mamdani, M. (2018) 'The African University'. *London Review of Books*, pp. 29–32.

Mannheim, B. (1991) *The Language of the Inkha: Since the European invasion*. Austin: University of Texas.

Marshall, Z. (2012) *Anansi's Journey: A story of Jamaican cultural resistance*. Kingston, Jamaica: University of West Indies Press.

Martin, K. & Mirraboopa, B. (2003) 'Ways of knowing, being and doing: A theoretical framework and methods for indigenous and indigenist research'. *Journal of Australian Studies* 27(76), 203–214.

Martin-Jones, M., Blackledge, A. & Creese, A. (Eds.) (2012) *The Routledge Handbook of Multilingualism*. London: Routledge.

Mathews, G. & Vega, C. A. (2012) 'Introduction: What is globalization from below?' In G. Mathews, G. L. Ribeiro & C. A. Vega (Eds.) *Globalization from Below: The world's other economy*. London: Routledge.

May, S. (2001) *Language and Minority Rights: Ethnicity, nationalism and the politics of language*. Harlow: Longman.

May, S. (2005) 'Moving the language debates forward'. *Journal of Sociolinguistics* 9(3), 319–347.

May, S. (2012) 'Contesting hegemonic and monolithic constructions of language rights 'discourse''. *Journal of Multicultural Discourses* 7(1), 21–27.

May, S. (Ed.) (2014) *The Multilingual Turn: Implications for SLA, TESOL, and bilingual education*. London: Routledge.

May, S. (2019) 'Negotiating the multilingual turn in SLA'. *The Modern Language Journal* 103, 122–129.

Mazrui, A. (1975) 'The African university as a multinational corporation: Problems of penetration and dependency'. *Harvard Education Review* 45, 191–210.

Mazrui, A. (2017) 'Some dimensions of English and globalization: An Africanist afterword'. In M. Borjian (Ed.) *Language and Globalization: An autoethnographic approach*, pp. 211–218. New York: Routledge.

Mbembe, A. (2001) *On the Postcolony*. London: University of California Press.

Mbembe, A. (2016) 'Decolonizing the university: New directions'. *Arts and Humanities in Higher Education* 15(1), 29–45.

Mbembe, A. (2017) *A Critique of Black Reason* (Trans. Laurent Dubois). Durham and London: Duke University Press.

McDonald, D. (2010) 'Ubuntu bashing: The marketisation of 'African values' in South Africa'. *The Journal of African Review of Political Economy* 37, 139–152.

McGregor, K. (2016) 'The world needs strong higher education in Africa'. *University World News* 6(403).

McNamara, T. (2012) 'Language assessments as shibboleths: A poststructuralist perspective'. *Applied Linguistics* 33(5), 564–581.

Meder, T. & Illes, F. (2010) 'Anansi comes to Holland: The trickster spider as a dynamic icon of ethnic identity'. *Quotidian Journal for the Study of Everyday life* 2(1), 20–63.

Mengisteab, K. & Hagg, G. (2017) *Traditional Institutions in Contemporary African Governance*. New York: Routledge.

Merlan, F. (2009) 'Indigeneity: Global and local'. *Current Anthropology* 50(3), 303–333.

Metcalf, T. (1995) *Ideologies of the Raj*. Cambridge: Cambridge University Press.

Mignolo, W. (2000) *Local Histories/Global Designs: Coloniality, subaltern knowledges, and border thinking*. Princeton, NJ: Princeton University Press.

Mignolo, W. (2002) 'The geopolitics of knowledge and the colonial difference'. *The South Atlantic Quarterly* 101(1), 57–96.

Mignolo, W. (2008) 'La opcíon descolonial'. *Letral* 1, 4–22.

Mignolo, W. (2009) 'Epistemic disobedience, independent thought and decolonial freedom'. *Theory, Culture, Society* 26(7–8), 159–181.

Mignolo, W. (2010) 'Delinking: The rhetoric of modernity, the logic of coloniality and the grammar of de-coloniality'. In W. Mignolo & A. Escobar (Eds.) *Globalization and the Decolonial Option*, pp. 303–368. New York: Routledge.

Mignolo, W. (2011a) *The Darker Side of Western Modernity: Global futures, decolonial options*. Durham, NC: Duke University Press.

Mignolo, W. (2011b) 'The Global South and world dis/order'. *Journal of Anthropological Research* 67(2), 165–188.

Mignolo, W. (2014) 'The North of the South and the West of the East: A provocation to the question'. IBRAAZ Platform 008. www.ibraaz.org/essays/108.
Mignolo, W. (2018) 'The decolonial option' In W. Mignolo & C. Walsh (Eds.) *On Decoloniality: Concepts, analytics and praxis*, pp. 105–257. Durham, NC: Duke University Press.
Mignolo, W. & Walsh, C. (2018) *On Decoloniality: Concepts, analytics, praxis*. Durham, NC: Duke University Press.
Mika, C. (2016) 'Worlded object and its presentation: A Māori philosophy of language'. *AlterNative: An International Journal of Indigenous Peoples* 12(2), 165–175.
Milani, T. (2017) 'The politics of the margins: Multi-semiotic and affective strategies of voice and visibility'. In C. Kerfoot & K. Hyltenstam (Eds.) *Entangled Discourses: South-North orders of visibility*, pp. 173–188. New York: Routledge.
Milani, T. & Lazar, M. (2017) 'Seeing from the South: Discourse, gender and sexuality from southern perspectives'. *Journal of Sociolinguistics* 21(3), 307–319.
Mills, C. (2017) *Black Rights/ White Wrongs: The critique of racial liberalism*. Oxford: Oxford University Press.
Moita-Lopes, L. P. (2006) 'Lingüística aplicada e vida contemporânes: Problematização dos construtos que têm orientado a pesquisa'. In L. P. Moita-Lopes (Ed.) *Por Uma Lingüística Aplicada Indisciplinar*, pp. 85–105. São Paulo: Parabola.
Moita-Lopes, L. P. (2015) 'Introduction: Linguistic ideology: How Portuguese is being discursively constructed in late modernity'. In L. P. Moita-Lopes (Ed.) *Global Portuguese: Linguistic ideologies in late modernity*, pp. 1–26. New York: Routledge.
Møller, J. S. (2008) 'Polylingual performance among Turkish-Danes in late-modern Copenhagen'. *International Journal of Multilingualism* 5(3), 217–236.
Monaghan, P. (2012) 'Going for wombat – Transformations in Wirangu and the Scotdesco Community on the Far West Coast of South Australia'. *Oceania* 82(1), 45–61.
Moore, R. E., Pietikäinen, S. & Blommaert, J. (2010) 'Counting the losses: Numbers as the language of language endangerment'. *Sociolinguistic Studies* 4(1), 1–26.
Motha, S. (2014) *Race and Empire in English Language Teaching*. New York: Teachers College Press, Columbia University.
Moyo, D. (2009) *Dead Aid: Why aid is not working and how there is a better way for Africa*. New York: Farrar, Strauss and Giroux.
Mudimbe, V. (1988) *The Invention of Africa: Gnosis, philosophy, and the order of knowledge*. Bloomington: Indiana University Press.
Muehlmann, S. (2007) 'Defending diversity: Staking out a common global interest?' In A. Duchêne & M. Heller (Eds.) *Discourses of Endangerment: Ideology and interest in the defence of languages*, pp. 14–34. London: Continuum.
Muehlmann, S. (2009) 'How do real Indians fish? Neoliberal multiculturalism and contested Indigeneities in the Colorado Delta'. *American Anthropologist* 111(4), 468–479.
Muehlmann, S. (2012) 'Von Humboldt's parrot and the countdown of last speakers in the Colorado Delta'. *Language & Communication* 32(2), 160–168.
Muehlmann, S. & Duchêne, A. (2007) 'Beyond the nation-state: International agencies as new sites of discourse on bilingualism'. In M. Heller (Ed.) *Bilingualism: A social approach*, pp. 96–110. Basingstoke: Palgrave Macmillan.
Mufwene, S. (2001) *The Ecology of Language Evolution*. Cambridge: Cambridge University Press.
Mufwene, S. (2010) 'The role of mother-tongue schooling in eradicating poverty: A response to Language and poverty'. *Language* 86(4), 910–932.
Mufwene, S. (2016) 'A cost-and-benefit approach to language loss'. In L. Filipović & M. Pütz (Eds.) *Endangered Languages and Languages in Danger: Issues of documentation, policy, and language rights*, pp. 115–143. Amsterdam: John Benjamins.

Mufwene, S. (2017) 'Language vitality: The weak theoretical underpinnings of what can be an exciting research area'. *Language* 93(4), e202–e223.

Mühlhäusler, P. (2000) 'Language planning and language ecology'. *Current Issues in Language Planning* 1(3), 306–367.

Mwaniki, M. (2018) 'Language and literacy education in complexly multilingual contexts: Reflections for theory and practice'. In L. Makalela (Ed.) *Shifting Lenses: Multilanguaging, decolonisation and education in the Global South*, pp. 21–44. Cape Town: CASAS.

Nakata, M. (1999) 'History, cultural diversity and English language teaching'. In P. Wignell (Ed.) *Double Power: English literacy and indigenous education*, pp. 5–22. Canberra: NLLIA.

Nakata, M. (2007) *Disciplining the Savages: Savaging the disciplines*. Canberra: Aboriginal Studies Press.

Nandy, A. (1983) *The Intimate Enemy: Loss and recovery of self under colonialism*. Delhi: Oxford University Press.

Nannyonga-Tamusuza, S. (2005) *Baakisimba: Gender in the music and dance of the Banganda people of Uganda*. London & New York: Routledge.

Nassentein, N., Hollington, A. & Storch, A. (2018) 'Disinventing and demystifying youth language: Critical perspectives'. *The Mouth - Critical Studies on Language, Culture and Society* 30, 9–27.

Ndhlovu, F. (2017) 'Southern development discourse for Southern Africa: Linguistic and cultural imperatives.' *Journal of Multicultural Discourses* 12(2): 89–109. doi:10.1080/17447143.2016.1277733.

Ndhlovu, F. (2018) *Language, Vernacular Discourse and Nationalisms: Uncovering the myths of Transnational Worlds*. Cham: Palgrave Macmillan.

Nero, S. (2006) 'Language, identity and education of Caribbean English speakers'. *World Englishes* 25(3/4), 501–511.

Ngũgĩ wa Thiong'o (1986) *Decolonizing the Mind: The politics of language in African literature*. London: James Currey.

Ngũgĩ wa Thiong'o (2012a) 'Asia in my life'. *Frontline* 29(10) May 19–June 01, np.

Ngũgĩ wa Thiong'o (2012b) *Globalectics: Theory and the politics of knowing*. New York: Columbia University Press.

Nordstrom, C. (2009) 'The bard'. In A. Waterston & M. Vesperi (Eds.) *Anthropology off the Shelf: Anthropologists on writing*, pp. 35–45. Malden: Wiley-Blackwell.

Nyamnjoh, F. (2012) 'Potted plants in greenhouses: A critical reflection on the resilience of colonial education in Africa'. *Journal of Asian and African Studies* 47(2), 129–154.

Ober, R. (2017) 'Kapati time: Storytelling as a data collection method in Indigenous research'. *Learning Communities: International Journal of Learning in Social Contexts* [Special Issue: Decolonising Research Practices] 22, 8–15. doi:10.18793/LCJ2017.22.02.

Ortega, L. (2013) 'SLA for the 21st century: Disciplinary progress, transdisciplinary relevance, and the bi/multilingual turn'. *Language Learning* 63, 1–24. doi:10.1111/j.1467-9922.2012.00735.x.

Ortega, L. (2018) 'Ontologies of language, second language acquisition, and world Englishes'. *World Englishes* 37, 64–79.

Ortega, L. (2019) 'SLA and the study of equitable multilingualism'. *The Modern Language Journal* 103, 23–38.

Otheguy, R., García, O. & Reid, W. (2018) 'A translanguaging view of the linguistic system of bilinguals'. *Applied Linguistics Review*. doi:10.1515/applirev-2018-0020.

Otsuji, E. & Pennycook, A. (2010) 'Metrolingualism: Fixity, fluidity and language in flux'. *International Journal of Multilingualism* 7(3), 240–254.

Otsuji, E. & Pennycook, A. (2018) 'Sydney's intersecting worlds of languages and things'. In D. Smakman & P. Heinrich (Eds.) *Urban Sociolinguistics: The City as a Linguistic Process and Experience*. London: Routledge.
Parakrama, A. (1995) *De-Hegemonizing Language Standards: Learning from (post)colonial Englishes about 'English'*. Basingstoke: MacMillan.
Pennycook, A. (1989) 'The concept of Method, interested knowledge, and the politics of language teaching'. *TESOL Quarterly*, 23(4), 589–618.
Pennycook, A. (1998) *English and the Discourses of Colonialism*. London: Routledge.
Pennycook, A. (2001) *Critical Applied Linguistics: A critical introduction*. Mahwah, NJ: Lawrence Erlbaum.
Pennycook, A. (2004) 'Language policy and the ecological turn'. *Language Policy* 3, 213–239.
Pennycook, A. (2007a) *Global Englishes and Transcultural Flows*. London & New York: Routledge Press.
Pennycook, A. (2007b) 'The myth of English as an international language'. In S. Makoni & A. Pennycook (Eds.) *Disinventing and Reconstituting Languages*, pp. 90–115. Clevedon: Multilingual Matters.
Pennycook, A. (2007c) "'The rotation gets thick, the constraints get thin': Creativity, recontextualization and difference'. *Applied Linguistics* 28(4), 579–596.
Pennycook, A. (2007d) 'ELT and colonialism'. In J. Cummins & C. Davison (Eds.) *Kluwer International Handbook of Education. English Language Teaching*, pp. 13–24. Norwell MA: Kluwer Academic Publishers.
Pennycook, A. (2010) *Language as a Local Practice*. London: Routledge.
Pennycook, A. (2012) *Language and Mobility: Unexpected places*. Bristol: Multilingual Matters.
Pennycook, A. (2015) 'Early literacies and linguistic mobilities'. In C. Stroud & M. Prinsloo (Eds.) *Language, Literacy and Diversity: Moving words*, pp. 187–205. New York: Routledge.
Pennycook, A. (2016) 'Mobile times, mobile terms: The trans-super-poly-metro movement'. In N. Coupland (Ed.) *Sociolinguistics Theoretical Debates*, pp. 201–206. Cambridge: Cambridge University Press.
Pennycook, A. (2018a) *Posthumanist Applied Linguistics*. London: Routledge.
Pennycook, A. (2018b) 'Repertoires, registers, and linguistic diversity'. In A. Creese & A. Blackledge (Eds.) *The Routledge Handbook of Language and Superdiversity*. London: Routledge.
Pennycook, A. (2018c) 'Applied linguistics as epistemic assemblage'. *AILA Review* 31, 113–134.
Pennycook, A. & Otsuji, E. (2019) 'Lingoing and everyday metrolingual metalanguage'. In J. Jaspers & L. Madsen (Eds.) *Critical Perspectives on Linguistic Fixity and Fluidity: Languagised lives*, pp. 76–96. London: Routledge.
Perley, B. (2012) 'Zombie Linguistics: Experts, endangered languages and the curse of undead voices'. *Anthropological Forum*, 22(2), 133–149.
Peterson, V. S. (1990) Whose rights? A critique of the "givens" in human rights discourse. *Alternatives* XV, 303–344.
Phan, H. L. L. (2017) *Transnational Education Crossing 'the West' and 'Asia': Adjusted desire, transformative mediocrity, and neo-colonial disguise*. London and New York: Routledge.
Phillipson, R. (1992) *Linguistic Imperialism*. Oxford: Oxford University Press.
Phillipson, R. (1997) 'Realities and myths of linguistic imperialism'. *Journal of Multilingual and Multicultural Development* 18(3), 238–248.
Phipps, A. (2019) *Decolonising Multilingualism: Struggles to decreate*. Bristol: Multilingual Matters.
Pietari, K. (2016) 'Ecuador's constitutional rights of nature: Implementation, impacts, and lessons learned'. *Willamete Environmental Law Journal*, Fall, 37–94.

Piketty, T. (2014) *Capital in the Twenty-First Century*. (Trans. A. Goldhammer) Cambridge, Mass: Belknap Press.
Piller, I. (2016a) *Linguistic Diversity and Social Justice: An introduction to applied sociolinguistics*. Oxford: Oxford University Press.
Piller, I. (2016b) 'Monolingual ways of seeing multilingualism'. *Journal of Multicultural Discourses* 11:1, 25–33. doi:10.1080/17447143.2015.1102921.
Pinker, S. (2011) *The Better Angels of Our Nature: Why violence has declined*. New York: Penguin.
Pinker, S. (2018) *Enlightenment Now: The case for reason, science, humanism, and progress*. New York: Viking.
Poynting, S. & Noble, G. (2004) 'Living with racism: The experience and reporting by Arab and Muslim Australians of discrimination, abuse and violence since 11 September 2001'. Report to the HREOC. Centre for Cultural Research University of Western Sydney.
Prah, K. K. (2017) 'Has Rhodes fallen? Decolonizing the humanities in Africa and constructing intellectual sovereignty'. The Academy of Science of South Africa (ASSAF) Inaugural Humanities Lecture. HSRC, Pretoria. 20th October 2016.
Prah, K. K. (2018) 'Discourse on language and literacy for African development'. In Makalela, L. (Ed.) (2018) *Shifting Lenses: Multilanguaging, decolonisation and education in the Global South*, pp. 9–20. Cape Town: CASAS.
Preston, D. (1996) 'Whaddayaknow?: The modes of folk linguistic awareness'. *Language Awareness* 5, 40–74.
Preston, P. W. (1986) *Making Sense of Development*. London: Routledge & Kegan Paul.
Pugach, S. (2017) *Africa in Translation: A history of colonial linguistics in Germany and beyond 1814–1945*. Ann Arbor: University of Michigan Press.
Pupavac, V. (2012) *Language Rights: From free speech to linguistic governance*. Houndmills: Palgrave Macmillan.
Quijano, A. (1991) 'Colonialidad y modernidad/racionalidad'. *Perú Indígena* 29, 11–20.
Quijano, A. (1998) 'La colonialidad del poder y la experiencia cultural latinoamericana'. In R. Briceño-León & H. R. Sonntag (Eds.) *Pueblo, Epoca y Desarrollo: La sociología de América Latina*, pp. 139–155. Caracas: Nueva Sociedad.
Quijano, A. (2000) 'Coloniality of power, Eurocentrism, and Latin America' *Nepantla: Views from South* 1(3), 533–580.
Quijano, A. (2007) 'Coloniality and modernity/rationality'. *Cultural Studies* 21(2–3), 168–178.
Rajagopalan, K. (2007) 'Revisiting the nativity scene'. *Studies in Language* 31(1), 193–205.
Rajagopalan, K. (2020) 'Linguistics, colonialism and the urgent need to enact appropriate language policies to counteract its baleful fallout on former colonies'. In A. Abdelhay, S. Makoni & C. Severo (2020) *Language Planning and Policy: Ideologies, ethnicities and semiotic spaces*. Newcastle: Cambridge Scholars Publishers.
Rajan, R. S. (1992) 'Brokering English studies: The British Council in India'. In R. S. Rajan (Ed.) *The Lie of the Land: English literary studies in India*, pp. 130–155. Delhi: Oxford University Press.
Ramchiary, A. (2013) 'Gandhian concept of truth and violence'. *Journal of Humanities and Social Sciences* 18(4), 67–69.
Ranjan, D. (2017) 'Traditional story telling: An effective indigenous research methodology and its implications for environmental research'. *AlterNative: An International Journal of Indigenous Peoples* 14(1), 35–44.
Ray, S. H. (1907) Linguistics. In A. C. Haddon (Ed.) *Reports of the Cambridge Anthropological Expedition to Torres Straits: Vol III*. Cambridge: Cambridge University Press.
Reagan, T. (1996) *Non-Western Educational Traditions: Alternative approaches to educational thought and practice*. Mahwah, NJ: Lawrence Erlbaum.

Reagan, T. (2018) *Non-Western Educational Traditions: Indigenous approaches to educational thought and practice*. London: Routledge.

Report (1980) Report of the Independent Commission on International Development Issues North-South: A programme for survival ('The Brandt Report'). Cambridge, Massachusetts: The MIT Press.

Resende, V. de M. (2018) 'Decolonizing critical discourse studies: For a Latin American perspective'. *Critical Discourse Studies*, doi:10.1080/17405904.2018.1490654.

Richard, N. (1987) Postmodernism and periphery. *Third Text* 2, 5–12.

Richardson, W. (2018) 'Understanding Eurocentricism as a structural problem of "undone science"'. In G. Bhambra, D. Gebriel & K. Nisancioglu (Eds.) *Decolonizing the University*, pp. 231–247. London: Pluto Press.

Riemer, N. (2016a) 'Academics, the humanities and the enclosure of knowledge: The worm in the fruit'. *Australian Universities Review* 58(2), 33–41.

Riemer, N. (2016b) 'Diversity, linguistics and domination: How linguistic theory can feed a kind of politics most linguists would oppose'. *History and Philosophy of Language Sciences*. https://hiphilangsc.net/2016/05/11/diversity-linguistics-anddomination-how-linguisticth eory-can-feed-a-kind-of-politics-most-linguists-would-oppose (accessed 12/29/2018).

Rodney, W. (1972) *How Europe Underdeveloped Africa*. London: Bogle-L'Ouverture.

Romaine, S. (2015) 'The global extinction of languages and its consequences for cultural diversity'. In H. F. Marten, M. Rießler, J. Saarikivi & R. Toivanen (Eds.) *Cultural and Linguistic Minorities in the Russian Federation and the European Union*, pp. 31–46. Cham: Springer.

Rosa, J. (2018) *Looking Like a Language, Sounding Like a Race: Raciolinguistic Ideologies and the Learning of Latinidad*. Oxford: Oxford University Press.

Rosa, J. & Flores, N. (2017) 'Unsettling race and language: Toward a raciolinguistic perspective'. *Language and Society* 46(5), 621–647.

Rubdy, R. (2015) 'Unequal Englishes, the native speaker, and decolonization in TESOL'. In R. Tupas (Ed.) *Unequal Englishes: The politics of Englishes today*, pp. 42–58. Basingstoke: Palgrave MacMillan.

Sabino, R. (2018) *Languaging Without Languages: Beyond metro-, multi-, poly, pluri- and translanguaging*. Amsterdam: Brill.

Said, E. (1978) *Orientalism*. London: Penguin.

Said, E. (1999) *Out of Place: A memoir*. New York: Vintage Books.

Salö, L. & Karlander, D. (2018) 'Semilingualism: The life and afterlife of a sociolinguistic idea'. *Working Papers in Urban Language & Literacies* 247, 1–14.

Santos, B. de S. (2002) *A Critica da Razão Indolente: Contra o desperdício da experiência*. São Paulo: Cortês.

Santos, B. de S. (2004a) 'A critique of lazy reason: Against the waste of experience'. In I. Wallerstein (Ed.) *The Modern World System in the Longue Durée*. London: Paradigm Publishers.

Santos, B. de S. (2004b) *Do Pós-moderno ao Pós-colonial. E para além de um a de outro*. Coimbra: Centro de Estudos Sociais da Universidade de Coimbra.

Santos, B. de S. (2005) *Renovar a Teoria Crítica e Reinventar a Emancipacão Social*. São Paulo: Boitempo.

Santos, B. de S. (2007a) 'Conhecimento e transformação social: Para uma ecologia dos sabers'. *Somanlu: Revista de Estudos Amazônicos* 7(1), 175–189.

Santos, B. de S. (Ed.) (2007b) *Another Knowledge is Possible: Beyond northern epistemologies*. London: Verso.

Santos, B. de S. (2012) 'Public sphere and epistemologies of the south'. *Africa Development* 37 (1), 43–67.

Santos, B. de S. (2014) *Epistemologies of the South: Justice against epistemicide*. New York: Routledge.
Santos, B. de S. (2016) Epistemologies of the South and the future. *From the European South* 1, 17–29.
Santos, B. de S. (2018) *The End of the Cognitive Empire: The coming of age of epistemologies of the South*. Durham, NC: Duke University Press.
Sarkar, M. (2018) 'Ten years of Mi'gmaq language revitalization work: A non- Indigenous applied linguist reflects on building research relationships'. *The Canadian Modern Language Review/La Revue Canadienne des Langues Vivantes* 73(4), 488–508.
Savransky, M. (2017) 'A decolonial imagination: Sociology, anthropology and the politics of reality'. *Sociology* 51(1), 11–26.
Schemm, Y. (2013) 'Africa doubles research output, moves towards knowledge-based economy'. *Research Trends 35*. www.researchtrends.com/issue-35-december-2013/africa-doubles-research-output/ (accessed May 2019).
Scheurich, J. (1997) *Research Method in the Postmodern*. London and Washington DC: Falmer Press.
Schiefflien, B. (1990) *The Give and Take of Everyday Life: Language socialization of the Kaluli children*. New York, Cambridge: Cambridge University Press.
Schissel, J., Leung, C., López-Gopar, M. & Davis, J. (2018) 'Multilingual learners in language assessment: Assessment design for linguistically diverse communities'. *Language and Education*. doi:10.1080/09500782.2018.1429463.
Schultz, T. (1980) 'Nobel lecture: The economics of being poor'. *American Economic Review* 8(4) 639–652.
SCRGSP (Steering Committee for the Review of Government Service Provision) (2016) *Overcoming Indigenous Disadvantage: Key Indicators 2016*. Canberra: Productivity Commission.
Seargeant, P. (2009) *The Idea of English in Japan: Ideology and the evolution of a global language*. Bristol: Multilingual Matters.
Seidlhofer, B. (Ed.) (2003) *Controversies in Applied Linguistics*. Oxford: Oxford University Press.
Severo, C. & Makoni, S. (2014) 'Discourses of language in colonial and postcolonial Brazil'. *Language and Communication* 34, 95–104.
Severo, C. & Makoni, S. (forthcoming) 'Solidarity and Politics of 'Us': How far can individuals go in language policy? Research methods in non-Western contexts'. In J. McKinley & R. Heath (Eds.) *The Routledge Handbook of Research Methods in Applied Linguistics*. Oxford: Oxford University Press.
Sey, K. (1973) *Ghanaian English: An exploratory survey*. Accra: Macmillan.
Shilliam, R. (2015) *The Black Pacific: Anti-colonial struggles and oceanic connections*. London: Bloomsbury.
Shilliam, R. (2018a) 'Black academia'. In G. Bhambra, D. Gebriel & K. Nisancioglu (Eds.) *Decolonizing the University*, pp. 53–64. London: Pluto Press.
Shilliam, R. (2018b) *Race and the Undeserving Poor*. Newcastle: Agenda Publishing.
Shi-xu (2015) 'Cultural discourse studies'. *The International Encyclopedia of Language and Social Interaction*, pp. 1–9. Hoboken, NJ: John Wiley & Sons.
Shi-xu (2016) 'Cultural discourse studies through Journal of Multicultural Discourses ten years on'. *Journal of Multicultural Discourses* 11(1), 1–8.
Shi-xu, Prah, K. K. & Pardo, M. L. (2016) *Discourses of the Developing World: Researching properties, problems and potentials*. London: Routledge.
Shoba, J., Dako, K. & Orfson-Offei, E. (2013) ''Locally acquired foreign accent' (LAFA) in contemporary Ghana'. *World Englishes* 32(2) 230–242.

Shohamy, E. & Menken, K. (2015). 'Language assessment: Past and present misuses and future possibilities'. In W. Wright, B. Sovocheth & O. Garcia (Eds.) *The Routledge Handbook on Bilingual Education*. London and New York: Routledge.

Shohamy, E. & Pennycook, A. (2019) 'Extending fairness and justice in language tests'. In C. Roever & G. Wigglesworth (Eds.) *Social Perspectives on Language Testing: Papers in honour of Tim McNamara*. Berlin: Peter Lang.

Silverstein, M. (2014) 'Michael Silverstein in conversation: Translatability and the uses of standardization'. *Tilburg Papers* #121. Tilburg, NL: Tilburg University.

Singh, J. (1996) *Colonial Narratives/Cultural Dialogues: "Discoveries" of India in the Language of Colonialism*. London: Routledge.

Sistoeurs (2008) www.sistoeurs.net/spip.php?article446.

Sium, A., Desai, C. & Ritskes, E. (2012) 'Towards the "tangible unknown": Decolonization and the indigenous future'. *Decolonization: Indigeneity, Education & Society* 1(1), i–xiii.

Skutnabb-Kangas, T. (2000) *Linguistic Genocide in Education – Or worldwide diversity and human rights?* Mahwah, NJ: Lawrence Erlbaum.

Skutnabb-Kangas, T. (2003) 'Linguistic diversity and biodiversity: The threat from killer languages'. In C. Mair (Ed.) *The Politics of English as a World Language: New horizons in postcolonial cultural studies*, pp. 31–52. Amsterdam: Rodopi.

Slater, D. (2004) *Geopolitics and the Postcolonial: Rethinking North-South relations*. Oxford: Blackwell.

Smakman, D. & Heinrich, P. (2018) 'Introduction: Why cities matter for a globalising sociolinguistics'. In D. Smakman & P. Heinrich (Eds.) *Urban Sociolinguistics: The city as a linguistic process and experience*, pp. 1–11. London: Routledge.

Smith, L. (1999) *Decolonizing Methodologies: Research and Indigenous peoples*. London: Zed Books.

Smith, L. T. (2012) *Decolonizing Methodologies: Research and Indigenous peoples* (2nd edition). London: Zed Books.

Solón, P. (2017) 'Vivir Bien'. In P. Solón (Ed.) *Systemic Alternatives* (Alternativas Sistemicas), pp. 13–57. La Paz: Fundación Solón/Attac France/Focus on the Global South.

Sonntag, S. K. (2003) *The Local Politics of Global English: Case studies in linguistic globalization*. Lanham, MD: Lexington Books.

Spear, T. (2003) 'Neo-traditionalism and the limits of invention in British Colonial Africa'. *Journal of African History* 44: 3–27.

Spinner, P. (2010) 'Review article: Second language acquisition of Bantu languages (a mostly untapped opportunity)'. *Second Language Research* 27(3), 418–430.

Spolsky, B. (2012) *The Cambridge Handbook of Language Policy*. Cambridge: Cambridge University Press.

Springer, J. M. (1909) *The Heart of Central Africa: Mineral Wealth and Missionary Opportunity*. Cincinatti: Jennings.

Stebbins, T. (2014) 'Finding the languages we go looking for'. In P. Austin & J. Sallabank (Eds.) *Endangered Languages: Beliefs and ideologies in language documentation and revitalisation*, (pp. 293–312). Oxford: Oxford University Press.

Stein, S. & Andreotti, V. (2016) 'Decolonization and higher education'. In M. Peters (Ed.), *Encyclopedia of Educational Philosophy and Theory*, pp. 479–491. Singapore: Springer Science Media.

Steinmetz, G. (Ed.) (2013) *Sociology and Empire: The imperial entanglements of a discipline*. Durham, NC: Duke University Press.

Storch, A. (2018) 'At the fringes of language: On the semiotics of science'. *Language Sciences* 65, 48–57.

Stroud, C. (2004). Rinkeby Swedish and semilingualism in language ideological debates: A Bourdieuean perspective. *Journal of Sociolinguistics* 8(2), 196–214.
Sundberg, J. (2013) 'Decolonizing posthumanist geographies'. *Cultural Geographies* 21(1): 33–47.
Tanasecu, M. (2013) 'The rights of nature in Ecuador: The making of an idea'. *International Journal of Environmental Studies* 70(6), 846–861.
Taylor, A. C. (1993) 'Les bons ennemis et les mauvais parents: Le traitement symbolique de l'alliance dans les rituels de chasse aux têtes des Shuar (Jivaro) de l Équateur'. In E. Copet-Rougier & F. Héritier-Augé (Eds.) *Les Complexitiés de l'Alliance, Vol. 4: Économie, politiques et fondements symboliques de l'alliance*, pp. 73–105. Paris: Editions des Archives Contemporaines.
Thibault, P. J. (2011) 'First-order languaging dynamics and second-order language: The distributed language view'. *Ecol. Psychol.* 23(3), 1–36.
Thikoo, M. (2001) 'Sociocultural blindspots in language curriculum renewal: Causes, consequences, cures'. In W. Renandya & N. Sunga (Eds.) *Language Curriculum and Instruction in Multicultural Societies*, pp. 107–122. Singapore: SEAMEO RELC.
Thomas, D. (2011) *Exceptional violence: Embodied citizenship in transnational Jamaica*. Durham, NC: Duke University Press.
Thomas, J. (forthcoming) 'Everyday African multilingualism as Indigenous pedagogy: Teacher-led translanguaging across Swahili, Akan/Twi, and English with Ghanaian learners in Tanzania'. In E. Trentman & W. Diao (Eds.) *The Multilingual Turn in Study Abroad*. Bristol: Multilingual Matters.
Thurlow, C. (2016) 'Queering critical discourse studies or/and performing 'post-class' ideologies'. *Critical Discourse Studies* 13(5), 485–514.
Tochon, F. (2019) 'Decolonizing world language education: Toward multilingualism'. In D. Macedo (Ed.) *Decolonizing Foreign Language Education: The misteaching of English and other imperial languages*, pp. 264–280. London: Routledge Press.
Todd, Z. (2016) 'An Indigenous feminist's take on the ontological turn: 'Ontology' is just another word for colonialism'. *Journal of Historical Sociology* 29(1). doi:10.1111/johs.12124.
Tollefson, J. & Perez-Millans, M. (2018) *The Oxford Handbook of Language Policy and Planning*. Oxford: Oxford University Press.
Toolan, M. (2009) (Ed.) *Introduction: Language teaching and integrational linguistics*. London: Routledge.
Tuck, E. & Yang, K. W. (2012) 'Decolonization is not a metaphor'. *Decolonization: Indigeneity, Education & Society* 1(1), 1–40.
Tupas, R. & Rubdy, R. (2015) 'Introduction: From world Englishes to unequal Englishes'. In R. Tupas (Ed.) *Unequal Englishes: The politics of Englishes today*. Basingstoke: Palgrave MacMillan.
UNESCO. (2018) *Global Education Monitoring Report 2019: Migration, displacement and education – building bridges, not walls*. Paris, UNESCO.
van der Walt, C. (2013) *Multilingualism in Higher Education: Beyond English medium orientations*. Clevedon: Multilingual Matters.
Vaughan, J. & Singer, R. (2018) 'Indigenous multilingualisms past and present'. *Language & Communication* 62, 83–90.
Venn, C. (2000). *Occidentalism: Modernity and subjectivity*. London: Sage.
Venter, E. (2004) The notion of ubuntu and communalism in African educational discourse. *Studies in Philosophy and Education* 23(2), 149–160.
Viveiros de Castro, E. (2004a) 'Exchanging perspectives: The transformation of objects into subjects in Amerindian ontologies'. *Common Knowledge* 10, 463–484.

Viveiros de Castro, E. (2004b) 'Perspectival anthropology and the method of controlled equivocation'. *Tipiti: Journal of the Society for the Anthropology of Lowland South America* 2 (1), 3–20.

Viveiros de Castro, E. (2014) *Cannibal Metaphysics*. Minneapolis, MN: Univocal.

Vorster, J.-A. & Quinn, L. (2017) 'The "decolonial turn": What does it mean for academic staff development?' *Education as Change* 21(1), 31–49.

Wagner, R. (2015) *The Invention of Culture and Coyote Anthropology*. Lincoln, NE: University of Nebraska Press.

Wallerstein, I. (1996) 'Eurocentricism and its avatars: The dilemmas of social science'. *New Left Review* 226(1), 93–107.

Wallerstein, I. (2004) *World-Systems Analysis: An introduction*. Durham, NC: Duke University Press.

Walsh, C. (2018) 'Decoloniality in/as praxis'. In W. Mignolo & C. Walsh (Eds.) *On Decoloniality: Concepts, analytics, praxis*. Durham, NC: Duke University Press.

Walsh, C., Castro-Gomez, S. & Schiwy, F. (Eds.) (2002) *Indisciplinar las Ciencias Sociales: Geopolíticas del conocimiento y colonialidad del poder*. Quito: Abya Yala.

Walter, D. (2017) *Colonial Violence: European empires and the use of force* (Trans. P. Lewis). Oxford: Oxford University Press.

Watkins, M. & Schulman, H. (2017) *Toward Psychologies of Liberation*. Houndmills: Palgrave Macmillan.

Watts, V. (2013) 'Indigenous place-thought and agency amongst humans and non-humans (first woman and sky woman go on a European tour!)'. *DIES: Decolonization, Indigeneity, Education and Society* 2(1), 20–34.

Wheeler, A. (2014) 'Cultural diplomacy, language planning and the case of University of Nairobi Confucius Institute'. *Journal of Asian and African Studies* 49(1), 49–63.

White Face, C. (Zumila Wobaga) (2013) *Indigenous Nations' Rights in the Balance: An analysis of the Declaration on the Rights of Indigenous Peoples*. Minnesota, MN: Living Justice Press.

Whitinui, P., Rodriguez de France, C. & McIvor, O. (2018) *Promising Practices in Indigenous Teacher Education*. Singapore: Springer Nature.

Whorf, B. (1988) *Language, Thought, and Reality: Selected writings of Benjamin Lee Whorf*. J. Carroll (Ed.) Cambridge, MA: MIT Press.

Williams, Q. (2017) *Remix Multilingualism: Hip Hop, ethnography and performing marginalized voices*. London: Bloomsbury.

Wilson, K. (2004) *Pulling Together: A guide for Indigenization of post-secondary institutions. Professional learning series*. BC Campus: Creative Commons.

Woolard, K. (2004) 'Is the past a foreign country? Time, language origins, and the nation in early modern Spain'. *Journal of Linguistic Anthropology* 14(1), 57–80.

Working group (2016) 'Report of the working group on slavery, memory, and reconciliation to the president of Georgetown University'. Unpublished report. https://slavery.georgetown.edu/wp-content/uploads/2016/08/GU-WGSMR-Report-Web.pdf.

Zeleza, P. (2017) The Decolonization of African Knowledges. An address at the 9th Africa Day Lecture, University of Free State, Bloomfontein, South Africa.

Zeleza, P. & McConnaughay, P. (Eds.) (2007) *Human Rights, the Rule of Law, and Development in Africa*. Pennsylvania: University of Pennsylvania Press.

Zuckerman, G. (2009) 'Hybridity versus revivability: Multiple causation, forms and patterns'. *Journal of Language Contact – VARIA* 2, 40–67.

INDEX

abyssal line 86, 120; postabyssal line 86
Africa 1–4, 7, 15–16, 20, 22, 26–7 30, 48, 50, 70, 80, 84, 88, 90–4, 112–3, 117, 125
African Americans 15, 55
Albury, N. J. 14, 76, 93, 129, 138
Anthropocene 82, 124
Anzaldúa, G. 107, 125
Aotearoa/New Zealand 1, 14, 36–7, 76, 113; Māori 76, 113
Arctic Circle 4–5, 36
artisanal knowledge 3, 12, 93, 101
Australia 1, 4, 15–6, 57, 68, 80, 115; Indigenous (Aboriginal and Torres Strait Islanders) 5, 6, 30, 34, 36–8, 47, 68, 75, 88, 113–4

Bhambra, G. 83, 85, 102
Block, D. 20, 78, 106, 139–40
Blommaert, J. 21, 50, 54, 140
Bonfiglio, T. 50, 53
border thinking 107
Brazil 67, 74, 75, 108, 124–5

Canagarajah, S. 21, 28, 42, 60, 139, 140
capitalism 1, 2, 4, 21, 25, 28, 31, 33, 35, 40, 70, 100, 102, 132; neoliberalism 95, 135
Caribbean 22–3, 113, 125; Creole 52
Centre 12, 27, 34, 40
centre-periphery 21, 26, 29, 32, 124
Césaire, A. 22, 61, 140
China 1, 7, 21, 37, 128
Cohn, B. 47, 141

colonial history 5–6, 9, 24, 32, 49, 80, 116, 132–3, 136
colonialism 1–2, 4, 23–4, 30–2, 35, 40–1, 47–9, 65–6, 84–5, 87, 103–8 118, 121, 132–3, 136
Comaroff, J. & J. L. 2, 16, 34, 124–5, 141
Connell, R. 2, 22, 34, 36, 83, 99, 128, 132, 141
consciousness 22, 59, 104, 110, 123, 134; Indigenous consciousness 114, 118, 121
cosmovisions 7, 11, 105, 114, 117; Indigenous cosmovisions 102, 10–113, 117–8
Coupland, N. 4, 102, 141
Couzens, V. 77–9, 141
creole 45, 52–3, 57
Critical discourse analysis 97, 103, 129
Cusicanqui, S. R. 15, 32–3, 133, 141

Dasgupta, P. 13, 50, 124, 141, 144
De Korne, H. 38, 65, 76, 77, 141, 142
De Souza, L. M. 13, 67, 75, 134, 142
decolonial 2, 3, 7–9, 19, 23, 29–33, 40, 57–58, 60, 71, 81–83, 85, 86, 89, 93–95, 98–101 107, 118, 123, 127–8, 130–135; grammar of decoloniality 31, 99; imagination 9, 86, 100, 132; insurgency 83; option 19, 29, 30, 31, 32, 98, 99, 128, 135; thinking 40, 58, 118, 130; turn 7, 19, 82, 83, 101, 132, 134
decolonization 21, 40, 42, 118; epistemic 31; language in education 14, 64, 82–4, 87–9, 98, 100, 127, 128, 129; applied

linguistics 82–3, 87, 89, 94, 97–100, 127–8; university and higher education 89–91, 93
delinking 31, 40, 99, 123, 125
Dependency theory 2, 21
Deumert, A. 66, 124, 142
Development 9, 21, 25–9, 84, 87, 91–2, 98–9, 109, 118; Underdevelopment 7, 21, 26
Di Carlo, P. 12, 57, 142
disenfranchisement 1, 8, 122
disinvention 58–9
Douglas Fir Group 95, 99, 109
Duchêne, A. 41, 54, 67–8, 143, 146, 152
Dussel, E. 30–1, 107, 134–5, 143

education 10–11, 13, 17, 20, 27, 75, 99–100, 107, 117, 120
Eira, C. 77–9, 141
English 21, 28, 52, 98, 128; Indian English 15, 84; Ghanaian English 52, 124; language education 82, 87–8, 93, 99; World Englishes 6, 15, 30, 47, 52, 70, 95, 97–8, 124
epistemic 39, 58, 107–8; racism 102, 104–5; reconstitution 31, 33, 130
epistemicide 35, 104
epistemologies 2, 14, 75, 77, 79, 115, 117; African 52, 93; alternative 4, 9, 17, 131, 132; epistemological racism 103–5; epistemological repertoires 15, 130; Eurocentric 73, 83–4, 86, 95, 96; Northern 10, 63, 103, 105, 120; Seascape 110, 111; Southern 2, 4, 7–9, 11, 19, 33, 35, 40, 78, 100, 102, 105, 107, 110, 112, 114, 118, 122, 123, 127, 132, 135
epistemology 33, 64, 73, 85–6, 93, 100, 113, 115, 120
Errington, J. 47, 48, 65–6, 132, 143
ethno-philosophy 21

Fanon, F. 16, 22, 61, 104, 117, 135, 143
Finnegan, R. 66, 144
Flores, N. 10, 30, 53, 66, 95, 120, 135, 144, 156

Gal, S. 48, 75–6, 144, 147
García, O. 32, 42, 60, 98, 129, 144, 153, 80, 123
Geographical south 4–7, 49, 61, 115, 120, 134, 136
Ghana 16, 52, 80, 97, 124–5
Global 6–9, 12–3, 19, 23–4, 27–8, 35, 37, 59, 70, 82, 85, 89, 91, 96, 98–9, 104, 114, 120, 124, 128, 134–6; Global Inequalities 19–22, 28, 123; Global North 1, 4–6, 15–17, 20, 34, 49, 55, 61–2, 66, 82, 84, 85, 101, 102–3, 105, 107, 116, 118–121, 123, 126, 136; global Portuguese 29; Global South 1–12, 15–6, 20, 22–23, 26, 29, 30, 32, 34–6, 40, 43, 49, 53, 56–7, 60–2, 64, 69–70, 80–1, 84–5, 91–3, 99–100, 102–3, 105, 107, 113, 116, 118–121, 123, 125–6, 129, 131, 134, 136
Gogolin 42, 145
Gramling, D. 42, 51, 145
grammar 45, 48, 50, 56; of decoloniality 31, 99
Grosfoguel, R. 100, 104, 107, 121, 145

Hardt, M. and Negri, A. 24, 145
Harris, R. 14, 44, 45, 50, 51, 68, 145
Hauck, J. D. and Heurich, G.O. 71, 72, 131, 145
Haugen, E. 44
Heller, M. 9, 41, 42, 54, 61, 68, 132, 146
Heryanto, A. 46, 48, 49, 146
Heugh, K. 9, 32, 43, 60, 61, 124, 125, 133, 146
Hopi 75–6
Hopper, P. 45, 146

imperialism 24, 29, 41, 90, 103; linguistic 21, 23, 26, 28, 119, 124; structural theory of 26
Indigenous 1–7, 11, 36, 50, 58–9, 66–7, 71–80, 84–90, 94, 103–119, 128, 133; First Nations 36, 89; Indigeneity 23, 37, 39, 67, 104; communities 1, 47; politics and standpoints 2, 36–40; radical indigenism 39; research 39, 114, 115, 116
Indonesia 48–9
integrational linguistics 58
invention; of Africa 30; of the Americas 30, 135; of language 49, 59; of monolingualism 42, 50–51; of native speaker 53; and disinvention 58–9; reinventing 8, 35, 49, 91, 108, 116
Irvine, J. 46, 48, 50, 144, 147

Kamwangamalu, N. M. 88, 108, 116, 147
Khubchandani, L. 45, 50, 55, 61, 124, 147
Kubota, R. 29–30, 85, 95, 105, 118
Kumaravadivelu 31, 32, 98–9, 128, 132, 148
Kusters, A. 53, 59, 129, 142, 148

Language; decolonizing 21, 42, 67, 82–3, 87, 94, 98–100, 118, 127, 128; dialects 13, 49, 65, 125; ecology 64–5, 76;

emergent grammar 45; endangerment 63, 100; ideology 30, 41, 51, 71, 78–9, 87, 97, 128–130, 132; invention of 49, 59; and literacy 44, 65–6, 100; myth 43–4, 53, 66, 68; policy 8, 11, 40, 63, 65, 69, 99, 100, 103, 128–9, 136; preservation 17, 41, 49, 54, 64, 67–8, 70, 75–6, 79; reclamation 10, 13–14, 63, 67, 77–8, 127; rights 54, 59, 63–4, 69–71, 100, 127; sign languages 53, 129; standardization 10, 14, 50, 53, 65, 99; vitality 63, 76, 81
lazy thinking 13, 75–76
Le Page, R. 45, 148
Leonard, W. 11, 66, 76, 77, 81, 82, 127, 142, 148
Li Wei 32, 42, 60, 98, 129, 144
Liddicoat, T. 96–7
lingua franca 54, 55, 62, 127
linguicism 21, 23, 26, 28, 119, 124
linguistic genocide 63
linguistic imperialism 124
linguistics; applied linguistics 1, 3, 8–18, 20–3, 29–30, 33–4, 40–1, 47, 57, 59, 63, 65, 79, 81, 83–9, 94, 97, 99–114, 117–127, 129–137; reinventing applied linguistics 8; and colonialism 1, 3, 8, 17, 24, 28–33, 41, 47–50, 57, 61, 65–8, 71, 73–9, 87–9, 98, 100, 103, 105, 124, 128, 130, 132; folk 13, 14, 93; integrational 44, 58; sociolinguistics 4–5, 9, 12, 14, 16, 42–5, 50–2, 56–7, 61, 75, 95, 102, 116, 119, 124, 127, 129, 131, 136; zombie 67, 69
Locus of enunciation 7, 14–5, 38, 52, 60, 133
Love, N. 43, 44–6, 149
Lüpke, F. 57, 68, 79–81, 112, 127, 149

Macedo, D. 100, 128, 149
Magubane, Z. 83, 149
Makalela 9, 55, 58, 60–1, 89, 93, 108, 116, 124, 127, 133, 149
Makoni, S. 8, 15, 16, 30, 40, 45–6, 49, 50, 54–5, 58, 65, 69, 103, 108, 116, 119, 125, 127, 128, 138, 150, 157
Malay, Malaysia 6, 36, 37, 49
Maldonado-Torres, N. 2, 30–1, 82–3, 101, 118, 150
marginalization 35, 56, 105, 117, 121, 134
May, S. 9, 51, 54, 57, 70, 96, 151
Mazrui, A. 27, 56, 151
Mbembe, A. 91, 100, 111–3, 117, 125, 151
mestiza 113, 125–6, 130
metadiscursive regimes 59, 61

metrolingual practices 6
Mignolo, W. 2, 7, 14, 16–7, 20, 22, 24–5, 30–3, 38, 40, 57–8, 60, 80–2, 93–4, 98–100, 103, 107, 116, 118–9, 130, 134–5, 151–2
Milani, T. 35, 125, 134, 152
Moita-Lopes, L. P. 29, 130, 131, 152
Monaghan, P. 38, 47, 68, 81, 152
monolingual; habitus 42; mindset 42, 51, 62, 136
monolingualism 23, 43, 47, 50–1, 53–5, 61–2, 127; multiple monolingualisms 42, 50–1; and semilingualism 51; and zerolingualism 51
Mudimbe, V. 30, 36, 47, 152
Muehlmann, S. 67–70, 80, 152
Mufwene, S. 11, 52, 54, 63, 66, 69–70, 79–80, 152–3
multilingualism 43; egalitarian 57; multilanguaging 55, 59, 62, 93, 127; plurality of 30, 40, 43, 127; polylingualism 42; remixing 54–7, 59; as singular phenomenon 43; Southern 8, 10, 17, 32, 42, 59, 71, 81, 87–8; traditional 57; translingual practice 42, 60, 98; ubuntu translanguaging 9, 58, 60, 93, 127, 133
multilingual turn 9, 51, 96
Mwaniki, M. 51, 88

Nakata, M. 2, 38–40, 46, 68, 75–6, 88, 153
native speaker 31–2, 47, 52, 53, 99
Ndhlovu, F. 7, 54, 61–2, 64, 153
négritude 22, 28
Ngugi wa Thiong'o 119, 126, 128, 153
North America 1, 4–5, 17, 33, 43, 74, 75, 80, 89, 104

Ontology; of language 73, 81, 85–6, 113, 116; ontological Eurocentrism 73; ontological turn 72–5, 131
Orientalism 22, 29
Ortega, L. 9, 95–7, 153
Otsuji, E. 6, 80, 154

Pennycook, A. 6, 8, 15–6, 29, 40, 44–6, 54–5, 58, 60, 64–5, 67, 72, 76, 80, 87, 94–5, 99, 110–111, 117, 127, 131, 138–140, 150, 154, 158
Perley B. 69, 76, 81, 111, 154
perspectivism 72
Phillipson, R. 21, 23, 26, 28, 87, 119, 154
pluriversality 38, 126
positionality 5, 12, 14, 31, 35

postcolonial 5, 19, 22, 27, 29–34, 39, 59, 81, 87, 103, 114–6, 124; postcolonialism 29, 30, 135
posthumanism 73, 135
Prah, K. K. 2–3, 11, 22, 27, 88, 92, 136, 155, 157
provincializing 107

Quijano, A. 30, 31, 118, 130, 155

Race; raciolinguistic 11, 53, 66, 120
racism; epistemic 102, 104–5; institutional 3, 8, 96, 123; White ignorance 95, 118, 120
Rajagopolan, K. 46–8, 52, 132, 155
resistance 2, 19, 22, 24, 30, 50, 58, 59, 102, 113, 134
Richardson, W. 83–4, 89, 91
Rodney, W. 21, 156
Romani language 49
Rosa, J. 10, 53, 66, 95, 120, 144, 156

Sabino 46, 156
Said, E. 16, 22, 29, 156
Sámi 5, 36
Santos, B. de S. 2–4, 8–9, 11, 13, 19–20, 35, 40, 69, 75, 78, 86, 92–3, 96, 98, 100–3, 107–8, 115, 117–9, 120–3, 130, 133, 156–7
Sarkar, M. 78, 105, 157
Savransky 8–9, 33, 73, 75, 81, 86, 93, 101, 131–2, 136, 157
second language acquisition 11–12, 17, 40, 79, 94–7, 127, 129, 131
sign language 53, 59, 129
Skutnabb-Kangas, T. 63–4, 87, 158
Smith, L. 5, 30, 37, 39, 79, 105–6, 110, 113, 116–7, 158
social construction 49
sociolinguistics 4, 5, 9, 16, 44, 50, 56, 75, 102, 103, 116, 119, 124, 129, 131
sociology 83, 85, 99, 124, 131; of absences 23, 35

South Africa 15, 26, 55, 61, 90–1, 93, 108, 116–7, 125
South America 1, 4, 6, 30, 31, 50, 109, 119, 125, 126, 134
Southern perspectives 1–10, 14–17, 41, 51, 58, 74, 82, 115, 122, 126–7, 130, 132, 134, 136
Southern theories 2, 6, 16, 18–9, 22–4, 28–36, 40, 47, 124, 134, 135
Stebbins, T. 64, 77, 158
Storch, A. 56–7, 112, 127, 142, 149, 153, 159
Stroud, C. 9, 32, 43, 51, 60–1, 124, 133, 146, 159

Tabouret-Keller, A. 45, 148
thinking otherwise 83, 99, 128, 132
Third world 2, 5, 7, 17, 19, 21–9, 33–6, 53, 107, 124, 127
Todd, Z. 33, 39, 60, 73, 74, 117, 133, 159
translanguaging 32, 42, 60, 98; bilanguaging 32, 60; translingual practice 42, 60, 98; translingualism 42, 60; *Ubuntu* 9, 58, 60, 94, 127, 133

Ubuntu-Nepantla 18, 107, 109, 117, 126
universalism 3, 8, 10, 21, 28, 91, 136

Viveiros de Castro 72–3, 125, 129, 160
Vivir bien 109–10

Wallerstein, I. 21, 83, 160
Walsh, C. 2, 20, 31, 83, 100, 130, 132, 152, 160
White ignorance 95, 118, 120
Williams, Q. 55–6, 160
World Englishes 6, 15, 30, 47, 52, 95, 97–8, 124
world systems 21, 24

Zeleza 70, 84, 91, 160
zerolingualism 51

CPSIA information can be obtained
at www.ICGtesting.com
Printed in the USA
LVHW031702260320
651299LV00004B/15